Assessment and Case Formulation in Cognitive Behavioural Therapy

'This book is an important contribution to the development of cognitive therapy that synthesizes the best of traditional cognitive therapy with important new developments emerging from a range of different areas including postmodern and constructivist approaches, interpersonal and relational perspectives, positive psychology and research and thinking about the role of reflection-in-action in therapeutic expertise. Combining practical accessibility with theoretical sophistication, this book will be invaluable reading for both beginning therapists and experienced clinicians.'

Jeremy D. Safran, PhD, Professor and Director of Clinical Psychology, New School for Social Research, New York; Author of *Interpersonal Process in Cognitive Therapy and Negotiating the Therapeutic Alliance: A Relational Treatment Guide.*

'Like a powerful river with many tributaries, this book somehow manages to weave influences from all kinds of diverse sources into an exciting, coherent whole. It is everything you'd want of a new CBT book for students and practitioners – fresh, practical, accessible. And the authors have created something else as well: a unique voice in the CBT world, which combines radical ideas and mainstream approaches in a contemporary blend that would not have even been conceivable five years ago.'

James Bennett-Levy, Oxford Cognitive Therapy Centre, Warneford Hospital, Headington, Oxford.

Assessment and Case Formulation in Cognitive Behavioural Therapy

Alec Grant, Michael Townend, Jem Mills and Adrian Cockx

Los Angeles | London | New Delhi
Singapore | Washington DC

First published 2008
Reprinted 2011

SAGE Publications Ltd
1 Oliver's Yard
55 City Road
London EC1Y 1SP

SAGE Publications Inc.
2455 Teller Road
Thousand Oaks, California 91320

SAGE Publications India Pvt Ltd
B 1/I 1 Mohan Cooperative Industrial Area
Mathura Road
New Delhi 110 044

SAGE Publications Asia-Pacific Pte Ltd
33 Pekin Street #02-01
Far East Square
Singapore 048763

Library of Congress Control Number: 2007931743

British Library Cataloguing in Publication data

A catalogue record for this book is available from
the British Library

ISBN 978-1-4129-3506-7
ISBN 978-1-4129-3507-4 (pbk)

Typeset by C&M Digitals Pvt Ltd, Chennai, India
Printed in Great Britain by the MPG Books Group
Printed on paper from sustainable resources

FOR KAREN AND RICHARD MORGAN-JONES
Alec Grant

FOR LOU, ADAM, PATRICK AND MILES
Michael Townend

FOR SALLY, AND EVERYONE AT AURORA
Jem Mills

FOR BIJAL AND MY FAMILY
Adrian Cockx

Contents

Acknowledgements

Alison Poyner, Claire Reeve, Louise Wise, Claire Lipscomb and Katherine Haw from Sage guided us skilfully through this project, and we are especially grateful to Alison for coming up with the idea in the first place. Anni Telford, Chris Brannigan, Wendy Wood, Margot Levinson, Tony Gowlett and other colleagues at the University of Derby have been both supportive and encouraging. Many thanks also to the students on the MSc in Cognitive Psychotherapy, University of Brighton, and the MSc in Cognitive Behavioural Psychotherapy, University of Derby, from whom we never stop learning. Finally, we are indebted to the clients who have generously agreed to us using their experiences in therapy with us, as illustrative casework material in the text.

Foreword

Good assessment and formulation skills are the gateways to successful therapy. Clearly however assessment and formulation must match the therapeutic focus. Thus a psychodynamic, humanistic, existential or CBT therapist will construct and navigate through these processes in rather different ways. More challenging perhaps is that over the last 20 years CBT has greatly diversified in the approaches and conceptualisations of mental health problems and interventions. Such diversity will have a major impact on the styles and focus of assessment, formulation and interventions.

This book helps bring this diversity to life with clear expositions of the basic principles of formulation within various CBT frameworks. All therapies now recognise the centrality of the core elements of Bonds, Tasks and Goals. Although different therapies will approach these in different ways, the central fulcrum for helpful formulation in CBT is collaboration. This collaboration is built via dialogue (called Socratic), open sharing and mutual guided discovery. Psychotherapy, both in formulation and enactment is always a co-construction. This open, reflective and collaborative stance enables therapist and client to find new insights and understandings about the client's personal constructions of meaning. These will focus on things that are external to them (such as relationships) and things that are internal to them (such as their sensations, intrusive thoughts or feelings). Throughout the book, Grant, Townend, Mills and Cockx use simple and complex case scenarios and case examples to illustrate key points. These cover individuals, couples and families.

Grant, Townend, Mills and Cockx note any simple idea that CBT is not interested in or does not explore the past in the formulation is incorrect. Indeed for many people with mood and other problems, understanding how influences from the past, be this in the form of aversive emotion memories, early schema or safety behaviours, can create biased thoughts and feelings and be essential for appropriate formulation and therapy planning.

Grant, Townend, Mills and Cockx also give important attention to the qualities of the therapeutic relationship that enable people to explore and reveal their difficulties. Shame is a major source of suffering for many. Shame can affect the nature of the difficulties people have, how they share or conceal them and even in helping seeking behaviour itself. One key process then is shame sensitivity especially in the early stages of therapy and formulation.

This book offers an exciting and wide ranging approach to formulation, bringing together different models in highly informative and innovative ways. Many therapists, students and educationalists, both new and experienced, will find much to inspire them. I am sure this book will be high on people's 'must read list' for some time to come.

Paul Gilbert

Introduction

1

Alec Grant, Michael Townend, Jem Mills and Adrian Cockx

The representation of a single theoretical background is increasingly hard to find in our contemporary cognitive behavioural communities. This book is no exception and readers will discover our theoretical and empirical allegiances, commonalities and differences, as the text unfolds. A common strand throughout is our fundamental commitment to empirically underpinned and grounded cognitive behavioural psychotherapy (Moorey, 2007; Salkovskis, 2002; Scrimali and Grimaldi, 2004).

Historical and contemporary writers in cognitive behavioural psychotherapy have tended to take a disorder-based approach to formulation, or have used variations of the original clinical models of the emotional disorders or depression developed by Beck and Colleagues (Alford and Beck, 1997; Beck et al., 1979). Whilst we are influenced by traditional Beckian cognitive therapy and traditional behaviour therapy (Marks, 1987), when supported by evidence, we are also influenced by other, more recent and integrative developments and revisions in our knowledge and practice field. These include the postmodern turn in cognitive therapy (Hammack, 2003; Lyddon and Weill, 1997; Ramsay, 1998; Safran and Messer, 1997) and related client-led textual representation (Chase Grey and Grant, 2005; Short, 2005); the compassion paradigm (Gilbert, 2005); transdiagnostic (Harvey et al., 2004) and multi-level approaches to assessment and formulation (Barnard and Teasdale, 1991; Brewin et al., 1996; Power and Dalgleish, 1999); the role of creativity (James et al., 2004; Mahoney, 2003; Mooney and Padesky, 2000); the influence of positive psychology (Cheavans et al., 2006; Ingram and Snyder, 2006); classic and contemporary therapeutic relationship issues (Gilbert and Leahy, 2007) and, finally, self-practice, reflective development and clinical supervision in cognitive behavioural psychotherapy (Bennett-Levy and Thwaites, 2007; Bennett-Levy et al., 2001; Townend et al., 2002).

Each of the above developments is reflected in this text, and their application to assessment and formulation is detailed in a unique synthesis of contemporary ideas for the cognitive behavioural practitioner, supervisor and educator.

SOME KEY ISSUES AND ASSUMPTIONS

Assessment as a collaborative enterprise

The keys to effective therapeutic interventions in cognitive behavioural psychotherapy are the development of a therapeutic relationship, a detailed and systematic assessment and a formulation to guide practice. Curiosity and hopefulness are two vital attributes for a cognitive behavioural psychotherapist in this endeavour. This is especially so when assessing the motivations for the client in seeking therapy during an initial assessment interview, which according to Sanders and Wills (2005), ought to include:

- What are your exact goals at this time?
- What other solutions have you tried to help you overcome your problems?
- How hopeful are you that therapy can help you currently?

In addition to the above, we have become increasingly aware in our work of the need to carefully assess any fears that clients may have around change. These might well be about the therapy process, the emotions they are likely to experience, and how therapy might impact on them, their family and relationships with others. It may also be that clients fear the closeness of a therapeutic relationship if they have a history of abusive relationships or have had difficulty in forming appropriate relationships with others.

In order to engage clients in the therapeutic process from the outset, it is important that therapists role model curiosity and hopefulness to encourage a 'possibility focus' in clients. It is equally important for assessment to be a focused and collaborative process where the client is invited to make a contribution to initial, and subsequent, agenda setting and management of the therapeutic process as a whole. The aim is neither to 'label' nor 'diagnose' the client, but to reach early and provisional agreement around the nature of the current difficulties and pathways to change and recovery, and therefore what needs to be worked on in therapy. This is a two-way process, in that the therapist assesses the client in a way that demonstrates compassion and empathy for his or her distress while remaining sensitive to his or her thoughts and feelings about engagement in therapy. Such an approach explicitly invites the client to consider if the cognitive behavioural approach and the psychotherapist are right for them at this time and helps to identify any resistance or doubts that the client may have.

The assumption behind collaborative assessment is to build a comprehensive picture of the client's difficulties and goals, both in terms of how the difficulties arose, how they affect the client currently, and emerging future-directed strategies to help the client work towards overcoming them. Sanders and Wills (2005) stress that the outline of assessment is not intended to be fixed and immutable, but, rather, a series of 'coat hooks' on which to hang gradually assimilating information from the client's meaning-making through the utilisation of guided discovery as the basis of collaboration between therapist and client.

The client's personal meaning-making

Centrally important in the collaborative enterprise that characterises contemporary CBT assessment is the personal meaning-making of the client and the need for the therapist to adapt to this. The therapist takes the position that *the* focus is both at the phenomenological level, the client's inner life world (Alford and Beck, 1997) and of equal importance is the client's perception and experiences of the external world, such as conflicts at home, within relationships, experiences at work, and the coping behaviours used in these contexts.

The relational approach to case formulation

Within such a phenomenological focus on the internal and external worlds, therapists need to be mindful that they will be part of the client's interpersonal and external worlds and vice versa. So, just as the interpersonal issues and difficulties that the client has in her life are likely to be played out in the therapy session, the cognitive behavioural psychotherapist may well process interpersonal information in a distorted way at times of 'therapeutic alliance rupture'. In the words of Robert Leahy (2001: 5), 'in the therapeutic relationship, both patient and therapist are patients'. Because of this, in our view, all interventions – including assessment – make sense only in relational and co-constructional forms (Gilbert and Leahy, 2007; Safran, 1997; Safran and Segal, 1996). Essentially, the therapeutic alliance between client and therapist should be seen as a psychosocial laboratory, within which:

> **Both patient and therapist struggle to sort out how much they can accommodate to the other's views about treatment tasks and goals, without compromising themselves in some important way. (Safran, 1997: 459)**

Interpersonal meaning-making and case formulation

Table 1.1 overleaf illustrates the need for both client and therapist to accommodate to each other's viewpoint in order to help the client work through difficulties. This is likely to involve rule and core belief affirmation and violation for both parties in the therapeutic relationship (Haarhoff, 2006; James et al., 2004; Leahy, 2001, 2007; Rudd and Joiner, 1997), and may often be transferential in character (Miranda and Andersen, 2007). It is therefore important that cognitive behavioural psychotherapy is viewed as a relational rather than a simple technical or mechanistic endeavour. Therapists will thus need to pay close attention to the activation of their own cognitions throughout the process of therapy and seek to make sense of this within the developing therapeutic process and evolution of the formulation.

THE STRUCTURE OF THE BOOK

In exploring the above further, this text is divided into three parts: Part I introduces the reader to fundamental and advanced technical and process knowledge in cognitive behavioural assessment and case formulation. Part II provides practical illustration of aspects of the preceding discussion, in diagrammatic and narrative form, using eight case studies. These are drawn directly from the authors' recent clinical work and cover helping individuals with the following difficulties: obsessional compulsive disorder; borderline personality disorder; post-traumatic stress disorder and related difficulties; family difficulties; low self-esteem; psychosis; health anxiety and, finally, chronic depression. The last part of the book explores a long overdue issue in our cognitive behavioural communities – specifically around leadership and related scientific

Table 1.1

Level of thought	Focus of thought	As applied to the therapeutic relationship for client	As applied to the therapeutic relationship for therapist
Core belief	Self Others World	Possibility of core belief accommodation with therapist's core beliefs. Possibility of core belief violation by therapist.	Possibility of core belief accommodation with client's core beliefs. Possibility of core belief violation by client.
Rules for living (underlying assumptions)	Self Others World	Possibility of rule accommodation with therapist's rules. Possibility of rule violation by therapist.	Possibility of rule accommodation with client's rules. Possibility of rule violation by client.
Automatic thoughts (ATs)	Self Others World	Possibility of AT accommodation with therapist's ATs. Possibility of AT violation by therapist.	Possibility of AT accommodation with client's ATs. Possibility of AT violation by client.

paradigm awareness – and highlights the need for a future text to develop and clarify this and other professional development concerns.

A range of blank case formulation templates that we have found helpful are provided in the Appendices at the end of the book for the reader to use within their own practice.

Part I

Cognitive Behavioural Assessment and Case Formulation

Assessment in CBT: the ideographic approach

2

Michael Townend and Alec Grant

Learning objectives

After reading this chapter and completing the activities at the end of it you should be able to understand:

1 The place and relevance of classification systems in CBT.

2 The relevance of, and distinction between, nomothetic and ideographic approaches to assessment.

3 The overall aims of assessment from the perspectives of therapist and client.

4 The role of functional analysis.

5 The relationship between assessment and formulation.

6 The key areas for assessment in a cognitive behavioural context.

The cognitive behavioural approach to human difficulties provides the means to explore the personal meanings, emotions and behaviours of the individual. This understanding takes account of the contexts of clients' past experiences, biological and genetic influences and current environments. Through the process of guided discovery and Socratic questioning, both the therapist and their clients develop meaningful insights into what may have caused clients' problems, what is maintaining them and potential ways to restore or achieve recovery (Freeman et al., 2004).

This approach differs from the medical model of human distress, in that it strives to understand clients' idiosyncratic experiences, and how they or others might be contributing to their current problems. This contrasts with giving clients a diagnostic label based on the presentation and severity of a number of symptoms (Farrington and Telford, 1996). So, for example, two people with depression may have very different formulations, in contrast to two people with, say, lung cancer, who wouldn't. This is not to say that diagnostic classification is not useful, but that its limitations need to be recognised in the context of the cognitive behavioural assessment process.

NOMOTHETIC ASSESSMENT: DIAGNOSTIC CLASSIFICATION SYSTEMS

Nomothetic assessment refers to assessment based on the aggregated features of particular disorders. These are gathered from large scale and systematic studies of populations who are suffering from specific disorders. This form of assessment pays attention to the classification of a person's problem in the form of diagnosis and has its uses, for example, in medical care when a rapid diagnosis, understanding of underlying disease processes and application of the appropriate treatment or medicine is essential to preserve life.

The American Psychiatric Association's *Diagnostic and Statistical Manual* (4th edition) or *DSM-IV-TR* (APA, 2000) comprises five axes on which the individual may be assessed: clinical syndromes, personality disorders, general medical conditions, psychosocial and environmental problems, and global functioning. An alternative diagnostic framework is the World Health Organisation's (WHO) *International Statistical Classification of Diseases and Related Health Problems (ICD-10)* (WHO, 2002). The *ICD-10* is seen as an essential part of the effort to develop an international language, in order to allow global communication in the subject of mental health and facilitate research across cultures and countries. It is also the more widely used classification system within the National Health Service of the United Kingdom.

Although they may be helpful in identifying the characteristics of specific problems – for example, post-traumatic stress disorder or the variants of, so-called, 'personality disorder – there is a major disadvantage for cognitive behavioural psychotherapists in the over-reliance of the above classification systems in assessment. This is that the search for similarities across conditions to make classification decisions means that differences and idiosyncrasies at the individual level become lost or obscured.

COGNITIVE BEHAVIOURAL ASSESSMENT: THE IDEOGRAPHIC APPROACH

The ideographic approach is sometimes referred to as functional analysis. In contrast to nomothetic assessment, ideographic assessment is concerned with understanding the person's own characteristics which contribute to their difficulties rather than a broad classification of what disorder they might have. It is also personal rather than disease-focused which, in our view, is essential in a psychotherapeutic context. It can also help to overcome the categorical limitations of diagnostic classification by accommodating more dimensional and contextual factors.

The initial goal of therapy is usually to work in collaboration with the client in order to break the vicious cycles which are sustaining or intensifying their problems. This employs, for example, behavioural strategies to increase activity levels, exposure-based experiments to reduce anxiety, or tackling unhelpful thinking with cognitive reappraisal strategies and a variety of appropriate behavioural experiments. Such strategies enable the client to begin to take control over their difficulties, although if cognitive behavioural psychotherapists only worked with these surface issues, clients might remain at risk of future relapse. They thus also use a range of strategies to identify and bring about change in clients' unhelpful assumptions and core beliefs in order to achieve, hopefully, more lasting positive changes (Beck et al., 1979; Bennett-Levy et al., 2004; Young, 1990; Young et al., 2003).

'DEBRA'

Debra is 25 years old and despite consuming around 3000 calories per day, eats a health conscious diet and has a weight with a body mass index within the normal range – BMI 22. Her doctor is very concerned about her physical health as she is repeatedly visiting him with pulled muscles, shin splints, back pain and complaints of tiredness and concerns about her ability to cope with her post-graduate university course. She has a history of innumerable diets. On the one hand it might be argued that she is eating a balanced diet with exercise, is prone to injury, and is experiencing the normal pressures of university life, therefore simply needs some support and reassurance. However, an idiographic assessment reveals that Debra was of a normal weight until the age of 13. A rather shy and quiet person, she started to stay at home and eat excessively when some girls at the school began to bully her. She gained weight rapidly, her self-worth reduced (emotional state) and the bullying worsened as a consequence. She comes from a high achieving family and consequently sets herself very high standards in order to compete (emotional state) with her siblings. She now finds it very difficult to trust people (emotional state) and this causes problems when she does try to socialise, which she avoids (behaviour) as a result of her anxiety (emotion). She is constantly worrying about what other people think of her (thought process), with a particular concern about her body shape (self-focussed attention). She responds extremely badly to criticism (emotion) and any suggestion of censor from others causes her to feel hopeless about herself, her shape and the future (emotion). She also tries to cope through excessive exercise and sometimes works out or runs and walks for several hours per day. Simply exhorting Debra to reduce her exercise, maintain a healthy diet and reassure her would have little effect as the primary cause of her unhealthy eating pattern is her emotional state.

The example of Debra above highlights the dangers of simply naming her symptoms, or producing a diagnosis of physical injury and reactive stress, rather than trying to understand her in the context of her overall life history and current circumstances.

Ideographic assessment comes into its own when working with people at the individual level, within a psychotherapeutic context. It is also particularly useful in helping people with more chronic or complex psychological or medical conditions. In these conditions, a wide range of psychological or physical factors will have an effect on the person and must be factored into cognitive behavioural psychotherapy assessment. This is particularly true for individuals with chronic conditions such as severe and relapsing depression, dysthymia, psychosis, bi-polar disorder or so-called personality disorders (Mills et al., 2004a), and in physical problems with psychological consequences such as heart disease, diabetes, chronic pain in all its forms where individual factors will play a part in how well the individual conforms to the self-management or health education guidance given (Kitchiner and Short, 2004).

AIMS OF THE ASSESSMENT PROCESS

There are a number of overall aims that the therapist in cognitive behavioural psychotherapy needs to work towards, and be mindful of, throughout the assessment process. These aims emerge from a collaborative process between therapist and client and should result in clients' increased understanding of the approach, as summarised below:

1 Give a detailed breakdown of the client's problems in terms of environmental triggers, thoughts, behaviours, emotions and physiological reactions.
2 Give a detailed account of the factors from the client's background and past which have contributed to the development of their main problems.
3 Give a detailed account of what factors are helping maintain the client's problems.
4 Describe the nature and strength of the therapeutic relationship.
5 Define the strengths of the client.
6 Define and utilise clinical measures that give an indication of severity and provide a baseline.
7 Provide a reasoned and research-based outline of how they will be able to work with the client based on the formulation emerging from assessment.

What clients should be able to do as the assessment process develops is as follows:

1 Understand and relate to the collaboratively developing formulation of what helped contribute to the emergence of their problems.
2 Understand and relate to the thoughts, behaviours, emotional and physiological reactions that are helping maintain their problems.
3 Contribute to, and understand, the plan for working on problem areas.
4 Understand the nature and place of measurement within the therapeutic process.
5 Understand the collaborative nature of the therapy process and the mutual expectations within this.

FUNCTIONAL ANALYSIS IN ASSESSMENT

Historically within the context of behaviour therapy, one of the cornerstones of practice was the 'behavioural analysis'. The term was originally stressed by Skinner and was meant to distinguish the field as one that focuses on behaviour as a subject in its own right rather than as an index or manifestation of something happening at some other level (cognitive or emotional). Skinner also believed that thinking and feeling were in fact covert (internal) forms of behaviour (Clark and Fairburn, 2005; Hawton et al., 1989).

The terms functional and behavioural analysis have been used incorrectly and interchangeably within the cognitive and behavioural literature. Functional analysis is the process of determining the cause (or 'function') of unwelcome or unhelpful behaviour before developing an appropriate intervention for it.

Unfortunately, it is now rare to see functional analysis considered within contemporary cognitive behavioural psychotherapy texts. What is surprising about this is that it still remains a fundamental part of competent assessment practice, in order to define and understand the client's problems as tightly as possible. This neglect of functional analysis is probably due to its behavioural heritage. Its importance is that it is simply not enough to know that someone is socially anxious; we need to understand the content and the processes of his thinking, as well as what he is focusing on and attending to. In addition we also need to identify avoidance and safety behaviours involved, along with antecedents and the characteristics of stimuli which lead to his distress and discomfort.

It is only through carrying out detailed functional analyses that hypotheses for the maintenance of client problems can be developed, and individualised client-centred cognitive and behavioural techniques be tailored to individual need on the basis of a full and systematically developed formulation.

RELATIONSHIP BETWEEN ASSESSMENT AND FORMULATION

A formulation is the means by which cognitive behavioural psychotherapists link theory with information about their clients, from the assessment process to practice and inform the choice of therapeutic interventions. This is shown in Figure 2.1 below.

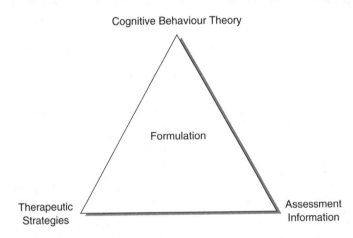

Figure 2.1   Relationship between assessment, theory, formulation and therapeutic strategies

Cognitive behavioural psychotherapy students frequently ask us 'when does the assessment phase end, and formulation and then therapy phases start?' There is of course no simple answer to this question as all the stages overlap with each other, and the dynamic therapeutic process means that each of the phases is returned to time and time again. This process is most frequently played out in complex cases. So, for example, if a depressed client did not respond to behavioural activation with an improvement in mood, a reassessment and revisions to the formulation would need to take place.

A thorough and detailed assessment and an appropriate formulation does, in our view, help the therapist and the client to understand that problems which originally seemed never ending, intractable, unpredictable and incomprehensible can be understood, explained and tackled (Sanders and Wills, 2005). Breaking down problems into more manageable parts, and 'shoulder to shoulder' explanations with the aid of diagrams, maintenance cycles and cognitive behavioural interventions, helps the client feel that the therapist understands them and their difficulties. Crucially, this also instils an important feeling of optimism and hope (Cheavans et al., 2006; Snyder, 2002) and helps to motivate the client to change unhelpful thinking, emotions and behaviours (Grant et al., 2004a, Sanders and Wills, 2005).

The assessment process and the subsequent development of the formulation are also powerful therapeutic strategies in themselves. Cognitive behavioural psychotherapists continually help clients make links between their thoughts, feelings, behaviour and their environments and interpersonal contexts. This is achieved through frequent summaries given by the therapist during assessment (Blackburn et al., 2001). This can enable clients to spot for themselves self-defeating strategies that they have been using, including unhelpful beliefs and behaviours. Once clients are aware of these, they are more likely to be empowered towards optimism and the view that their problems are solvable. Moreover, importantly, this process can help people to begin to recognise and overcome meta-cognitive beliefs – that is to say beliefs that they hold about their own thoughts and beliefs, which may also be helping to maintain their emotional difficulties (Dalgleish, 2004; Wells, 1997).

A summary of the value of assessment and formulation can be seen in Table 2.1.

Table 2.1   The value of assessment and formulation in cognitive behavioural psychotherapy

Assessment	Formulation
1 Has an educational role and focuses the client on external and internal factors or processes that may have not been seen as relevant to the problem.	1 Helps the client to make links between thoughts, emotions, behaviours and the environment.
2 Increases the possibility of change through a process of clarifying and differentiating the problem or problems into manageable parts.	2 Helps the client and therapist to recognise the vicious circles that are maintaining their difficulties.
3 Focuses on 'what can be done' instead of the continuity of the problem.	3 Helps both the therapist and client to set therapeutic priorities.
4 Sets reasonable limits on what can be achieved.	4 Informs and guides the therapeutic plan.
5 Suggests that distress can be predictable, therefore controllable or changeable.	5 Further instils a sense and feeling of hope and optimism for the client.
6 Instils a sense of feeling of hope and optimism.	6 Helps to motivate the client.
7 Helps to motivate the client.	7 Helps the therapist and client to understand any predispositions or experiences that led up to the problem developing.
8 Enables the therapist to demonstrate understanding, warmth and empathy for the client's distress and build a collaborative relationship.	
9 Helps the client to make links between thoughts, feelings, behaviours and the environment.	
10 Helps the client to recognise vicious circles of factors that are maintaining their difficulties.	

THE PRACTICE OF FUNCTIONAL ANALYSIS AND ASSESSMENT

Functional analysis is the cornerstone of assessment practice within cognitive behavioural psychotherapy. The problem assessment initially concentrates on the 'here and now' of the client's identified areas of experiences and difficulties. This is then contextualised by the identification of earlier formative events and experiences which have influenced the client's beliefs systems, emotions and behaviours.

It is important to remember that an assessment process is not about a rigid list of questions, each being fired off one after the other. Assessment should, like therapy, be a collaborative process of joint discovery, albeit led by the therapist. Sanders and Wills (2005) sum up the process in a clear and informed way while acknowledging that different professional groups might apply the assessment process in different ways:

> **The outline of assessment is not intended to be a fixed rota for therapists to stick to. Rather it is a series of coat hooks on which to hang information as it is assimilated, and people will use it according to their core training. (Sanders and Wills, 2005: 80)**

In structural terms, a cross-sectional assessment is carried out of all the problems or issues that the client (or therapist) believes are relevant. Then a specific focus is applied to a detailed assessment of each of these areas and both proximal (recent) and distal (more distant) aspects are assessed.

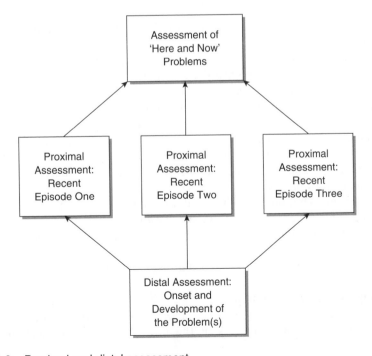

Figure 2.2   Proximal and distal assessment

An example of distal aspects might be a list of triggers for panic, typical cognitions and physiological responses and behaviours. The proximal aspects include an episodic analysis perhaps of the last time the person panicked or felt low. Further information should also be gathered regarding frequency, intensity and duration of the problematic problems being assessed. The key areas of assessment are detailed below.

Assessment information (to adapt to therapist style and client needs)

Functional analysis

1 **Five Ws**
   What is the main problem or problems?
   Where does the problem occur?
   When does the problem occur?
   Why (what is the feared consequence or belief)?
   With whom does the problem occur?

2 **FIND**
   What is the FREQUENCY of the problem?
   How INTENSE are the symptoms or how depressed is the individual (using a scale of 0–8 or 0–100%)?
   What NUMBER of times does the problem occur?
   How long does the problem or episode last – DURATION?

3 **ABC analyses**
   Antecedents: What are the triggers to the problem: internal/external and proximal/distal?
   Autonomic/Physical: What physical symptoms are present?
   Behaviour: What does the person do? Avoidance, checking, reassurance seeking, rituals, safety behaviours, escape.
   Cognitive content, Cognitive process and emotions: What is the person thinking – before during and after an episode? Are there any images? What is the meaning associated with the images? Identification of processes: self-focused attention, thinking errors, worry, thought suppression; inflated sense of risk or threat. What emotions are evident: anger, guilt, shame, depression, fear, embarrassment, shame; what core beliefs and rules are evident?
   Consequences: What happens afterwards in terms of reduced or increased anxiety, improved or worsened mood, others reactions and interactions?
   Coping strategies: what does the client do to cope and what coping skills and assets do they possess?
   Modifiers: What makes the problem better and what makes it worse?

4 **Development of the problem**
   Onset: When did the problem first start? What happened at the time? What was going on at home or work at the time? Were any stressors present at the time?

Formative: Are any key themes, rules, beliefs or assumptions evident from the individual's background, upbringing life both past and present; is there any history of trauma or abuse?

Fluctuations: Is the problem lifelong or recurring? Is the problem static or has it changed over time?

5 Goals and expectations from therapy

What do you want to achieve from therapy?

What are you expecting from therapy?

What are your hopes or fears about therapy or the therapeutic process?

Why are you seeking therapy at this point in time?

6 Medication and Substance Use

Medication and side effects: What medication is being taken? Are any side effects present?

Alcohol intake: How many units of alcohol consumed in a week? Does the client drink to self-medicate or cope?

Caffeine intake: What is the client's intake of coffee, soft drinks that contain caffeine?

Smoking: Does the client smoke tobacco?

Non-prescribed drugs: Does the client take illegal substances? If yes, what do they take? Are they taken for recreational or self-medication purposes?

7 Assets and strengths

What coping resources – personal/social/environmental – are available to the client?

What are the client's strengths?

8 Impact of the problems on the client's life

What has been the effect of the problems on the client's work, home, leisure and relationships?

9 Mental status

Appearance: How does the client appear? Are they caring for themselves? Do they appear anxious or agitated or depressed?

Speech: What is the form and flow of the client's verbal communication?

Mood: Does the client feel low or depressed? Do they feel anxious? Do they experience any other emotions such as guilt and shame? Are there any fluctuations to the mood during the day and evening – diurnal variation?

Appetite: Have there been any changes in appetite? Has the client lost or gained weight recently?

Sleep: How many hours sleep is the client getting? Are there any difficulties getting off to sleep? Do they wake during the night? What time do they awake in the morning? Have there been any recent changes? Does the client have nightmares?

Libido: Have there been any changes in the client's sex drive?

Anhedonia: Is the client able to enjoy life or activities?

Irritability: Does the client feel irritable or agitated?

Self-worth and self-image: Does the client have low self-esteem? How do they view themselves as a person? How do they think others see them? Are there any body image issues?

Hopelessness: How does the client view the future in terms of optimism or pessimism?

Risk/self-harm/suicide: Are any indicators of risk present for self-neglect/self-harm/abuse/suicide? Does the client have suicidal thoughts or wishes? Has the client made any plans for suicide? Does the client have access to means for suicide? Is the client a danger to others?

Psychosis: Does the client experience hallucinations or delusional beliefs or over-valued ideas? Is there any evidence of thought disorder?

Concentration: What is the client's level of concentration? Have there been any recent changes?

Orientation: Is the client aware of the time, location and know the name of key individuals?

Memory: What is the client's memory like? Have there been any recent changes?

10 Medical history

Details of previous therapy for the main problem.
Medical and psychiatric history.

11 Ethico-legal

Does the client have any convictions?
Are there any legal cases currently in progress?
Are there any child protection issues?
Is the client currently seeking compensation for injury or negligence?

12 Personal history

What type of accommodation does the client have?
Is there any uncertainty about the accommodation?
Who does the client live with?
Are there any problems at home?
Does the client work/unemployed/go to college or university/school?
What does the client do in their leisure time?
How does the client describe their personality?
Any changes to personality?
Are there any relationship or sexual problems?
How does the client describe their relationships?
Do they have any children? What are their ages? Any problems?

13 Family history

Parents: relationship, changes, work.
Siblings: relationship, changes, work.
Is there a family psychiatric history?
Are there any inherited disorders in the family?

14 Developmental history

Childhood and adolescence: Were there any important events? What was the atmosphere like at home? How did they get on with others? Were they abused? Were they happy?

Schooling and education: Was their schooling normal? Were there any long absences? How did they get on with their teachers and peers? How well did they do at school? What further education have they had? How did they do?

Work: What have they done in terms of work since leaving school? Any significant future plans?

THREE SYSTEMS AND FIVE ASPECTS ANALYSIS IN ASSESSMENT

The three systems analysis approach, originating in the 1960s (Hugdahl, 1981; Lang, 1968), is a useful framework for understanding and assessing clients' emotions within an assessment process in terms of three linked systems (Grant et al., 2004a; Hawton et al., 1989). These are:

Behavioural – what does the person do?
Cognitive – what thoughts and images occur and how is information processed?
Physiological – what physical sensations or reactions occur?

The above behavioural, cognitive and physiological systems together make up an emotional experience. This today seems a simple or even simplistic idea, but was revolutionary when it was first presented and developed. It is still important for the assessment of individual emotion and explaining emotions within an individual formulation.

In the three systems model, all the systems relate to each other. Cognitive theories emphasise that environmental triggers – be they external or internal to the individual – will activate an emotional response if they are significantly meaningful for the individual. Once the three systems are activated, how an emotionally distressed person behaves will be influenced by what they are thinking and feeling physiologically and vice versa. For example, a person who is socially anxious may experience the emotion of shame due to their excessive sweating in public, with a related range of thoughts and images, avoidance and safety behaviours and inhibited social behaviours, as well as physiological symptoms such as palpitations and sweating. This is demonstrated in Figure 2.3 overleaf.

An important point of this model is that it can help therapists and clients to understand different response patterns to stressors or activating events. For example, one person might appear more 'cognitive' than another in terms of self-reported cognitions or distressing images whilst in others the physiological system might be emphasised more. People with generalised anxiety often talk about worry, whilst people with a panic problem pay particular attention to the physical symptoms that they fear. The three systems model also helps to explain the phenomena known as synchrony, where all the three systems change together, and desynchrony whereby a client might improve in one or more of the systems but more slowly or not at all in the others (Hodgson and Rachman, 1974).

An understanding of these processes in assessment is crucial for formulation and conceptualising the client's problems. They are important as they can indicate or emphasise the reasons why someone might have improved in one area or system but not in another. Additional therapeutic strategies can be used to target the unresolved system in order to bring about overall change in the emotive state.

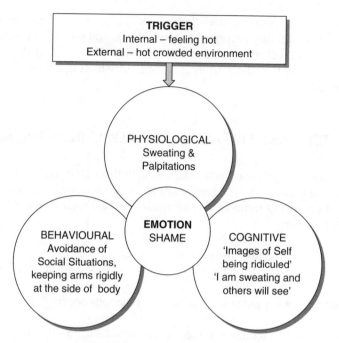

Figure 2.3   Three systems and five aspects analysis in assessment

THE FIVE ASPECTS MODEL

The five aspects model is an uncomplicated framework that is useful within both assessment and formulation (Greenberger and Padesky, 1995). It is valuable at the proximal level of assessment with regard to specific episodes of a problem. The example below of 'Ewan's' panic problem demonstrates this, illustrating the situational specific information and episodic vicious circle formulation for him using an adapted five aspect framework. Ewan was referred following repeated panic at work which on one occasion had led to him making an excuse and leaving an important meeting. When seen for therapy he was continuously anxious that he would panic at work and was panicking daily, but remained at work with extreme effort.

By assessing single episodes of panic it was possible to assess all the environmental triggers for panic and resultant cognitive, emotional, behavioural and physical responses.

STANDARDISED CLINICAL INTERVIEWS

Emerging from the context of a scientist-practitioner approach to therapy, case formulations arose in part as an alternative to traditional psychiatric diagnoses. However, there is, in our view, no inherent reason why diagnosis and case formulation should be viewed or remain as mutually exclusive (Scott and Sembi, 2006). The assessment process in cognitive behavioural psychotherapy typically follows a

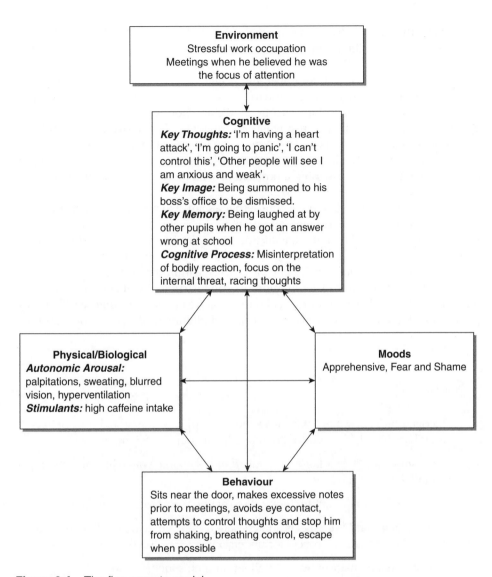

Figure 2.4   The five aspects model

semi-structured approach and for most therapists will reflect the way they were taught as trainees. What this means is that there is probably a variation in both assessment processes and content within the cognitive behavioural practice field. The range and extent of this variation is unclear, as to our knowledge no research has been carried out in this area of therapists' practice. Scott and Sembi (2006) have suggested that the lack of standardisation of assessment practice may lead to diagnostic inaccuracy. These authors thus recommended that the first session should include a structured interview, followed by standardised assessment in the middle and end of therapy.

We agree that standardised interviews, such as the Structured Clinical Interview for Depression (SCID) (Zimmerman and Mattia, 1999) and the Anxiety Disorders Interview Schedule for *DSM-IV* (ADIS-IV) (Brown et al., 1994), are necessary where the accuracy of a diagnosis is an imperative – such as in the context of psychological reports for legal reporting, within a research study or in medical practice with the pre-scriptions of pharmacological interventions. We are, however, less convinced of their value within routine daily practice when an experienced cognitive behavioural psy-chotherapist is assessing a client. However, it can be argued that practice with a stan-dardised interview schedule can be extremely valuable to a less experienced therapist, or where the therapist is assessing a problem of which they have little or no previous experience (Antony and Barlow, 2002).

In all cases, we suggest that in selecting either a semi-structured diagnostic interview or outcome assessment instrument, attention must be paid to its psychometric proper-ties in terms of its validity and reliability, degree of structure (and how this might fit with the needs of the client), breadth of diagnostic coverage and the utility of the instrument in terms of its viability and ease of use within the particular clinical envi-ronment. It also needs to be kept in mind that no instrument will best fit the require-ment of all clients, therapists or clinical settings so we also suggest that specific needs, priorities and resources also need to be considered (Summerfeldt and Antony, 2002).

Summary

1   Ideographic assessment based on the principles of functional and behav-ioural analysis is the core of cognitive behavioural assessment.

2   Assessment and formulation are linked in a dynamic way with each having an influence on the other.

3   Key areas of assessment include cross-sectional and longitudinal elements.

4   Three systems and five aspects analyses are useful frameworks within the con-text of the assessment process for understanding cross-sectional problems.

5   Assessment and measurement of client problems includes both ideographic and nomothetic approaches.

Activities

1   Consider the way that you utilise diagnosis in therapy and its usefulness.

2   Examine the balance between ideographic and nomothetic approaches in your practice.

3   Consider how you might make the best use of five aspect analysis within the assess-ment process.

Further reading

Antony, M. and Barlow, D.H. (2002) *Handbook of Assessment and Treatment Planning for Psychological Disorders*. New York: Guildford Press.
This edited text provides an authoritative review of assessment strategies and tools.

Grant, A., Mills, J., Mulhern, R. and Short, N. (2004) *Cognitive Behavioural Therapy in Mental Health Care*. London: SAGE Publications Ltd.
An excellent introductory text that covers basic processes and procedures within cognitive behavioural psychotherapy and a range of problem areas.

Process and related issues in cognitive behavioural assessment

3

Michael Townend and Alec Grant

Learning objectives

After reading this chapter and completing the activities at the end of it you should be able to:

1 Understand the theoretical underpinning of cognitive behavioural assessment.

2 Apply to practice the important processes within cognitive behavioural assessment.

3 Appreciate the role of the therapeutic relationship, power and emotions in the assessment process.

4 Understand the factors that might make someone more likely to respond well to a cognitive behavioural approach and the influence of diversity in cognitive behavioural assessment.

The descriptions of functional analysis and assessment described in the last chapter may sound rather formulaic. However, a skilled interviewer can gently but firmly lead the client through all the above information collection areas whilst enabling her to express her ideas in her own words, using her own language. Skilled interviewers would also ensure that, regardless of the order these stages are dealt with, they are all covered and that they have as clear and detailed a picture of the problems, the person, their history and the interplay between all three, as is needed.

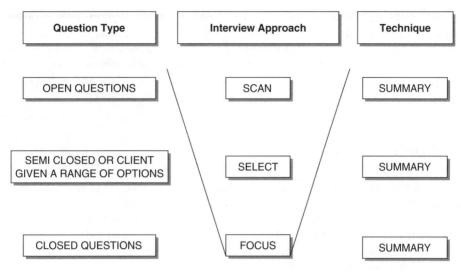

Figure 3.1   Funnelling

FUNNELLING

The behavioural questioning format which is perhaps most helpful in eliciting all this information is known as 'funnelling', or 'scan, select and focus'. Using this approach to interviewing, cognitive behavioural psychotherapists move from the general to the specific questioning and back again as they gather each set of information. This is illustrated in Figure 3.1.

The process is repeated over and over again until sufficient information is gathered to achieve the aims of the assessment. It is important to stress that information does *not* have to be collected in a single assessment session, or through the process of interview. Data gathered through observation, for example of the client in his problem situation, is equally important (Mulhern et al., 2004), as is information from significant others in the client's life.

LANGUAGE

Constructivist psychotherapists would argue that language is what defines meaning for the individual and how society defines the individual (see, for example, Neimeyer and Mahoney, 1999). Whether or not this position is accepted, it remains important for cognitive behavioural psychotherapists to be very specific in their use of language and give an explanation of any technical language (or avoid it altogether) during the assessment process. This allows clients to know precisely what therapists mean and to ensure that anything which might have an ambiguous meaning is clarified.

It is also important that the language used in the psychotherapeutic process does not label the client as a 'walking pathology' or blame them for their difficulties. For example, if you look at most historical and many contemporary cognitive behavioural psychotherapy texts you will see them peppered with words such as 'dysfunctional', 'negative automatic thoughts', 'depressive' and so forth (including in this text to a degree). We believe that it is important that therapists are aware of their use of language in the psychotherapeutic context, and are careful around the meanings that clients might attribute to themselves as a consequent of the words and phrases used during the assessment and formulation process (Grant et al., 2004a).

HANDLING EMOTIONS

It is also important for cognitive behavioural psychotherapists to be aware of and make therapeutic use of the emotional content of their interviews in a constructive and meaningful way. For example identifying affect changes in sessions, often from subtle cues, are used as a prompt to check out how the client is appraising the situation and their emotions (Greenberg, 2007). A number of other strategies are also routinely used by therapists as well, including normalisation and containment.

Normalisation

When people see any therapist they are usually distressed by their experiences or inability to deal with their problems and difficulties themselves. Many clients believe that they are the only ones to have experienced the difficulty, or believe that everyone else can deal with things much better than they can. This can be recognised in cognitive terms as unhelpful thinking processes and content. During assessment and formulation it can be useful for therapists to normalise clients' experiences for them in such a way that they are not minimised or trivialised but, instead, help clients feel that they are not alone with their problems. This in turn can foster a sense of hope that they can be helped to overcome them.

'SAM'

Sam was referred with an eating disorder that involved binge eating. She was particularly distressed each Saturday, as she would have a takeaway followed by some confectionery and a glass of wine on a Friday night with her partner. She considered this to represent a total lack of control, demonstrating her weakness and worthlessness. When this was discussed, in terms of what other people do at the end of the week to wind down, she was able to recognise that some dietary flexibility was a normal part of life. This was further reinforced by asking other people about their Friday night eating habits and similar self-disclosure by the therapist. Recognition of this reduced her distress and reduced the frequency of actual binge eating over her subsequent weekends.

Containment

There are two parts to helping clients contain emotion within the cognitive behavioural psychotherapy assessment and formulation processes. The first part concerns the situation where people who come for therapy become very upset or distressed about their difficulties, particularly when talking about them for the first time or if they concern difficult experiences or trauma. Whilst it is crucial to acknowledge clients' distress, it is important to help people who are expressing strong emotions, of whatever kind, regain sufficient control of them in order to work productively with them.

For many clients it is the very fear of the emotion itself which is maintaining the problem, through meta-cognitive processes (Leahy, 2007; Wells, 1997). They might have a fear of fear in panic or about being depressed in depression. They thus seek to suppress their emotions, rather than experience them to the full and learn that they are not harmful and that they can cope with them. During the initial assessment process, it is usually better in our experience to help the client contain the emotion initially, until it is understood in terms of the overall formulation.

The second part of containment concerns the therapist's own emotions. The therapeutic process frequently involves working with upsetting experiences, such as child abuse, rape, violence, self-harm and other trauma, or asking about and assessing intimate personal details about people's sexual activities and diversities. A therapist may become upset, embarrassed or distressed by what their client is discussing with them. Showing this to the client, often through inadvertently displayed facial or verbal expression, may evoke shame or embarrassment in the client and inhibit their subsequent openness and truthfulness (Greenberg, 2007).

Even without facial or verbal displays, the client may also become concerned that the therapist is judging them or dislikes them. Equally, the client may feel that the therapist is too fragile to hear the truth, and might therefore withhold important information in order to protect the therapist. In our experience, this can seriously damage the therapeutic relationship, can lead to clients dropping out of therapy or, ultimately, prevent the therapist and therapy from being effective.

We advocate a number of strategies that therapists could utilise to prevent these possibilities. When they recognise strong emotions in themselves it is important to recognise their meanings and triggers and engage it 'in the moment'. Containment can be achieved through immediate self-work, and self-work beyond the session. Throughout, it is important for the therapist to remind themselves of the professional imperative for self-management of emotional responses while at the same time maintaining a focus on the needs of the client. This is difficult to do, but with increased experience becomes easier. However, there are occasions where emotional arousal is so automatic, rapid and unexpected that it overwhelms therapists before they can spot and manage their experience.

It is helpful therefore for therapists to discuss those feelings during clinical supervision sessions, and if the material any particular client is dealing with is too distressing then the ethical action might be to pass the client over to another therapist who does not have the same issues. In such circumstances it would then be appropriate for the therapist to work on these issues themselves either through self-practice and reflection, or with another therapist, to ensure that they do not continue to interfere with therapeutic work (Bennett-Levy et al., 2003; Sinason, 1999; Sutton et al., 2007).

MEASURING THERAPY OUTCOME

Measuring therapy outcome is arguably essential with all clients in order to evaluate the effectiveness of interventions used. It is best to approach the issue of outcome assessment with each client from three different perspectives: idiosyncratic or person-specific measures; standardised symptom measures; and quality of life measures. In each case measurement should take place at the beginning of therapy, mid-point of therapy or where a change in therapeutic strategy is made, at the end of therapy and at 1 month, 3 months and 6 months after the end of therapy during a follow-up phase. The follow-up phase is important in order to monitor progress and provide any assistance with relapse prevention.

Person-specific measures

Person-specific measures include problem and goal ratings. Problem ratings deal with the specific problems the client is expressing. After defining them in a measurable way, the therapist asks the client to rate each one in terms of the amount of discomfort or interference with normal activities the problem causes. End of therapy goal ratings apply to the goals which the therapist and the client negotiate together. These are usually specific, measurable, realistic and within a specified time frame (SMART). In both problem and goal statements the scaling system often used is a nine point scale (0–8).

Other person-centred measures can also be used. These include the frequency of a particular behaviour, such as panic or anger outbursts, or its duration: for example, the length of time spent hand-washing in someone with an obsessive compulsive disorder. Individualised diaries are usually developed by the therapist for this form of self-monitoring measurement.

Personal distress ratings (in the literature referred to as subjective units of discomfort – SUDS) or belief or conviction ratings using a 0–8 scale (where 0 = no distress/no belief and 8 = worst level of distress possible/complete conviction) are also a useful, minimally intrusive and common feature of assessment, formulation and measurement practice (Anthony and Barlow, 2002; Hawton et al., 1989).

Standardised symptom measures

Standard symptom measures have been specifically developed and designed to measure the symptoms of a problem, syndrome or concept, such as depression, self-esteem, hopelessness, shame, panic or anxiety. There are now thousands of such measures available for use by the cognitive behavioural psychotherapist, which can be rather overwhelming. It is an important and legal responsibility to check the measure's copyright status before making copies as often these need to be purchased from the copyright holders or publishing company. Commonly used measures include the Beck Depression Inventory (for depression) (Beck, 1996), Beck Anxiety Inventory (for anxiety) (Beck and Steer, 1990), Fear Questionnaire (for phobic avoidance and dysphoria) (Marks and Mathews, 1979), Yale Brown Obsessive Compulsive Scale (for Obsessive Compulsive Disorder) (Goodman et al., 1989) and the Impact of Events Scale (for Post-traumatic Stress Disorder) (Weiss and Marmar, 1997). (The interested reader may wish to further consult Anthony and Barlow (2002) for a review of contemporary scales.)

Quality of life measures

Quality of life measures are also an important part of the outcome measurement process because they evaluate improvements in the overall functioning of the individual. One of the most commonly used scales and one that can be routinely used because of its ease of use in routine practice is the Work and Social Adjustment Scale (Mundt et al., 2002). This measures the global impact of the problem on the person's life over the following five areas: work; home management; social activity; private leisure activity; family and relationships.

The use of detailed questionnaires and measures

Using detailed questionnaires and measures is often helpful in the extended assessment process, and squares with the role of the cognitive behavioural psychotherapist as 'scientist-practitioner'. However, it may be that the perception of the need for precision from the outset of therapy relates somewhat more to the core profession of the cognitive behavioural therapist gathering the information (Sanders and Wills, 2005). So, for example, according to these authors, psychiatrists and psychologists may be keener to use structured interviews and standardised measures early, based on the perceived need to gather precise current data. In contrast, those with a core background in counselling or psychotherapy may be more interested in qualitative issues, emerging from the historical and interpersonal story unfolding from the dialogue with clients, prior to using questionnaires.

The use of standardised measures may arguably be better used a little later after the first session, when a good enough therapeutic bond has been developed between client and therapist. Some therapists do however advocate weekly completion of questionnaires, even within or after the first assessment session, but care does have to be taken as client resistance to completing questionnaires can become seen in a 'pathologising' way. Beck (1995: 30), for example, advises that 'If the patient resists filling out forms, the therapist adds this problem to the agenda so that he can help her identify and evaluate her automatic thoughts about completing forms'. Equally, there may well be a moral imperative to encouraging clients to complete standardised questionnaires as part of the assessment process to identifying risk. Persons (1989), for example, argues that, for depressed clients, assessment of suicidal intent is vital – item 9 on the BDI II being important here, as well as other scales and items contained within them that assess levels of risk.

However, the 'demand characteristics' of measurement may well influence the client's emerging story, so caution should be exercised. Sanders and Wills (2005) argue that long and detailed questionnaires might prove off-putting to some individuals, especially to those who have literacy difficulties. In addition, an over-reliance on outcome measures *only* in making assumptions about problem level and goal achievement by clients is problematic (Townend and Grant, 2006). Clients may complete these measures in such a way as to 'fake good' to please their therapist in the spirit of impression management (Goffman, 1969). Equally, patients may 'fake bad' for a number of reasons, including the wish to extend the duration of the therapeutic relationship. This may account for the fact that not all writers of cognitive behavioural therapy value the use of quantitative measurement in their work (see, for example, Nezu and DelliCarpinni, 1998). Qualitative measures may be used in acknowledgement of these issues, such as direct observation of clients in problem and goal scenarios. However, direct observation is not without methodological problems since the presence of the therapist may constitute a safety signal which reassures the patient, thus contributing to a reduction in their anxiety (Short et al., 2004).

ASSESSMENT OF SUITABILITY FOR COGNITIVE BEHAVIOURAL PSYCHOTHERAPY

The rapid development of cognitive behavioural psychotherapy has facilitated the adaptation of the cognitive behavioural approach to a wide range of clinical problems (Sanders and Wills, 2005). This is not to say that the indiscriminate application of cognitive behavioural psychotherapy is supported or is in any way justifiable. In all cases a decision has to be made as to the suitability of the approach for the client, given their current presentation, motivation and situation.

Addressing the question of suitability is important for a number of reasons. First, if the therapy is offered when it is not indicated then the chances of a successful outcome for the client is reduced and the therapist might be acting in an unethical way. It might also be unethical on the grounds that an appropriate intervention may have further negative effects on the client and the reputation of the therapeutic approach as a whole. Offering therapy to clients in inappropriate circumstances also denies therapy to other clients who might benefit to a much greater degree or through more rapid improvement.

There are thus clinical, ethical and economic reasons for giving careful consideration to the issue of suitability and this is therefore a question that ought to be revisited time and again throughout the therapeutic processes, but particularly during the assessment and formulation phases and during clinical supervision. This raises the question of what criteria or what frameworks should be used to make such important decisions.

Behaviour therapists have historically used the following set of questions to help guide their decisions:

- Are the presenting problems observable?
- Are the problems current?
- Are the problems predictable?
- Can clear behavioural goals be agreed between therapist and client?
- Does the client understand, and is she able to consent and agree to therapy?
- Are any contra indications for behaviour therapy present?

These questions well serve the needs of behaviourally orientated therapists who, for example, focus on clients with anxiety problems such as phobic and obsessive compulsive difficulties. However, they don't tend to work as well when applied to the wider range of clients who can now be helped with cognitive behavioural psychotherapy. For example, in terms of the first question, not all problems that clients suffer are observable; worry is not observable and neither are obsessional thoughts, but both are now routinely addressed.

The question of the problem being current is also problematic: therapy for trauma using reliving and rescripting focuses on 'recapturing' the original traumatic incident (Ehlers and Clark, 2000). Schema therapy and compassionate focused therapy also use approaches that, while grounded in the 'here and now', draw heavily on past experiences (Gilbert, 2005; Young, 1990; Young et al., 2003).

The third question concerning the predictability of the problem is also a tricky one if applied to cognitive behavioural psychotherapy in an inflexible way. Many client problems encountered by cognitive behavioural psychotherapists are predictable if appropriate theory is considered, but not all problems are predictable all of the time. On some occasions, working with the client on making the problems more predictable, and developing coping strategies for unpredictability, are useful therapy goals.

The fourth question of clear behavioural goals is partly relevant to a certain degree, as goals are important. However, goals might not necessarily be behavioural, relating more to cognitive-affective components such as reducing the distress from delusional beliefs.

The fifth question of consent and agreement is still very much relevant, whilst the sixth – absence of contra-indications – has necessarily changed in the context of developments taking place over the last 20 or 30 years. In the past, individuals with psychosis, personality disorders, learning disabilities, substance misuse or severe depression would routinely have been excluded from therapy. Now specific approaches have been developed to help people with these difficulties (Tarrier, 2006).

Given the above criticisms of behavioural criteria, further frameworks have been developed to help the cognitive behavioural psychotherapist with suitability decisions. It has been suggested (Sanders and Wills, 2005) that the criteria outlined in the list below (which we have adapted and developed further) are particularly useful for inexperienced and beginning therapists. We would extend this recommendation to experienced therapists as they too must remain mindful of these criteria and refer back to them from time to time. This is recommended in order to prevent 'therapeutic drift'. This phenomenon refers to the therapist slowing moving away from accepted practice without realising that this has in fact occurred. We would always recommend that decisions about suitability are contextualised in team meetings, when appropriate, and are routinely considered in clinical supervision.

Acceptability of the model/approach to therapy

The client

- Can recognise automatic thoughts or images
- Can recognise and distinguish changes in affect or emotions
- Can recognise helpful and unhelpful behaviour for self or on others
- The approach and formulation make sense to the client

Therapeutic relationship

The client

- Can, or has the potential to, form a therapeutic relationship
- Is able to tolerate the therapeutic process
- Her coping strategies such as intellectualising or avoidance are not so extreme or excessive that they would impede engagement in therapy

Individual and attitudinal factors

The client

- Has some optimism regarding therapy
- Accepts both responsibility and the need for change
- Is willing to carry out homework assignments

- Is able to make the time for therapy sessions and homework assignments
- Is able to concentrate and focus on an agreed agenda
- Has problems which are not too severe or chronic
- Is able to contribute to establishing goals and a problem list

Physical

The client

- Has no medical contra-indications to therapy or underlying medical problems (see below)

Ethical

- Therapy won't lead to harm coming to the client or to another person
- The client is able to give informed consent (or others are able to do so legally for the client)

Economic

- Therapy is justified on clinical grounds in order that others are not denied a service
- The private client is able to afford the fees
- The client can afford the sundry costs of therapy such as exposure materials or travel

Contextual

- The client is not in the middle of an unrelated crisis
- The type of problem can be contained or worked with within the specific setting proposed

PHYSICAL PROBLEMS

An important issue with regards to decisions as to suitability for cognitive behavioural psychotherapy is to ensure that the problem is not due to underlying physical problems or being maintained at least in part by such problems. This is because certain physical and psychological conditions inhibit psychotherapeutic approaches and some physical problems present as psychological difficulties. In such circumstances, not only would the psychotherapeutic approach not be helpful, but the underlying physical problem might be quite serious and need immediate medical treatment. For example, hyperthyroidism (an overactive thyroid gland) is often mistaken for anxiety, whilst hypothyroidism (underactive thyroid) can be mistaken for depression. Both these problems are fairly common, serious and need medical assessment.

Certain medications can also inhibit the effects of the therapy. For example, benzodiazepines such as diazepam can prevent anxiety reduction when exposure approaches are being used in phobic or obsessive compulsive problems, thus preventing progress being made. An effect called 'state dependent learning' may also be observed, where the effects of psychotherapeutic work are only apparent when the client is taking drugs or alcohol. In the case of sedative drugs (benzodiazepines) a commitment to gradual withdrawal, under medical supervision, is often needed before psychotherapeutic work can commence (Marks, 1987).

The effects of stimulants such as caffeine is something that anyone engaged in psychotherapeutic work must be aware of and routinely assess, particularly in people who are seeking help with an anxiety problem. Caffeine occurs in coffee, tea, coca-cola, some analgesic preparations and some cold remedies. Usual suggestions are that if a client is consuming more than 500mg of caffeine daily, they might need to reduce the amounts. This should, however, be done gradually as one of the common symptoms of caffeine withdrawal is a severe headache.

Table 3.1 gives some of the biological causes that can mimic anxiety or depression (differential diagnosis).

Table 3.1   The physical causes that mimic anxiety and depression

Physical problem	Mimicked psychological problem	Symptoms	Differentiating characteristics
Hyperthyroidism	Anxiety	Tachycardia, diarrhoea, sweating, weight loss, irritability.	Preferences for cold weather; weight loss despite increased appetite; Bulging eyes (some cases).
Hypothyroidism	Depression	Lethargy with reduced energy levels.	Difficult to identify through observation or interview. Blood test needed before therapy for depression should commence; little daily variability in mood or energy levels.
Excessive caffeine	Anxiety and/or panic	Irritability, headaches, tachycardia, tremor, palpitations, insomnia.	Symptoms reduce or are eliminated on caffeine reduction.
Hypoglycaemia	Anxiety	Disturbed out of character behaviour, tremor, periods of unexplained fatigue.	Specific periodic anxiety, especially when having not eaten.
Hyperventilation	Anxiety and/or panic	Most anxiety symptoms but with tingling and dizziness particularly prominent.	Dizziness; ringing in the ears.

DIVERSITY IN ASSESSMENT

It has been acknowledged in principle that those who provide counselling or support should respect differences and the diversity inherent within any society or culture.(Cowie and Rivers, 2000: 3)

What this quotation means is that the therapist's own personal material and worries need to remain firmly outside of the interaction, such as ensuring that any prejudices the therapist may hold do not intrude into the relationship. These prejudices might include, for example, disapproval of attempted suicide or abortion. Another problem might be when the client's issues are too close to home for the therapist. For example, if the therapist has recently experienced bereavement, it may be too painful for them to work with a client suffering from the same problem. It might also be difficult for some therapists to work with people with particular religious or other personally relevant beliefs.

Cognitive behavioural approaches have been criticised for adopting and promoting culturally insensitive eurocentric, white and middle-class positions in regard to both research and practice (see, for example, Hoshmand, 2006). It is our view that an understanding of diversity and related issues are essential prerequisites to effective therapy (LaTaillade, 2006; Martell et al., 2004). Within the assessment process it is important to be able to assess protective factors and coping strategies (for example, positive self and self-others core beliefs, and assertive challenging of discrimination). Such strengths, even in the face of continued stress, can promote positive therapeutic outcomes.

Other important protective factors might include forms of family, community or other social support, spiritual or religious beliefs and a strong sense of ethical identity commitment to a particular sexual orientation, such as being gay or lesbian (Padesky, 1989). These all provide an individual with resources for challenging negative messages and stereotypes (LaTaillade, 2006).

Clients are likely to carry with them any individual experiences of therapy of racism or other discriminatory behaviours that might be projected onto them by therapists, knowingly or unknowingly (Bernard and Goodyear, 2004).

It is our view that therapists must be prepared to work in such a way that their own beliefs and experiences do not knowingly or unwittingly interfere with their therapeutic work, which should be adapted to the individual diversity needs of the client. To be able to work in a way that avoids discrimination is of course far easier to say than do. Evidence from work on social cognition suggests that to be human is to be biased and therefore prejudiced in one way or another (Augoustinos et al., 2006). This point is made not in the spirit of condoning or agreeing with sexism, ageism, racism or any other 'isms', but to simply state that therapists are not discrimination-immune.

We have also found it useful, and most of the time essential, to consult with our clients, therapists, community and spiritual leaders and read about the experiences of others who have been subject to discrimination in order to know how to adapt our therapeutic work with particular clients or client groups. Equally, we have found it essential to challenge discriminatory beliefs in ourselves and continually revisit this issue by asking ourselves:

1　Do I manifest an ideology that promotes a biased attitude on the grounds of age, culture, race, religion or sexuality?
2　How have or might I have internalised or developed an attitude or behaviours that reflect bias or prejudice in some way?
3　What past or recent experiences or events including media portrayals might have influenced me and biased me?

At the level of organisational social cognition and related identity construction (Augoustinos et al., 2006), we have also noted recently that 'political correctness' may make it difficult for therapists, experienced or otherwise, to admit to some form of bias through a fear of criticism or professional censure. Clearly, some therapists are more comfortable than others with discussions concerning diversity, discrimination and bias. In our view, it is far better to acknowledge and work with biased therapist beliefs which might inhibit therapeutic work, either in clinical supervision or through other developmental processes, rather than to simply ignore them or pretend that they do not exist. This may be difficult for some therapists; it might be difficult to acknowledge in some contexts but we maintain that it is an essential professional obligation and one worth striving to achieve.

THERAPEUTIC RELATIONSHIPS IN ASSESSMENT

The therapeutic relationship is of as much central importance to cognitive behavioural psychotherapy as it is within other forms of counselling and psychotherapy (Gilbert and Leahy, 2007; Lambert and Barley, 2002; Mahoney, 2003). Relationship factors within cognitive behavioural texts, research and practice are sometimes, in our view erroneously, referred to as 'non-specific factors' in therapy (also known as common factors). Factors such as the quality of the therapeutic relationship, the therapeutic alliance, empathy, warmth, genuineness, conditional and unconditional regard, are very specific and crucial to the effectiveness of therapy.

Lambert and Barley (2002), in summarising the contribution of factors based on decades of research and years of reviewing research studies on psychotherapeutic outcomes, argue that 30 per cent of improvement can be attributed to common factors, 15 per cent to expectancy (placebo effect), 40 per cent to extratherapeutic change (improvements that would occur without formal professional therapy but might include self-help) and 15 per cent to specific therapeutic techniques.

The therapeutic relationship starts to build and develop from the very first moment the therapist meets the client. How the therapist appears to the client and even the words the therapist uses have a direct effect on how the therapist is perceived and thus on how the person will relate to them initially and how the relationship will develop over time.

Cognitive behavioural therapists, responding flexibly to their client's interpersonal style (Schaap et al., 1993), embrace the idea that the better the relationship the more likely the client is to share openly and honestly with their therapist, allow trust to develop and agreement on goals, tasks and bonds (Bordin, 1979). Thus, the relationship underpins all cognitive behavioural psychotherapeutic techniques and strategies and is the foundation on which the approach is based.

Gilbert and Leahy (2007) importantly draw our attention to four key aspects of the therapeutic relationship within cognitive behavioural psychotherapy:

1   The early stages of relationship development and the forming of a safe place for the client.
2   The conceptualisation and handling of problems in the therapeutic relationship, such as maintenance of boundaries, working to prevent or repair alliance ruptures.

3   Attunement to the effect that the therapeutic process is having on the therapist herself and how this influences the work with the client and the overall conceptualisation.
4   Attention to the ending of the therapeutic relationship.

In light of the above, at this stage in the narrative, it may be helpful to consider the therapeutic relationship from the perspective of therapist variables and characteristics and then process issues occurring between client and therapist. Goldstein and Myers (1988) identified several therapist variables which, they argue, help facilitate change. These are discussed below, alongside related issues from the cognitive behavioural psychotherapy therapeutic relationship literature.

EXPERTISE IN ASSESSMENT

There are various ways in which cognitive behavioural psychotherapists can enhance their expertise. From perspectives including social influence theory (Gilbert and Leahy, 2007; Schaap et al., 1993), these include ensuring appropriate environments for working with clients. Therapists who achieve this are able to demonstrate the status they hold within the employing organisation and, within health and social care environments at least, this supports the impression that the higher the status the more expert the individual.

It has also been suggested that displaying appropriate books and certificates can also enhance the client's perception of expertise. The amount of self-confidence conveyed by the therapist, through their verbal and non-verbal communication, is also important. A firm handshake, positive eye contact and clear introductions can convey a great deal of expertise with very little effort. We would argue that although these may seem insignificant issues they are extremely important. Expertise can also be enhanced by predicting the symptoms or experiences or responses of the client, and explaining the ways in which other clients with similar problems have been successfully helped or what hindered their recovery (Schaap et al., 1993).

CREDIBILITY IN ASSESSMENT

Credibility is perceived by the client through the therapist's ability to be knowledgeable about what is happening to him/her, and also by the therapist's motivation to impart knowledge and information. See Table 3.2 for four components which enhance credibility.

MOTIVATION, TRANSPARENCY AND PSYCHO EDUCATION

The therapist as a source of valued information is an important notion within an ideographic approach to assessment and formulation. Motivations and intentions of the therapist in this regard can also be linked to the concept of transparency. Within the practice of cognitive behavioural psychotherapy, it is important that full explanations are given regarding what is being done or considered during the therapeutic process,

Table 3.2   Four components which enhance credibility

1 The level of expertise demonstrated by the therapist.
2 The reliability of the therapist as a source of information, including qualities such as being
   dependable, behaving in a predictable way and remaining consistent throughout the therapeutic
   relationship.
3 The therapist's motivation and intentions, which must be demonstrated as always having the client's
   interests at the forefront of the relationship and having no other inappropriate motivations.
4 The dynamism or charisma of the therapist, which can be defined as attention to detail, working to
   instill confidence and optimism and being proactive when dealing with the client or their issues.

and the rationale for the way they are being done. This demonstrates to the client both the therapeutic principles and reasoning behind each of the therapist's actions and ethical decisions in practice.

For example, it is often the case that behavioural experiments are woven into the assessment and formulation processes (Bennett-Levy et al., 2004; Grant et al., 2004b). These are incorporated to either gather further assessment information or to demonstrate, illustrate and test out various aspects of the formulation. It would not normally be appropriate to launch into these without an open discussion of, and preparation for, the experiment and check out that there are no contraindications to what is being discussed and negotiated (Bennett-Levy et a., 2004; Grant et al., 2004b). This transparent way of using experimentation is linked to the notion of cognitive behavioural psychotherapists as working collaboratively and empirically with their clients.

COLLABORATIVE EMPIRICISM

Beck et al. (1979) used the term collaborative empiricism to signify therapists' work with clients based on transparent agendas and partnership relationships. Cognitive behavioural therapists are also empiricists in that, with their clients, they are in effect testing out the realities of what is and is not real or factual from clients' perspectives. This also means that the therapeutic relationship itself can often be a topic of analysis and discussion, with no fear that honesty from the client will distress the therapist.

The therapist must be able to discuss with the person any factors within the relationship which may be blocking progress, such as not carrying out homework tasks that they have agreed in a previous therapy session. Thus a difficult line frequently has to be walked between being non-judgemental, with support accorded to the client in achieving their desired outcomes, and open and honest exploratory feedback. The therapist should not aim to blame the client for perceived failures or lack of co-operation, but instead seek a mutual understanding of the meaning of, for example, homework non-completion (Leahy, 2001). In guided discovery terms (Padesky, 1993), the therapist explores the possible significance of this in the client's life and social relationships outside of therapy and in the therapeutic relationship itself.

Within the ongoing assessment and formulation process, the above is simply one example of how the cognitive behavioural therapeutic relationship can also be seen as a social laboratory where different ways of relating to others can be experimented with, tested out and rehearsed with the therapist.

WARMTH AND EMPATHY

Warmth

Communicating relational warmth unconditionally and with deep regard for the client responds to her right as a human being to be treated empathically and appropriately in relation to making decisions about her own life (Gilbert, 2007; Greenberg, 2007). This provides a more secure foundation for cognitive behavioural practice at the level of existential ethics (Buber, 1958). In addition to ethical considerations, demonstrating warmth and empathy facilitates the client to feel free to talk about themselves in an open and honest manner, without fear of rejection from the therapist.

According to Gilbert (2007), writing from an evolutionary and compassion perspective, the key element of warmth is that it provides a stimuli that is coded as safe which then activates innate soothing systems.

Cognitive behavioural psychotherapists can learn and need to display warmth in a number of different ways. Warmth can be demonstrated through both non-verbal and verbal forms of communication, such as shaking hands with perhaps a slightly longer hold than would be the case for a more general handshake. Some therapists would also shake hands with one hand and also touch the client's lower arm at the same time or shake hands using a double handshake. Such a willingness to make physical contact signals acceptance, but care also needs to be taken, depending on the respective genders of the client and therapist and the client's psychological difficulties.

Other non-verbal means of communicating warmth are maintaining eye contact when the client is speaking, sitting with the body orientated towards the client, and mirroring their posture (whilst not having the chair directly facing them as most people would find this too threatening) and, where appropriate, revealing facets of self to the person which demonstrate therapists' humanity and similarity to the client.

Warmth can also be conveyed in the use of appropriate humour, and some cognitive behavioural psychotherapists develop a style of working with their clients that includes gentle and humorous teasing. This does require great skill and can only be used within the context of an already established therapeutic relationship, but is valuable to lighten the mood in a therapy session. It can also, when used appropriately, demonstrate a deep and caring understanding of the client and their difficulties.

Capella and Street (1985) suggest that smooth and fluid speech patterns, in a voice which is not heavily accented, and which is neither too loud nor too soft, also has a positive effect on how clients relate to therapists. All of these various actions send a message to the client that the therapist is a warm and humane individual who is on their side and wishes to support and help them.

Empathy

Cognitive behavioural psychotherapists consider empathy to be an important part of the therapeutic process in demonstrating understanding at the emotive level for the client and acknowledgement of their distress (Gilbert and Leahy, 2007; Thwaites and Bennett-Levy, 2007). Empathy, according to a relatively recent meta-analysis, can account for between 7 and 10 per cent of the variance in therapeutic outcome (Bohart et al., 2002).

Therapists who are empathic help clients to notice their own emotions and habitual behaviour patterns and help them to change those when they are unhelpful. Attunement to the client experience also helps therapists more fully appreciate their clients' emotions, appraisals, goals and which therapeutic strategies might be most useful for them (Greenberg, 2007).

There are several definitions of empathy which are worth consideration within the context of the therapeutic process. One of the earliest was the concept of 'einfuhlung' or 'feeling into', which was proposed by Lipps in 1903 (cited in Preston and de Waal, 2002). The concept centred on the notion that we can feel into and thus somehow experience the emotional life of another person and thus more fully understand them.

Later, Rogers defined empathy as:

(Perceiving) the internal frame of reference of another with accuracy and with the emotional components and meanings which pertain thereto as if one were the person, but without ever losing the 'as if' condition. Thus, it means to sense the hurt or the pleasure of another as he senses it and to perceive the causes thereof as he perceives them, but without ever losing the recognition that it is as if I were hurt or pleased or so forth. (Rogers, 1959: 210–11)

Recent research suggests that empathy may be a generalised proprioceptive phenomenon that functions and emerges from many different areas of the brain and allows us to transform what we see into the experience of what it would be like to be there in that moment. Gilbert (2007), drawing on research from neuroscience, suggests that:

Empathy involves a particular capacity to be emotionally resonant with the other, which may depend on mirror neurones. We are then able to process and think about these feelings that have been stimulated within us. So empathy involves both this emotional communication and abilities to think about our emotions. (Gilbert, 2007: 131)

What the above ideas suggest is that therapeutic relationships which are strong on empathy might have a direct impact on processing centres in the brain. If handled appropriately, empathy can be utilised by the skilled cognitive behavioural psychotherapist to create the safe environment needed for therapeutic work using Socratic dialogic approaches. In turn, this helps the client to explore and uncover meanings and engage in new learning through behavioural experiments and other strategies of change.

It is also argued that empathy helps the client to begin to regulate their own affect, through self-soothing, within the context of the therapeutic relationship. This enables the client to become more empathic to themselves, more willing to engage in self-exploration and take goal-directed risks (Greenberg, 2007).

Demonstrating empathy

The ability to be empathic can be learned (Burns and Auerbach, 1996) and the experience understood in a therapeutic and clinical supervision context (Waddington, 2002). In order to be empathic it is important for therapists to be able to recognise and feel both what is said and also what is not said or avoided. It is also about going beyond simple ideas of active listening, and one's own mind and own responses to the situation or event, to be there in that moment with the client, see and feel things as they do and then convey this to them.

When working empathically, cognitive behavioural psychotherapists do need to take care to attend to their own verbal and non-verbal communication. Clients are often hyperaware of the responses of others (including therapists), so these do need to be congruent with and appropriate with the empathy that the therapist is trying to convey.

With respect to verbal aspects of Socratic communication, for example, therapists should ensure that their voice tones rise towards the end of statements to indicate a constant exploratory, tentative and questioning style. This also ensures that the client has the opportunity to refute what they are saying which is important because, in spite of what many therapists believe, their empathic responses may often be incorrect (Burns and Aeurbach, 1996) and clients need the opportunity to say when therapists are off the mark. Such feedback is important as it may lead to further assessment or a revised formulation.

It is also important that therapists do not habitually complete sentences for clients, which in some texts is regarded as a way of demonstrating empathy. Although this can be useful at times, it equally carries the danger of being intrusive, or signalling not listening, or demonstrating that the therapist does not really understand the client's perspective (Gilbert, 2007). The real hallmark of empathy is thus when a cognitive behavioural psychotherapist is able to convey that she knows what the client is feeling and what they are going to say, and that in that moment the client deepens his understanding and continues to explore his or her meanings and experiences (Gilbert, 2007).

Thwaites and Bennett-Levy (2007) have also recently developed a potentially very valuable approach to conceptualising empathy in the context of cognitive behavioural psychotherapy, that may help therapists to understand empathy and help educationalists to teach therapists how to become more empathic. They propose a cogent integrated model of therapeutic empathy with four key related aspects: empathic attunement, empathic attitude/stance, empathic communication and empathic knowledge. The model also emphasises self-reflection of the therapist with the development of therapeutic empathy; and describes how the specific contribution of cognitive behavioural knowledge and skills can help therapists understand clients' personal and idiosyncratic experiences.

INTERPERSONAL PROCESSES WITHIN ASSESSMENT AND FORMULATION

When we talk about interpersonal processes, we are referring to those aspects of the therapeutic relationship that occur between two or more people. Within this context there are at least three concepts that are important. These concepts are expectation, power and resistance (Farrington and Telford, 1996; Leahy, 2001; Safran and Muran, 2000; Safran and Segal, 1996).

Expectations

Both the client and the therapist bring expectations into the relationship and the assessment and formulation process. Clients, for example, might have a view of therapists as relatively passive recipients of information whose role is to listen and occasionally give advice. They may also have more or less tacitly held expectations that therapists will somehow miraculously make their lives better or happier simply by talking to them. It sometimes surprises clients in assessment that a key expectation is that they engage in the process of therapy and actively work outside of the sessions to make change happen for themselves, with therapists' help and support.

Equally, novice, and sometimes more experienced, therapists frequently have expectations about how their clients should behave within therapy sessions. Tacitly held, but over-idealised, expectations are that they will be co-operative, willing to enter into a collaborative relationship and won't be influenced by their own defensive thoughts and behaviours. Whilst for some clients these are reasonable expectations, those with more complex difficulties, including those with so-called personality disorders (Beck et al., 1990; Mills et al., 2004a; Young, 1990; Young et al., 2003), frequently 'play out' or enact in therapy sessions many of the unhelpful and self-defeating interpersonal strategies which they employ, more or less unconsciously, in their relationships outside of therapy. The expectations that clients will always do their homework and will agree with strategies put forward by the therapist, understand what is being proposed, or indeed even turn up for every appointment, are all problematic. The unprepared cognitive behavioural therapist in these situations will feel frustrated, whilst the more experienced practitioner will seek to understand the behaviours in terms of the client's cognitive systems and beliefs, and incorporate these into the formulation and therapeutic plan.

These issues make checking out the *theory of therapy* held by both the therapist and client a useful enterprise, to include beliefs about each other within the process (Leahy, 2001, 2007; Miranda and Andersen, 2007; Padesky, 1999; Rudd and Joiner, 1997). To counter the effect that unrealised expectations of both the client and therapist can have in the therapeutic relationship, it is important that mutually held theories of therapy beliefs are fully explored right at the start of the assessment and formulation process.

If the client is not engaged from the start of the work then the outlook for the relationship and goal attainment may be poor. To assist this process, the list below details issues that may usefully be covered as part of the assessment and formulation process to help minimise mismatched expectations. What follows should be explored with the client using unambiguous and appropriate language.

Therapist explaining to client:

1 How the therapist works: this should include the cognitive behavioural model and its basic assumptions.
2 That each session will commence with a review of progress, mood check and agenda setting.
3 That between-session 'homework' is a feature of therapy and that there is a link between attempts at homework and therapeutic outcome.

4 That attendance at therapy sessions is essential.
5 That the client should raise with the therapist any issues of concern, if the therapist does not raise them first.

Therapist asking of client:

1 If they have seen anyone else for the difficulty, how useful they found this and what was/was not achieved?
2 What therapeutic model that person used?
3 What does the client think is going to happen during their time in therapy?
4 What does the client hope to achieve?

Joint exploration:

1 What are the common goals for therapy?
2 How will progress be measured?
3 How will the process for therapeutic tasks be negotiated and agreed?
4 How frequently will sessions take place?
5 How long will the sessions last?
6 Where will the client be seen for therapy sessions?
7 Roughly how many sessions are likely to be required to achieve the goals set?
8 What are the arrangements for contacting each other if either therapist or client needs to cancel and rearrange an appointment?
9 There are some other situational expectations which will sometimes need to be explored, such as fees, or if the therapy work is being carried out in the private sector.

Power

An immense amount of power resides in the understanding of the matrix of information transmission between the cognitive behavioural psychotherapist and their clients. Social influence theory (Milgram, 1983) can provide a theoretical model to understand the power and processes within a therapeutic context and how the therapist chooses to ethically use information within the context of a trust-based therapeutic relationship. This marks the difference between use and abuse of power and the choices the therapist has to make.

The analysis and use of power within cognitive behavioural relationships is based on the idea that therapists are experts who have theoretical knowledge of the sorts of problems clients present with and ways of helping overcome them. This is a very different way of thinking about power than might be advocated by many of the other schools of psychotherapy or counselling who claim no expertise for the client but view them as the total expert for and on themselves. As cognitive behavioural psychotherapists, we would not dispute that obvious fact that the client knows a great deal about how they are thinking, feeling and functioning and their own past experiences. However, it seems to us that they will not normally fully understand the genetic, biological, cognitive, behavioural and affective mechanisms at play in the subjective totality of their experience. They are also not likely to have a developed theory about how their problems came about, or were influenced by their past, the meaning of the various experiences they are having, or what cognitive behavioural strategies might be useful to aid their recovery.

Cognitive behavioural models thus accept the notions of expert and other forms of power-influence within the therapeutic, assessment and formulation processes. It is also one of the aims of the cognitive behavioural approach to gradually transfer power from the therapist as expert to the client. People seek therapy usually for the simple reason that things are not going well for them in some area of their life and they don't quite know what to do about it. They therefore look to the therapist to give them therapy to make them 'better' or help them to cope. This in itself can be a problem for cognitive behavioural psychotherapists, as the whole process is not about making things better for people in the traditional sense of the term. Rather it is about helping the client to:

...take control of his or her own problems and for him or her to manage his/her life in such a way that future problems are dealt with in an adaptive way. (Marshall, 1996: 32)

Strong and Matross (1973), further supported by Farrington and Telford (1996), described five power bases: expert, referent, legitimate, informational and ecological. These have influenced cognitive behavioural practice and teaching on the relationship between the therapeutic relationship and power.

The therapist is often viewed by the client as an expert with very specific professional knowledge and experience which they can use to assist the client. The expert power base is exemplified by the use of educational strategies, as well as explaining and developing formulations with the client and suggestions regarding therapeutic strategies and approaches to coping. The expert power base gives explanations and suggestions 'weight' and therefore makes the client more likely to listen to and react to them with changes in thinking and behaviour, particularly during the early stages of therapy.

The referent power base refers to how much the therapist is seen as someone who the client can relate to, admires and would like to be like. It is influenced by the warmth and empathy of the therapist and by their willingness to self-disclose relevant information about themselves and reveal their humanness and their intrinsic similarity to the client. It is also influenced by the amount of positive feedback (conditional regard) given to the client. Referent power thus relies on the interpersonal and empathic abilities of the cognitive behavioural psychotherapist as discussed earlier.

The legitimate power base refers to the expectation of clients, that their therapists will be able to help them. How well cognitive behavioural psychotherapists match up to this expectation is dependent on how well these expectations were negotiated in the first place. Matching up to such expectations is also dependent on how well the cognitive behavioural psychotherapist manages to involve the client in the therapeutic process.

Legitimate power can also be used productively by offering and discussing the research evidence data behind the decisions that are being made within the assessment and formulation process. This can also be supported by providing 'bibliotherapy', or guided reading, or video, DVD and website references that speak to the problems covered, and the theories and strategies behind what is being done in therapy. Finally, legitimate power can be exercised by offering clients a range of options about possible courses of action, when more than one option is viable.

Informational power refers to a key therapeutic task of simply providing information. Within the therapeutic relationship there is an asynchrony of information. That is to say the therapist has far more knowledge and information than the client about practice matters. In order to enhance the positive use of this power difference, it can be useful to make available the detail and research base of the information that cognitive behavioural psychotherapists use in practice. The consistency of the information, and the clarity and confidence with which explanations about procedures and techniques are given, will all have an influence on how effectively this is used for the benefit of the client within the assessment and formulation process.

Ecological power is the ability of the cognitive behavioural psychotherapist to influence the environment around the client. This might, for instance, include mediating or liaising between other professionals, or with relatives or immediate family members. Ecological power can also be used by helping the client to work with and influence others around them. Within a cognitive behavioural context this might mean learning to be assertive or improve social skills, or simply the development of a personal bill of rights to empower the individual.

Resistance

Another important area that is increasingly being recognised, assessed and formulated by cognitive behavioural psychotherapists is that of resistance within the therapeutic process. Not all cognitive behavioural therapists find the concept of 'resistance' useful, as it conjures up notions of a single-person (the client) rather than relational (client and therapist) psychology. Padesky (2006, personal communication), for instance, prefers to unpack the interpersonal meaning of the therapeutic roadblock or alliance rupture without labelling it as resistance.

Newman (1984) suggested that there were four different ways in which clients demonstrated their resistance to change, with some of these occurring within the assessment and formulation process:

1   Homework or tasks which the client agreed to do are not completed.
2   The client expresses scepticism about changes which have been achieved and attributes the change elsewhere – for example to changes in others or to medication.
3   The client expresses strong emotions towards the therapist, suggesting for example that it is something that the therapist is or is not doing that is negatively affecting the change process.
4   The client/patient avoids engaging in certain activities or answering certain questions within the session itself.

Newman (1984) has helpfully also suggested instead that the best way to respond to a resistance is to treat it as a problem in itself. In other words, to reassess and formulate it in terms of the client's overall difficulties and the context of the therapeutic process. In shifting the terms of the 'resistance' problem more explicitly to a relational picture of ongoing assessment and formulation, there are useful questions deriving from the work of Newman (1984, 2007) and Leahy (2001, 2007) that could be asked. Engagement with the following set of questions might help the therapist in the assessment and formulation of resistance:

1   Where is the site of the resistance (in the client solely, or in the core beliefs, rules and automatic thoughts of the client, or in the core beliefs, rules and automatic thought mismatch between the client and the therapist, or in mismatched expectations/ theories of what therapy is about between them)?
2   What form is the resistance taking?

3 When and with whom is the resistance occurring (in the therapeutic relationship solely, or in both the relationship and 'outside' relationships)?
4 What is the function of the client resistance?
5 How does the form of the resistance match how the person has behaved in the past and fit into the formulation of their current problems?
6 What is it the client is afraid may happen if they go along with the therapist's requests or suggestions?

Hopefully, engaging with the above questions might lead to 'resistance' being discussed, operationalised, recognised for its interpersonal significance, and included in the overall developing formulation of the problem. This may then enable client and therapist to move forward in a meaningful and useful way.

ALLIANCE FRACTURES OR RUPTURES

Another important idea within cognitive behavioural psychotherapy, very similar to the notions of Newman (1984), is that the therapeutic relationship is an important arena for facilitating change. Problems in the therapeutic relationship need to be understood and worked through and it is by attending to this that therapists have an opportunity to engage with, explore and understand the client's unique world of experiences. This new information can then be used to help the client to develop or expand their range of cognitive, affective and interpersonal dialogues and behaviours (Katzow and Safran, 2007).

RECORDING SESSIONS AND ACTIVE WORK BETWEEN SESSIONS

Finally, an import issue of collaboration from the outset of the assessment process, and throughout the course of therapy, is tape recording of each session for the benefit of the client. Salkovskis (2002) argued, on the basis of research into memory, that much of the dialogue in sessions is lost to recall. Encouraging the client to allow audiotaping of sessions, where the client keeps the tape and listens to it afterwards, is a good way to control for this. As well as being useful for relapse prevention (the client amassing an audio record of the complete therapy process), clients can be encouraged to actively reflect on the session while listening to the tape. James Bennett-Levy and his colleagues at the Oxford Cognitive Therapy Centre have developed the following series of post-session reflection questions, which we have also found helpful in our own therapeutic work:

Session reflection questions (To be undertaken in first 24 hours after session, or immediately after listening to session tape)

1 What did you learn about yourself during the session? Did anything become clearer? Or surprise you? What new perspectives did you gain?
2 What are the implications of this learning for the way you (i) do things (ii) view yourself and/or other people (iii) view the future?
3 If the implications are that you will be doing things differently, what difference will this make in your life? How will it impact on the way you feel ... and think about yourself?

4   What difference will that make?
5   What are your first steps towards bringing this new learning into your life? On a
     regular basis?
6   What do you actually intend to do before the next session? What will be an indica-
     tor that you have done this successfully?

Summary

1   The assessment process is designed to establish therapeutic relationships,
     and can also provide further the information from which a formulation can
     be developed.

2   Not everyone is suitable for cognitive behaviour therapy and criteria can be
     applied to identify people who are likely to be helped with the approach.

3   The therapeutic relationship that helps the client to feel safe, with an
     empathic therapist, is the bedrock of cognitive behavioural psychotherapy.

4   The appropriate utilisation of power in the therapeutic relationship is both
     a therapeutic skill and an ethical imperative.

Activities

1   Consider the ways in which your current practice of assessment is structured, problem-
     oriented and collaborative. Are there ways in which you could improve in these areas?
2   Practise recording sessions with your clients and invite them to use the associated
     reflection questions while listening to the audiotapes. Consider the extent to which
     this improves your clinical work.
3   Consider the ways in which your own automatic thoughts, rules for living and core
     beliefs affect your clinical work with your clients.
4   In at least one therapy session reflect on the use of language and its impact on the
     therapeutic relationship and therapy process.

Further reading

Beck, J. (1995) *Cognitive Therapy: Basics and Beyond.* New York and London: The
     Guilford Press.
Chapters 3 and 4 of this book will help the reader immensely in structuring assessment.

Sanders, D. and Wills, F. (2005) *Cognitive Therapy. An Introduction,* 2nd edn. London:
     SAGE Publications Ltd.
Chapter 4 of this excellent text will develop collaborative assessment ideas further for
the reader.

The fundamentals of case formulation

4

Alec Grant and Michael Townend

Learning objectives

After reading this chapter and completing the activities at the end of it you should be able to:

1 Understand and describe the SETB cycle.

2 Explain the function of cognitive behavioural case formulation.

3 Distinguish between generic, problem-specific and idiosyncratic formulation models.

4 Articulate the levels of case formulation and related belief structures.

5 Consider the importance of hope and culturally informed beliefs in formulation development.

6 Understand the relationship between case formulation and Beck's cognitive theory of psychopathology.

7 Evaluate the arguments for the levels of thinking that case formulation should be targeted at.

8 Describe the structure of case formulation in terms of its various components.

The basis for the structure of cognitive case formulation, and for subsequent therapeutic interventions, derives from the cognitive model. This hypothesises that the emotions and behaviour of people are influenced by their *perception* of events rather than by events directly (Beck, 1964; Ellis, 1962). Gathering information around personal meaning-making by both client and therapist constitutes developing a collaborative case formulation, and is by its very nature ongoing and always incomplete. Case formulation has thus been defined as follows:

> A provisional map of a person's presenting problems that describes the territory of the problems and explains the processes that caused and maintained the problems. (Beiling and Kuyken, 2003: 53)

The emerging and ongoing formulation should contain a strong positive and optimistic focus. Padesky (2006b) argues that problems are described using *deconstructive* language, or in the past tense. In contrast, goals are stated *constructively*. This means that the clients' goals should represent their vision of how they would like things to be different in their life. By engaging in this kind of future-oriented dialogue, the therapist strives to role model and inculcate curiosity and hopefulness in the client.

As well as attending to what the client says, the therapist should keep a 'third ear' out for the shape, style as well as the content of the client's narrative. The process of good assessment and formulation building pays as much attention to what is not said as well as that which is made explicit. For example, it can be very instructive to observe what the client tends to talk most about and what is marginalised in her narrative. Marginalised issues are often outside of the awareness of practitioners, but become more accessible as a function of reflective developmental practice and related clinical supervision utilising videotapes of clinical work (Bennett-Levy, 2006; Townend et al., 2002).

THE ARCHITECTURE OF COGNITIVE BEHAVIOURAL CASE FORMULATION

The SETB cycle

The cycle of situation-emotion-thought-behaviour (SETB) is the most familiar and central feature of cognitive behavioural case formulation (Beiling and Kuyken, 2003). This cycle forms the basis for all generic and specific models of case formulation. In keeping with the cognitive model, the assumption behind this cycle is that a client's interpretation of an event, rather than the event itself, leads to emotional distress.

The function of cognitive behavioural case formulation

A case formulation is an individualised theory about a person's problems, based on a more general cognitive behavioural theory (Persons and Davidson, 2001). Specifically, in tandem with a comprehensive assessment of the client, a case formulation marries individual knowledge of problems with knowledge of the intricacies of the cognitive model and with research and theoretical literature related to the difficulties (Needleman, 1999). Its chief function is to help a therapist devise an effective therapy plan, via a credible, systematic and collaboratively developed formulation framework. From this framework, the therapist can understand the client (Beck, 1995) and the client can understand how her problems, and possible solutions to those, hang together (Grant et al., 2004a; Needleman, 1999).

In the development of this framework, the therapist needs to balance the goals of immediacy and comprehensiveness. He or she must efficiently identify what is needed to help the client, and avoid areas that may be intriguing or interesting but which have little direct relevance in helping the client tackle his/her problems (Eells, 1997). Eells argues that the more complex a case formulation the more difficult it may be to demonstrate its reliability and validity. Thus, a balance between complexity and simplicity is an important aim in case formulation construction.

It is important to remember that the theory about a client's difficulties emerging from a case formulation is simply a 'best guess' as to the ways in which underlying cognitions maintain problematic behaviours. From this viewpoint, decisions around amending or discarding elements of the formulation are based on whether emerging interventions seem to help the client achieve his/her therapy goals.

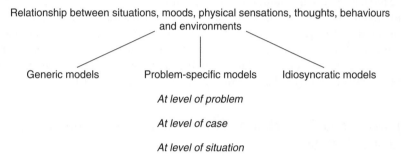

Figure 4.1   Models of case formulation

See also Chapter 6 and Part II of this text.

Generic models   Generic models, such as the 5-aspect model (Greenberger and Padesky, 1995), the SETB model (Beiling and Kuyken, 2003), and the Beckian linear formulation (see model in use in Grant et al., 2004a) can be used in forms of cognitive behavioural therapy when clients present with more diffuse life difficulties rather than clinically significant problems. It is also helpful to use one or more of these in the early stages of therapy, to help socialise the client to the cognitive behavioural approach. Padesky and Mooney (1990), for example, use their 5-aspect model in the early stages of therapy to help clients understand how their difficulties hang together in terms of the relationship between thoughts, physical symptoms, mood, behaviour and environment, irrespective of what their difficulties may be (this can be downloaded from www.padesky.com).

Problem-specific models   From the perspective of evidence-based practice, it has been argued that therapists have an ethical duty to work with clients using problem-specific, or validated models of case formulation for specific problems, where and when those exist (Persons, 1989; Persons and Davidson, 2001). It is beyond the scope of this chapter to explore in-depth, validated models of case formulation and these will be discussed in greater detail in Chapter 6. However, it is important to say at this point in the text that the variety of diagnosis or problem-specific formulation models may well seem bewildering to the newcomer until the structural similarities and common theories between them become clear. Each separate formulation model includes connections between most if not all of the factors listed below, with the distinctions between them existing in the emphasis placed on particular connections (see Chapter 6):

- Situations or events (often referred to in the CBT literature as triggers)
- Thoughts
- Emotions
- Physiological sensations
- Behaviour
- The environmental and interpersonal context of the problem

Idiosyncratic models   One of the potential problems associated with problem-specific models of case formulation is that in clinical practice environments individuals tend to increasingly present for help with multiple problems or, again as in the indication for the use of generic models, with problems for which no validated model exists. Because of this, it is often necessary to work collaboratively with clients in the production of either idiosyncratic formulations or formulations which constitute and function as hybrids between validated and idiosyncratic formulations (see Chapter 6).

'Shoulder to shoulder' sharing of the cognitive behavioural formulation with the client

Arguably because of the shifting contextual nature of cognitive behavioural psychotherapy (Safran and Messer, 1997), and because of the fact that assessment-in-relation-to-formulation is an ongoing process, the development of the case formulation should begin at the first session of therapy and should be increasingly refined until the last session (Beck, 1995). It should be done, ideally, 'shoulder to shoulder' (Padesky, 2003). In clarification of this phrase, Padesky argues that it is a matter of good practice for the cognitive behavioural case formulation to be shared with the client at all stages of its development.

However, care should be taken by the therapist to *pace* the sharing of the formulation development in line with the unique learning speed and learning cycle of his or her client. Bennett-Levy et al. (2004) suggest that clients need time to reflect on developing information, inherent in the case formulation, combined with carefully tailored behavioural experiments emerging from it. In illustration of this point, Kuyken (2006) uses the analogy of the navigator who hinders the driver by showing him the whole road map rather than the specific information relevant to the current driving task. For this reason, 'shoulder to shoulder' collaboration combined with gradualness are essential in the development of the case formulation.

PRACTICALITIES AND PROCESSES OF CASE FORMULATION DEVELOPMENT

Whilst the pace of sharing the formulation is important, how the sharing occurs is also of importance. Development of the formulation is not a simple form filling and didactic exercise, but a guided activity. By guided activity we mean that in our experience the formulation should be developed through the Socratic method of guided discovery, with the client encouraged to write down on a formulation sheet their findings and discoveries as the session (or sessions) progress. Some therapists prefer to use white boards or flip charts as aids in this process, but by doing so a student–teacher relationship can be fostered, rather than a relationship based on collaboration, if care is not taken with the process.

We have also found it useful to enlarge formulation templates (examples of which can be found at the end of this book) from A4 to A3 size to give the client lots of space for recording and making notes. This can then be photocopied for the clients, therapy records (with the client retaining their copy) and reduced in size again if required. We also routinely, as homework, ask clients to reflect on the formulation and make adjustments based on prospective experiences between sessions in order to test the ecological validity of the initial formulation, thus further demonstrating relational and collaborative formulation.

Levels of cognitive behavioural case formulation

Persons and Davidson (2001) specify three levels of case formulation:

1   The level of the case: a formulation of the person's problems as a whole, explaining the relationships among and between the client's problems.
2   The level of the problem: a formulation of a particular problem or syndrome – for example Ehlers and Clark's (2000) formulation of post-traumatic stress disorder.
3   The level of the situation: a mini formulation of the client's responses in a particular situation. The thought record is ideal for this as it includes columns for the central components of the cognitive model of emotional disorder: situation, emotion, thought and behaviour.

At a case level, Persons (1989) argues that problems manifest as *overt difficulties* and *underlying psychological mechanisms*. Overt difficulties constitute problems which the client experiences on a day-to-day basis, and which could relatively easily be described using a simple triggering situation, event, automatic thoughts and behaviours (SETB) formulation. Underlying psychological mechanisms refer to the core beliefs and rules for living which guide overt difficulties (Beck et al., 1990; Grant et al., 2004a; James et al., 2004; Needleman, 1999).

BELIEFS AT THE LEVEL OF UNDERLYING PSYCHOLOGICAL MECHANISMS

Core beliefs

Core beliefs represent fundamental and tacitly held beliefs about ourself, others, the world and the future (James et al., 2004). Mostly (with the exception of new beliefs occurring as a result of trauma in adulthood), those beliefs emerge from our early life experiences ' ... from the first and enduring lessons that life has taught us' (Grant et al., 2004a: 17).

According to cognitive theory, children learn to construct reality through early experiences in their social and material environment, especially with significant others. Sometimes these early experiences lead children to develop attitudes and beliefs that will later prove maladaptive. Children who are brought up in 'good enough' supportive and nurturing environments, with appropriate boundaries and unconditional love, are likely to grow up with balanced and flexible core beliefs and underlying assumptions. Conversely, children who experience 'toxic parenting' may well only have negative core beliefs and related assumptions to draw on and will process information in line with these (Padesky, 2003). This is an important basis for the cognitive theories of psychopathology.

Beck's cognitive theory of psychopathology   Cognitive behavioural case formulation draws heavily on the cognitive theory of psychopathology first articulated by Aaron Beck (Beck, 1976 in Persons and Tompkins, 1997). This theory states that psychopathological symptoms and problems result from the activation of core beliefs, acquired, mostly (but not exclusively), in childhood or adolescence.

The links between cognitive behavioural case formulation and Beck's cognitive theory can be seen in the fact that three elements of case formulation match the three components of Beck's model, namely the client's psychopathological symptoms and problems, the core beliefs underpinning these, and the life events activating the core beliefs. Since Beck's model also underscores the view that core beliefs are learned via early childhood experiences, case formulation, in diagrammatic and narrative form, includes a description of the origins of clients' core beliefs.

These cognitive structures both organise and process incoming information (Dobson and Dozois, 2001) in relation to memory (James et al., 2004) and related emotional and behavioural responses (Needleman, 1999). The cognitive model proposes that the core beliefs of well-adjusted people allow for an accurately realistic appraisal of life events. In contrast, those of maladjusted individuals result in the kinds of distortions of reality that give rise to psychological problems (Beck, 1976). It must be stressed that the terms 'adjusted' and 'maladjusted' refer to polar points on a continuum. In this sense, everyone is more or less influenced by early life experiences.

Freeman and Needleman (in Needleman, 1999) suggest that it is useful to follow an Eriksonian developmental typology to better understand the nature and range of fundamental core beliefs (Erikson, 1950. See also Young (1990) and Young et al. (2003) for a more contemporary view). The following Table 4.1 describes some of these, clinically relevant, core beliefs.

Table 4.1   Core beliefs

Core belief	Social significance
I am at risk (People are not to be trusted)	Basic trust vs mistrust
I am vulnerable to harm (I need someone to take care of me)	Autonomy vs shame and doubt
I am uncertain/unmotivated (I must feel absolutely certain that I like doing something before I put effort into it)	Initiative vs guilt
I am vulnerable to exploitation (I've got to look out for myself because good guys get walked over)	Generativity vs stagnation
I'm incompetent	Industry vs inferiority

Culturally shared core beliefs   With reference to life in the USA, and perhaps, by extrapolation, other western developed societies, Needleman (1999) makes the point that individuals may be socialised into traditional large-scale, culturally shared core beliefs. He gives three examples of these, shown in Table 4.2.

Socialisation into culturally shared core beliefs may also occur on a smaller scale, in communities that vary as a function of ethnicity and/or religious or spiritual grouping. Family and peer groups may also carry their own transmitted core beliefs. Whatever the reference group – large- or small-scale – culturally shared core beliefs can have a profound effect on how individuals view themselves in the context of the world around them.

Table 4.2   Culturally shared core beliefs

Culturally shared core belief	Risk to the individual
Living happily ever after	Fairy tales abound with stories of rags to riches, or frogs turning into princes. The symbolic and ideological function of these stories is that individuals can somehow magically and quickly transcend their life and personal circumstances. People may waste much of their lives searching for the mythical 'soul-mate'.
The rugged individual	This belief refers to 'going it alone'. The assumption is that people should be strong and independent. There is an added gender-related issue in that it may be harder for males to experience, or to be perceived to be, needing help. This can lead to isolation and feelings of failure.
Material wealth defines worth	Individuals may have low self-esteem because they feel they do not measure up to perceptions of worth as measured by material possessions.

Disorder-specific core beliefs   According to the cognitive model, the *cognitive-content specificity hypothesis* proposes that each psychological disorder has its own unique belief structure (Beck, 1967; Beck et al., 1990; Beiling and Kuyken, 2003; Needleman, 1999; Wells, 1997), as described in Table 4.3.

It may be apparent from the above that core beliefs are *absolute, global* statements of self-worth: the individual damns her or himself in the accepted knowledge that he/she is, for example 'worthless', 'useless' or 'unlovable'; that others are 'predatory', 'malign', 'dangerous' or 'exploitative', and that the world is 'cruel', 'merciless' or 'unforgiving'.

Rules for living

Rules for living are sometimes referred to as 'underlying assumptions' (Grant et al., 2004b), 'intermediate beliefs' (Beck, 1995), 'conditional beliefs' (Persons, 1989), or 'conditional assumptions' (Needleman, 1999). It is useful to regard them as having an intermediate place between core beliefs and automatic thoughts. Closely related to core beliefs, in terms

Table 4.3   Core belief themes in relation to specific psychological disorders

Psychological disorder/Issue	Associated core belief themes
Depression	Loss (I have lost everything) Failure (I am a failure) Deprivation (I do not deserve anything)
Anxiety	Threat (My safety is threatened) Danger (I am in danger) Coping (I cannot cope)
Panic Disorder	Danger (I am in danger of dying of a heart attack or a stroke; I am in danger of going mad)
Obsessional compulsive disorder	Responsibility (I will harm myself or others unless I take action to prevent this)
Social Phobia	Failure (I will be socially rejected, humiliated or criticised)
Anger	Personal violation (Someone else breaking one's own rules)
Guilt	Moral lapse (I have broken my own rules)

of thematic content, they are more tied into specifying an individual's worth against some relatively specific aspect of their lives, the world or others. Whereas core beliefs are generally tacitly held by individuals and are thus the least accessible of the three cognitive structures, rules for living are relatively more accessible and can be sub-divided into conditional assumptions, central goals and implicit rules (Needleman, 1999).

Conditional assumptions   These can be usefully thought of in the form of 'if–then' statements (Beck et al., 1990; Grant et al., 2004b). For example, a woman whose core belief is that she is unlovable may have a conditional assumption such as '*If* I please men all the time, and satisfy their every need, *then* one of them might love me'.

Some 'if–then' conditional assumptions may thus be seen to both confirm and compensate for thematically related core beliefs. Using the above example, problems may occur when such rules are violated: if, for instance, men-pleasing becomes a strategy to actually push potential partners away.

Central goals   Deriving from core beliefs, these are goals that people use to guide their behaviour in order to achieve or accomplish what they perceive to be most important to them. For example, someone who is materially deprived in childhood may make material possessions the single most important thing to them in their adult life. This can, for example, result in compulsive hoarding: the individual never throws anything away so that their house becomes packed with possessions and junk, and becomes uninhabitable. Another example can be found in individuals who fulfil the criteria for avoidant personality disorder (APA, 2000). If safety and freedom from emotional pain are the most important goals for an individual, they may avoid all social and life-demand situations and become friendless and unfulfilled as a result.

It may be clear why individuals with compulsive hoarding problems and avoidance issues seek help. Although central goals, as derivatives of core beliefs, may guide their behaviour, other aspects of their lives and life goals are made forfeit as a result of this.

Implicit rules   These are beliefs characterised by the words 'should', 'must' or 'ought to' with regard to clients' views about right and proper behaviour, and thoughts and feelings about themselves and others. Clearly, there are benefits that can accrue to people from having implicit rules if they are held as flexible guides, and equally costs if these rules are held as dogmatic absolutes. For example, the individual with the implicit rule 'I must be successful in everything I do', in turn deriving from and compensating for the core self-belief 'I'm a failure', is likely to be unsuccessful some of the time, with negative emotional consequences.

BELIEFS AT THE LEVEL OF OVERT PROBLEMS

Automatic thoughts

Automatic thoughts, sometimes termed 'negative automatic thoughts' are, relatively speaking, the most accessible of all three levels of cognitive structure. In contrast to rules for living and core beliefs, they are much less durable and central although they relate thematically to both these structures. Automatic thoughts emerge in conscious awareness in the form of words or images. They may be fleeting – coming and going very quickly in a fraction of a second – or sustained. This characteristic determines whether they are noticed or not. Further, they may be self-enhancing and accurate or they may be distorted and contribute to emotional distress and dysfunctional behaviour. It is striking that automatic thoughts are often accepted as real as opposed to hypothetical, in that they may or may not be true. To this extent, prior to coming into therapy, clients usually do not subject their thoughts to rigorous testing (Grant et al., 2004b; Needleman, 1999; Sanders and Wills, 2005).

To recapitulate, Persons (1989) argues that automatic thoughts are central to the 'situation level' of case formulation and can be captured well in thought records. Mills et al. (2004a: 44–5) provided the case example of 'Walter', who came for help for his long-term problem of lack of confidence and low self-esteem. He spent some time recording his thoughts in situations where he felt anxious. Standing outside a restaurant thinking about entering and joining a party (situation), he felt anxious (emotion) and had the cryptic automatic thoughts 'I can't go in' and 'it's too much'. These were a form of shorthand for the more complete and clarifying thought 'everyone will see that I'm anxious as I enter and decide not to talk to me'. Prior to successfully engaging in cognitive behavioural therapy, these thoughts and related distressing feelings would result in Walter either avoiding these kinds of events or 'bolting' for safety before going into them.

WHICH LEVEL OF THINKING SHOULD CB CASE FORMULATIONS BE TARGETED AT?

This is a contentious issue in CB theory and therapy, and views are informed by issues of parsimony, relevance and relapse prevention. Writers such as Persons (1989) stress the importance of identifying and working with clients' core beliefs in order to leave clients less vulnerable to future difficulties post-therapy. Persons and Davidson (2001) argue that since Beck's theory of psychopathology emphasises the importance of understanding clients' beliefs about their selves, others, the world and the future, the therapist may wish to provide hypotheses about all four of these levels of belief or focus on only two or three. Persons and Tompkins (1997) further argue that therapists can only understand clients' surface problems by having knowledge of their core beliefs.

James (2001), however, urges caution – especially with regard to students of cognitive behavioural psychotherapy who may identify core beliefs in their work with clients without either having identified client resources or having the necessary skills to help the client engage with the unhelpful nature of the core beliefs.

Padesky's (2006b, personal communication) view is that therapists should work with the level of belief most *relevant* to the client's difficulties. These do not always include core beliefs and sometimes don't include underlying assumptions. This standpoint seems to sit comfortably with the view that the goal of case formulation is clinical utility rather than exhaustive explanation.

We are influenced by the relevance argument, but would concur with James (2001) in agreeing that cognitive therapists need thorough and rigorous education, supervision and classroom practice in core belief and underlying assumption-focused work to prepare them for making the transition from classroom to real-life practice.

RELATIONSHIPS AMONG AND BETWEEN THE LEVELS OF UNDERLYING MECHANISMS AND OVERT PROBLEMS

Synchrony

Persons (1989) argues that a problem in one element at the level of overt difficulties usually indicates that problems in the other two elements are also present. She further clarifies that a problem at the level of underlying psychological mechanism is likely to manifest in all three elements at the overt difficulty level that is at the level of emotions, thoughts and behaviours.

Interdependence

From Person's perspective, the synchronous relationship between the three elements of the overt difficulties indicate that a change in any one component is likely to produce changes in the other two. A classic example is that if a depressed, inactive person increases his/her activity level, a reduction in negative thinking and an improvement in mood would be expected.

Cognitive behavioural case formulation components

Case formulation schemes usually also have the following core elements: a description of presenting issues or problem list, and predisposing factors, including recent or *proximal* factors and factors more distant in time, termed *distal* factors. Case formulation schemes also describe perpetuating factors which serve to maintain the presenting problems, protective factors which function as personal and social resources, and explicit guides for intervention (see, for example, Beck, 1995; Persons, 1989).

In addition to the above, it is important for therapists to form explicit sets of hypotheses about the nature of clients' problems, and versions of case formulations in diagrammatic and narrative forms (see examples in Part II of this book). These guide both their interventions and their clinical supervision. Hypotheses, which can be tested out via, for example, behavioural experiments, serve as tests of the usefulness of the case formulation for the client. This view of cognitive behavioural therapy for an individual client constitutes a single-case empirical study, in which case formulation, therapy planning, monitoring of outcome and revision of the formulation are part of an iterative process (Persons and Tompkins, 1997).

Problem and goal-focused assessment

In addition to having a list of goals to work towards, stated in specific, operational and concrete terms, it is important to develop a problem list with clients. The problem list can be revisited at regular intervals to monitor client change over the course of therapy. Persons (1989) argues that specifying the problem list is the first step in therapy, because it focuses the therapeutic intervention without which therapy might proceed aimlessly. Equally, the goal list allows both the client and clinician to have a 'destination' during the therapy process, and the potential for agency and pathway development to achieve these goals from a positive psychological hopeful basis (Cheavens et al., 2006; Snyder, 2002).

Hope, agency and goals

Snyder (2002) defines hope as a positive motivational state, based on an interactively derived sense of successful goal-directed agency and pathways planning. This is conceptualised in Figure 4.2.

Figure 4.2   The hope trilogy model

Snyder (2002) distinguishes between type 1 and 2 goals, as follows:

Type 1   Positive goal outcome
    A. Reaching for the first time
    B. Sustaining present goal outcome
    C. Increasing that which already has been initiated

Type 2   Negative goal outcome
    A. Deterring so that it never appears
    B. Deterring so that its presence is delayed

Pathway thinking, pathway dialogues

We typically think about how we can link our present to imagined futures. However, goals remain but unanswered calls without the requisite means to reach them. For a high-hope person pursuing a specific goal, pathway thinking entails the production of one plausible route, with a concomitant sense of confidence in this route. For a low-hope person, pathway thinking is tenuous and the resulting route is not well articulated.

Agency thinking, agency dialogues

According to Snyder (2002), agency thought – the perceived capacity to use one's pathways to reach desired goals – is the motivational component in hope theory. These self-referential thoughts involve the mental energy to begin and continue using a pathway through all stages of the goal pursuit. Related to this point, we have found that high-hope people use agency phrases such as 'I can do this' and 'I am not going to be stopped'.

Agency thinking is important in all goal-directed thought, but it takes on special significance when people encounter impediments. During such blockages, agency helps people to channel the requisite motivation to the best alternate pathway.

Characteristics of high- and low-hope thinkers

In summary, the relative characteristics of high- and low-hope thinkers are as follows:

High-hope thinkers

- Pathway decisive
- Pathway clear
- Well-articulated route
- Affirming and positive internal pathways messages (self-talk)
- Able to produce alternative routes
- Increasingly refined and tailored pathways thinking

Low-hope thinkers

- Pathway indecisive
- Pathway tenuous
- Poorly articulated route
- Negative internal pathways messages
- Inflexibility about alternative routes
- Difficulty in refining and tailoring pathways thinking

The development of the problem and goal list

As with all other aspects of assessment, the development of the problem and goal list is ongoing throughout the course of therapy. New, hitherto undiscussed, problems and goals may emerge as therapy progresses.

According to Persons and Tompkins (1997), the problem list as the first task in formulation work helps the therapist and client to see emerging connecting themes and causal relationships. An effective case formulation will make apparent causal relationships both between problems and between problems and deeper cognitive levels. This will allow the therapist and client to develop a working hypothesis about how the client's problems hang together – essentially, what the relationship is between them.

The straightforward process of making a problem list can also be containing for both client and therapist, allowing them to work collaboratively in several problem domains and allowing therapy to have a central theme. Finally, a comprehensive problem list minimises the risk of issues being overlooked, while simultaneously ensuring that both client and therapist feel less overwhelmed by the former's difficulties.

While opinions about this vary between cognitive behavioural texts, Persons and Tompkins (1997) argue compellingly that the problem list should be an exhaustive list of the patient's difficulties, stated in concrete, behavioural terms. It should contain reference to behaviours, moods and cognitions since these are the fundamental building block of a cognitive behavioural case formulation:

> ...we suggest that problems be described in these terms whenever possible. For example, through careful questioning the problem 'My job performance is slipping' can become any of the following: 'I'm not returning phone calls'(behaviour); 'I don't enjoy my job so at times I don't show up for work at all'(mood and behaviour); or 'I feel guilty because I know my co-workers think I'm a real flake' (mood and cognition). (Persons and Tompkins, 1997: 323)

Diagnosis

Persons and Davidson (2001) argue that a psychiatric diagnosis, while not strictly speaking part of a cognitive behavioural case formulation, can lead to an initial formulation, citing the case of major depression. In addition, the diagnosis can give some information about helpful treatment interventions which will be useful to the evidence-based therapist. Persons and Davidson's rationale is that randomised control trials suggest appropriate interventions given that these trials are based around diagnosis. (See also Chapter 2 for a discussion of diagnosis in relation to assessment.)

The working hypothesis

Persons and Davidson (2001) argue that the working hypothesis is at the heart of the formulation. It is essentially a mini-theory of the person and their problems, arguing from general case formulation to the specific details of the client's unique presentation. The working hypothesis describes the relationship between problems on the problem list. This relationship can be linked to events activating schemas, and related automatic thoughts, emotions and behaviours, or to experiences causing events, such as depressive feelings resulting in social withdrawal. Finally, the relationship can be between problems and environmental or biological events or issues which trigger them, such as being made redundant from one's job.

According to Persons and Davidson (2001), the first section of the working hypothesis should address the core beliefs which are causing or serving to maintain the problem, via underlying assumptions or rules for living and automatic thoughts. Following Beck's theoretical emphasis on beliefs about the self, world and future, the therapist may wish to focus on these. However, it should be remembered that the overall goal as suggested earlier is *clinical utility rather than exhaustive explanation.*

Measures

Standardised and person-specific measures are argued as a helpful and necessary component of case formulation (Beck, 1995; Grant et al., 2004b; Persons, 1989; Persons and Davidson, 2001). Appropriate (that is mood and thought-specific) measures, taken at the start of the therapy process, and at regular intervals subsequently, provide an important adjunct to the qualitative data emerging from the therapist–client dialogue. (See also measures in the context of assessment in Chapter 2.)

The frequency at which measures should be taken remains a moot point in the cognitive behavioural community. Some (for example Beck, 1995) advocate weekly measures, taken at each therapy session. However, this view should arguably be balanced by the social context of measurement – specifically, the meaning of such data collection for the client. Some clients, for example, may be put off by what they see as an unnecessary amount of form filling. Others may use the event of measurement as an opportunity to 'fake good' or 'fake bad' depending on the overall meaning for them of the therapeutic relationship and being in therapy. Faking good and bad refer to scoring deliberately high on a measure to stay in therapy, or scoring low to get out of it. There may be many reasons for this, which may, in turn, be useful information for the case formulation, and can be formulated by, for example, using the 'downward arrow' techniques (Mills et al., 2004b):

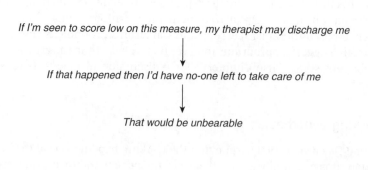

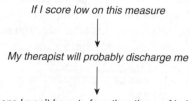

Strengths and assets

Stressing strengths and assets can assist in the working hypothesis in several ways. At a fundamental level, a focus on client strengths or resilience building integrates positive psychology with cognitive behavioural psychotherapy, thus remedying a long-standing perception and stance of cognitive behavioural psychotherapy as a 'deficit model' (Mooney and Padesky, 2000). Moreover, the linking of client strengths and assets can consolidate and strengthen the hope in change as a possibility (Cheavens et al., 2006; Ingram and Snyder, 2006; Snyder, 2002; Snyder et al., 1999), and can thus be used in the service of developing client creativity for positive change (Mooney and Padesky, 2000).

THE RELATIONSHIP BETWEEN CASE FORMULATION AND EMERGING INTERVENTIONS

The tension between case formulation-driven therapy and therapy supported by randomised control trials may have become apparent to some readers at this stage. The case for one form of approach or the other is represented in the views of Persons and Davidson (2001) and Needleman (1999) respectively. As stated earlier, Persons and Davidson (2001) assert that cognitive behavioural therapists have a professional and ethical duty to provide interventions that have been shown to be effective in controlled studies. These authors recommend *individualising* standard protocols (problem- or diagnosis-specific formulations) to take account of the individual client's unique behavioural, cognitive and emotional experiences and presentation. In some degree of contrast to this, Needleman argues, using the example of panic disorder, that overt problems often belie very different underlying psychological mechanisms between individuals sharing apparently the same or similar overt problems (see also Marzillier, 2004 in support of this position).

Our view is that while it is of course important to be aware of, and where appropriate, collaboratively utilise empirically supported problem-specific interventions and related formulations, there are several problems with the *totalising* claims implicit in Persons and Davidson's argument. One is the problem of extrapolating from the tightly controlled selection criteria of individuals for randomised control trials to the 'messiness' of client problems in real-life clinical settings – the problems of so-called 'external' and 'ecological' validity (Mace et al., 2001; Norcross et al., 2005; Roth and Fonagy, 1996; Rowland and Goss, 2000). Another is the ontological and epistemological assumptions guiding Persons and Davidson's argument. 'Ontology' refers to what counts as the reality of (in this case of this argument) the client's problems and 'epistemology' to the theory of knowledge of the client's problems.

From Persons and Davidson's standpoint, which may be termed a 'realist' one, what is *real* is awareness of the client's problems perceived unproblematically, clearly and transparently by a neutral, observing and assessing therapist. From a constructivist position (Leahy, 2001, 2007; Safran, 1998), such assumptions are naïve in that both the reality and knowledge taking place in and emerging from the psychotherapeutic relationship are co-constructed and perceived through the grids of meaning of both client and therapist. That is to say, the problem(s) and solution to the problem(s) are interpersonally discussed and constructed.

As highlighted in Chapter 1, the implications emerging from the constructivist position are that both client and therapist will have thoughts about therapy and each other which may or may not be facilitative of a good outcome (Leahy, 2001, 2007; Miranda and Andersen, 2007; Rudd and Joiner, 1997; Safran, 1998). For this reason, case formulations should, in our view, always be individualised to take account of those beliefs where possible. Essentially, the therapist, as complex human being, is dealing, interpersonally, with another complex human being, not with a coherent problem that needs fixing. In this human context, cognitive therapy amounts to two individuals sitting down talking with, and getting to know, each other (Leahy, 2001). There are clear implications emerging from this for good quality clinical supervision for cognitive behavioural therapists, and for the vexed question of whether or not these therapists should undergo personal psychotherapy themselves as part of their reflective development (Bennett-Levy, 2006).

A final and related reason for individualising case formulations is the contextual bases of clients' difficulties. These might include the interpersonal context and history of clients' social environments and relationships which may, in turn, be replicated in clients' relationship with their therapists (Leahy, 2001; Miranda and Andersen, 2007; Safran, 1998; Safran and Segal, 1996). Such a thorough contextual and relational understanding of a client and their problems, via a carefully tailored, constantly developing case formulation, is likely to constitute a more effective, contextually appropriate basis for the selection of appropriate therapeutic interventions:

> ...**case conceptualization (formulation) involves placing a psychological problem in its context. Understanding the context in which a problem arises permits appropriate selection of interventions. Although novice therapists may be aware of many techniques for addressing a particular clinical problem, they often choose inappropriate approaches. This results from failing to have a clear understanding of the underlying mechanisms that produced the problem. (Needleman, 1999: 3)**

Summary

1 The SETB cycle constitutes the essential components of case formulation and relates to its functions as a central pillar in cognitive behavioural psychotherapy.

2 There are key distinctions between generic, problem-specific and idiosyncratic formulation models which relate to their various uses.

3 The structure and function of cognitive behavioural case formulation coheres with Beck's cognitive theory of psychopathology.

4 A debate exists around which levels of thinking case formulation should be targeted at. Hope and culturally formed beliefs structures inform case formulation development.

Activities

1   Choose a suitable client and attempt to formulate her/his difficulties using generic and problem-specific models.
2   Having done the above, consider the implications for targeting levels of thinking in your clinical work with this client.

Further reading

Needleman, L.D. (1999) *Cognitive Case Conceptualization. A Guidebook for Practitioners.* Mahwah, NJ: Lawrence Erlbaum Associates.
An excellent comprehensive overview of case formulation in cognitive behavioural psychotherapy.

Key issues in cognitive behavioural case formulation

5

Alec Grant and Michael Townend

Learning objectives

After reading this chapter and completing the activities at the end of it you should be able to:

1 Describe the ways in which case formulation is said to improve cognitive behavioural practice.

2 Understand key issues related to the evidence-base for case formulation.

3 Explain the role, and advantages and disadvantages, of heuristic decision making in case formulation development.

4 Describe some common therapists' mistakes, and ways of strengthening confidence in case formulation and its development.

5 Evaluate the significance of described emerging implications, including the role of self-practice.

Case formulation has been described as the cornerstone of evidence-based cognitive behavioural practice (Kuyken et al., 2005). These authors argue that formulation functions as a bridge between practice, theory and research in the execution of cognitive behavioural therapy. In this context, the individual aspects of a client's presenting problems are synthesised with relevant cognitive behavioural theory and research.

COGNITIVE BEHAVIOURAL CASE FORMULATION AS A PSYCHOLOGICAL MAP

The overall aim of case formulation is to describe the client's problems in the form of a 'psychological map', in terms of not only what his/her problems are but why he/she is having them at this present time (Kuyken, 2006). Cognitive behavioural theory is used to make explanatory inferences about what is causing and maintaining the client's problems and to inform the strategies needed to help the client reach her therapeutic goals. The resulting picture contributes to the emergence of contextually appropriate interventions; these feed back on the formulation in constituting hypotheses to test its collaboratively developed appropriateness, usefulness and meaningfulness for the client.

HOW CASE FORMULATION IS SAID TO IMPROVE COGNITIVE BEHAVIOURAL PRACTICE

According to Kuyken (2006), cognitive behavioural case formulation improves clinical practice in several other ways. Firstly, therapy as an empathic endeavour is realised because the client's problems are 'normalised' as being understandable reactions to life circumstances rather than pathologised. Secondly, the case formulation enables large amounts of otherwise complex information to be utilised collaboratively and in a more straightforward diagrammatic form. Thirdly, the case formulation as work-in-progress lends itself to high quality clinical supervision thus strengthening the validity of the formulation. Fourthly, cognitive behavioural case formulation informs therapy by selecting, focusing and sequencing interventions. Fifthly, a good formulation will take into account a client's preferred way of working towards change and, conversely, suggest probable 'therapy-interfering' behaviours and strategies. Finally, in keeping with the need for case formulation to be parsimonious (that is, to use the least number of necessary explanatory elements), formulation enables the simplest and most cost-efficient interventions.

THE EVIDENCE-BASE FOR COGNITIVE BEHAVIOURAL CASE FORMULATION

In spite of the claims made for the benefits of case formulation, Beiling and Kuyken (2003) point out that there has, as yet, been a marked lack of evaluation of these claims. It is assumed rather than proven that case formulation provides:

- a systematic cognitive theory framework for making hypotheses about the client's problems;
- individualised cognitive therapy protocols;
- improved understanding of presenting problems for both therapist and client;
- improved therapeutic alliance;

- more focused therapeutic interventions; and
- enhanced treatment outcomes.

There has been relatively little research regarding formulation in cognitive behavioural psychotherapy, despite its central place in contemporary practice. This may at first seem surprising, but less so when seen against the backdrop of most research in the field of cognitive behavioural psychotherapy being based on standardised protocols emerging from randomised controlled trials. It is also the case that research into the efficacy of formulation is likely to be a low priority for funding. This is because most research funding is allocated on a disorder basis to test the relative efficacy or effectiveness of interventions rather than to test or examine process or component variables within an intervention.

However, because case formulation draws on appropriate cognitive behavioural psychotherapy theories, training courses spend a lot of time on formulation and related clinical supervision. It could thus reasonably be expected that two clinicians who have had similar training would generate similar formulations. This hypothesis has been tested in several studies, using a variety of methods (Flitcroft et al., 2007; Kuyken et al., 2005; Mumma and Smith, 2001; Persons and Bertagnolli, 1999; Persons et al., 1995). Overall, these studies broadly indicate that similar formulations are developed between clinicians under test conditions. However, when clinicians are asked about the reasoning behind their formulation development decisions, their responses indicate much greater variability than would be expected. The research also indicates that when more experienced therapists are compared there is a trend towards slightly better inter-rater reliability.

In terms of the evidence base, it seems overall that clinicians tend more to agree on surface, manifest problems – what the client directly expresses – than they do on underlying, inferred mechanisms (i.e. core beliefs and rules for living) (Beiling and Kuyken, 2003; Kuyken et al., 2005). However, reliability seems to improve as a result of training, systematic case formulation gathering methods (see, for example, Beck, 1995; Persons, 1989), levels of clinical experience and accreditation status (Kuyken et al., 2005).

Kuyken (2006) suggests that variability in formulation might be due to a number of factors. These include:

1   Training differences
2   Heuristic decision-making biases (to be discussed further below)
3   A lack of application of systematic frameworks

These suggestions are important as they give an indication of strategies that can be used in training and by individual practitioners to improve the validity and reliability of formulation. This might be achieved through standardised training, identification of decision-making biases and understanding how these may have arisen, and the teaching and utilisation of standardised frameworks of formulation and underpinning theory.

Top-down and bottom-up evaluation

According to Beiling and Kuyken (2003), evaluating the scientific basis of cognitive behavioural case formulation draws on two approaches: top-down and bottom-up. The top-down approach refers to using generalisations from theory and research to apply to individual cases, for example for clients who have been traumatised, are socially phobic, or suffer from generalised anxiety disorder or psychosis.

The bottom-up approach refers to the following set of criteria:

- Is the formulation reliable? In other words, is the formulation based on inferences that several clinicians can agree with?
- Is the formulation valid? This question refers to the extent to which it squares with the client's experiences, with standardised measures, with the therapist's clinical impressions and with the therapist's clinical supervisor's impressions.
- Does the formulation improve the intervention and the therapy outcomes?
- Is the formulation acceptable and useful to the client?

Beiling and Kuyken (2003) argue in related terms that, within the scientist-practitioner model of cognitive behavioural practice, the following question should be applied to each element of the case formulation: are the constructs underpinning the cognitive case formulation substantiated by evidence?

The reliability of cognitive behavioural case formulation

Cognitive behavioural psychotherapists tend to agree well about clients' presenting problems, but less well about what has been described as the 'inferential aspects': clients' underlying assumptions and core beliefs (Kuyken, 2006; Kuyken et al., 2005). This problem refers to the *reliability* of cognitive behavioural case formulation. Good reliability would amount to a high level of agreement between clinicians at all levels of the case formulation, whereas poor reliability would constitute the opposite. However Beiling and Kuyken (2003) argue that reliability is not the same as quality. Even in situations where there is a high degree of agreement among several clinicians for one particular client, the resulting case formulation may be a poor quality one in terms of being incoherent and unhelpful in planning interventions. For this reason:

> **...it may be more important for a formulation to be a coherent and justifiable account of a person's presenting problems than for it to be replicable in similar form by other cognitive therapists. (Beiling and Kuyken, 2003: 191)**

In this context, despite the scientific status of case formulation, it is arguably important to have a therapeutic road map to increase collaboration between client and therapist, and to provide a rationale for emerging interventions. As has already been argued, from a relational psychotherapeutic perspective, techniques only make sense in the context of the developing alliance, the story that emerges from the dialogue between client and therapist, and how the therapist fits into this story. In this sense (somewhat ironically given scientific concerns), the case formulation could be considered a necessary 'healing ritual' (Hubble et al., 1999) which gives important context to related interventions (Sanders and Wills, 2005).

Beiling and Kuyken (2003) also point out that good quality case formulations may not be reliable because a client's problems change across time, and the theoretical orientations between clinicians may differ. For example, it is probable that a case formulation for the same client would differ between cognitively and behaviourally oriented therapists. However, both may be of good quality in generating verifiable hypotheses and having good treatment utility.

A further confounding factor is around the argument that cognitive behavioural case formulation allows the most appropriate interventions at the most appropriate time. Some potentially problematic questions arise from this assumption which suggests that formulations may work indirectly rather than directly, as follows (Kuyken, 2006):

- Does case formulation directly impact on outcome or does it affect outcome solely through the selection of appropriate interventions (Beiling and Kuyken, 2003)?
- Does case formulation 'work' by anticipating upcoming problems?
- Is the benefit of case formulation merely about facilitating high quality clinical supervision?
- Does having a developed case formulation enhance cognitive behavioural therapists' confidence?
- Does having a case formulation encourage therapist accountability?
- Does a combination of the above factors make CB case formulation 'work'?

CASE FORMULATION AS AN ACT OF FAITH

In conclusion of this section, currently, in the absence of knowledge about the reliability and validity of case formulation, its use constitutes an act of faith on the part of both therapist and client – in our view, a worthwhile one. At a round table discussion at the European Association for Behavioural and Cognitive Therapies XXXIV Annual Congress in September 2004, the august body on the stage expressed the view that the reliability of case formulation is less important than its believability by therapist and client. In addition to this, the consensus was that a good case formulation helps the client to see that their problems are understandable, in the light of core beliefs, rules for living and triggering situations.

Process issues in the evidence-base for case formulation in cognitive behavioural therapy

As indicated above, some of the problems of inter-therapist reliability may be due to difficulties in the formulation process: specifically to what Kuyken (2006) describes as 'heuristic decision-making biases'. Beiling and Kuyken (2003) and Kuyken (2006), supported by Eells (1997), argue that cognitive behavioural therapists use heuristics, or cognitive shortcuts, to make efficient decisions in the face of complex information. This may be an adaptive process, since humans use a discrete number of heuristic principles to make a 'good enough' interpretation when faced with a large amount of often incomplete and ambiguous information (Augoustinos et al., 2006). According to Kuyken (2006), heuristic decision making can provide both opportunities and constraints with busy clinicians, inevitably, taking cognitive shortcuts in response to information complexity. In this context, 'good enough' rather than 'the best' case formulation may be the emergent product.

The following categories of heuristics are argued to affect the reasoning process of cognitive behavioural therapists in the form of cognitive biases (Kuyken, 2006): *representativeness*, *availability* and *anchoring/adjustment*. The representative bias refers to seeing presenting issues (A) as representative of another set of issues (B). These may be inferred but end up as ultimately irrelevant. The availability bias suggests that clinicians make use of information that comes more readily to mind, which they regard as relevant, in decision making. This information may also be irrelevant. Finally, the anchoring/adjustment bias refers to the tendency to make judgements solely on the basis of an initial hypothesis, or organising hypotheses around a core idea – a form of 'sticking to your guns' or resisting u-turns.

In related terms, Eells (1997) argues that clinicians may over-pathologise clients on the basis of their difference from the clinician or, conversely, under-pathologise them on the basis of their sameness. Equally, if a clinician relies too heavily on observable behaviour they may overlook meaningful patterns organising the elements of a client's problems. For example, attributing a client's panic symptoms entirely to catastrophic interpretations of bodily sensations (Clark, 1988) may neglect significant life history events or relationship patterns that also contribute to the onset and maintenance of the problems, as well as to the meaning they have for the client (Needleman, 1999).

Such over-generalising can also result from stereotyping clients on the basis of ethnicity, age, gender, appearance, socioeconomic background or education (see Chapter 2 of this text).

Kuyken (2006) argues that professional training may result in greater confidence in clinical decision making, thereby increasing the proneness of cognitive behavioural therapists towards anchoring effects. However, as argued above, 'good enough' rather than optimal formulations may be of good quality and treatment utility, especially if supported by high quality clinical supervision.

Some common mistakes in case formulation

Further problems impacting decision-making processes in cognitive behavioural case formulation were described by Melanie Fennell (2004). She itemised key mistakes which student cognitive therapists are prone to make in formulation construction, including the following:

- Being unfamiliar with relevant theory: for example the existence of a specific model or protocol for a specific disorder.
- Misunderstanding or misapplication of a theory: for example using an over-complex formulation for straightforward problems or, conversely, using an over-simple formulation for more complex problems.
- 'Jumping ship' in the face of therapeutic difficulties or 'road blocks': for example abandoning a developed formulation in favour of a totally different one without adequately testing out the original formulation.
- Failing to regard the formulation as a hypothesis to be tested out.
- Being blinded by theory. This includes the tendency of clinicians to exhibit 'halo effects' in relation to 'off the shelf' formulations. In our experience, students often, for example, over-apply Fennell's (1998, 2006) Low Self-Esteem (LSE) formulation model without considering alternatives or adequately testing the model out.

- Being blinded by the brilliance of their own creation, thus failing to provide adequate tests of the formulation as a set of hypotheses or to develop it in the face of, sometimes contradictory, new information.
- Making the client feel summed up or 'rumbled', resulting in therapist triumphalism in the face of dents to the client's self-esteem.
- Using the case formulation as a personal (for the therapist) guide to understanding the client rather than sharing it with her.
- Adopting the expert position (inappropriately).
- Using client-unfriendly jargon in the development of the formulation.
- Rushing into therapy without an adequate formulation.
- Waiting until every detail of the formulation is gathered before starting therapy.
- Applying therapy protocols inflexibly, without taking adequate account of individual differences between clients which require individual 'tailoring' of protocols.

In the context of making mistakes in the case formulation construction process, Eells (1997) argues that therapists may over-individualise a formulation to the neglect of prior knowledge of psychology, empirical knowledge of psychopathology and past work with psychotherapy clients. Eells (1997) asserts that if each client is assumed to be a complete *tabula rasa*, with experiences that are so unique that the therapist must ignore all previous knowledge, then he is doing his client a disservice.

In support of this position, Persons and Davidson (2001) argue that clinicians have an ethical duty to base formulations on RCT-proven protocols first, where they exist. These authors assert that reconciliation is possible between idiosyncratic and protocol-driven formulations, in the following ways:

- Therapists necessarily have to individidualise nomothetic formulations to take account of an individual client's elements of the formulation, for activating events and maladaptive behaviours, which are unique to that individual.
- A distinction must be drawn between standardised protocols which treat disorders and individualised protocols which treat clients. The client's problem list is crucial in this regard.
- An individualised version of a nomothetic formulation is necessary to deal with the difficulties arising in the use of the protocol – including alliance ruptures.
- Because of RCT exclusion criteria, standardised protocols are strong on internal, but not so strong on external validity. Therapists working with clients with multiple disorders necessarily have to use two or three different nomothetically validated protocols individualised in a hybrid fashion.
- Finally, therapists are forced to use individualised formulations where there exist no RCT-validated therapies for a client's problems.

Compared with Person and Davidson's (2001) implicit adherence to the ethics of evidence-based case formulation practice, Padesky (2006a) seems to be in favour of a more liberal stance. This is illustrated in the following dialogue between Padesky and Grant:

Grant: ...if (RCT-derived) protocols already exist for particular disorders – ...given your stance on guided discovery and not knowing where the client is going to lead with you

following – how do you reconcile an emerging ideographic formulation with existing nomothetic ones?

Padesky: ...one's questions will be informed by existing theories and models but it is important to stay open to the unexpected in client's answers. Sometimes idiosyncratic responses can be fitted with existing models and sometimes not. Also, as therapists we can share our models with clients and get client feedback... every interaction is not via guided discovery.

Essentially, what emerges from the above discussion is that a balance must be struck between an individual and a general formulation (Eells, 1997). Eells argues that humility is an asset in this respect. As stated earlier in this text, the 'match' between any model and any individual is inherently imperfect and the case formulation is never more than an approximation of the individual in distress.

THE COGNITIVE BEHAVIOURAL THERAPIST AS A FLAWED INFORMATION PROCESSOR

From the above, it can be seen that cognitive behavioural therapists may make fundamental errors in formulation construction and/or use information processing heuristics and biases. These may undermine both the quality and treatment utility of the case formulation. This points to the benefits of *triangulation* in the case formulation development process. Triangulation is a term borrowed from empirical research which refers to the need to have as many points of reference as possible to ensure the robustness of a particular proposition or hypothesis. So, it is arguably important for cognitive behavioural therapists to do the following:

- Adhere to a consistent framework for the construction of the case formulation, both in narrative form and diagrammatically (see, for example, Beck, 1995 and Persons, 1989).
- Test the appropriateness of the hypotheses emerging from the formulation for the client through, for example, the use of collaboratively developed behavioural experiments (Bennett-Levy et al., 2004).
- Have alternative hypotheses in mind and to bring the case formulation to clinical supervision, in the context of real-time equivalent observation of clinical work (supervision utilising video or DVD recordings). Group supervision is especially useful because several 'judges' are available to discuss the quality and treatment utility of the formulation (Grant and Townend, 2007).

All of the above are likely to minimise the negative impact of problematic heuristics in the development of the case formulation and maximise the likelihood of a 'good fit' of the formulation to the client. By this means, cognitive behavioural psychotherapists learn rigorous formulation skills through education and supervised practice which prepares them well for doing effective work.

USEFUL INFORMATION PROCESSING IN CASE FORMULATION

According to Kuyken (2006), decision-making research suggests two relatively independent cognitive systems at play in therapists' case formulation development: the intuitive and the rational. The intuitive system is fast, automatic, effortless, associative and implicit (that is, not so available to introspection). In contrast, the rational system is slower, serial, effortful, consciously monitored and deliberately controlled. The rational system monitors the outputs from the intuitive system, providing a critical overview of output judgements. Kuyken (2006) argues that a formulation might be initiated by an intuitive judgement which is then confirmed or altered by the rational system.

According to this model, novice therapists are much more likely to be reliant on the rational system, spending long periods of time in preparation of case formulations. In contrast, rigorously trained, highly experienced and clinically effective cognitive behavioural therapists may well operate intuitively in much of their practice. This reflects the learning rationale underpinning the use of the Cognitive Therapy Scale-Revised (James et al., 2001), and the view that the knowledge-base of professional expertise is derived from subjective reflection on experience as well as empirical research (Schon, 1983).

Kuyken (2006) argues that the balanced synthesis of the intuitive and rational cognitive systems can probably enable 'good enough' formulation. In his terms, those should not deviate too far on a continuum from optimal to frankly 'dangerous formulations'.

100	0	100
Extremely dangerous formulation		Optimal formulation

SOME EMERGING IMPLICATIONS

The overly rational nature of 'evidence-based practice' in cognitive behavioural therapy

Given the need for emerging case formulations to balance intuitive and rational systems, it is ironic that much of the dialogue in the British cognitive behavioural community is currently, arguably, overly rational (see, for example, the jiscmail discussion archives of members of the British Association for Behavioural and Cognitive Psychotherapies (BABCP) (www.babcp.com)). In large part, this may be because of the historical basis of cognitive behavioural therapy in positivist worldviews, within which quantitative-experimental studies are privileged over interpretive research using qualitative methods (Grant et al., 2004b). In jiscmail dialogues, a frequently asked question is 'does it work?' – the 'it' referring to empirically tested techniques.

In our view, this technique-focused brand of cognitive behavioural psychotherapy is epistemologically and ontologically naïve in giving insufficient attention to the significance of interpersonal issues and the therapeutic alliance between cognitive behavioural psychotherapists and their clients (Gilbert and Leahy, 2007; Leahy, 2001; Norcross, 2002; Safran, 1998; Safran and Segal, 1996). Earlier in this text, the discussion focused on the *relational* rather than the *realist* nature of cognitive behavioural therapeutic work with clients. From a relational position, the dialogue emerging between each unique configuration of therapist and client is based on the thoughts, feelings and behaviour of both (Leahy, 2001, 2007), in moment-by-moment interaction. It is from this relational basis that cognitive behavioural intervention techniques will both contextually emerge and be more or less contextually appropriate (Safran and Messer, 1997).

Thus, the therapeutic dialogue can never be *solely* informed by a supposedly objective stance taken by the therapist, based, in turn, on the quantitative-experimental evidence-base. Following Padesky (1993, 2006a), interventions emerging from guided discovery may be as surprising to the therapist as they are to the client. In this context, what emerges as 'intervention' will often not be rationally planned but will often be testament to the creativity of both client and therapist drawn from naturally occurring moments. This requires therapists to pay attention to what is going on, or not, in therapy, often 'between the lines' rather than solely focusing on treatment protocols.

The scope for creativity in cognitive behavioural therapy

From a basis in positive psychology, Mooney and Padesky (2000) have argued favourably for the role of forms of creativity in cognitive behavioural practice which take account of clients' resources and dispositional styles (see Part II of this text). Writing from a constructivist and integrative perspective, the importance of spontaneously occurring and unplanned creativity in psychotherapeutic practice was also underscored by Mahoney (2003, 2004).

A creative, sometimes uncertain, dialogue between client and therapist in the construction of a case formulation is arguably thus to be welcomed. The emergent product should ideally, of course, conform to a balanced synthesis of the intuitive and rational cognitive systems and pay due regard to the existing empirical evidence around 'what works' for specific disorders. This is quite a challenge for cognitive behavioural therapists, but equally, in the final analysis, an exciting and creative one.

TEACHING PROJECT ON RUNNING BEHAVIOURAL EXPERIMENTS

This chapter will conclude with a discussion about a teaching project run by one of the authors (Grant). Its aim was to enable students to use self-change methods, emerging from their own formulations, on themselves. Permission was sought and received to run this project from a cohort of MSc Cognitive Psychotherapy students at the University of Brighton, in 2005.

The students, who had for some time been working on cognitive self-exploration and identification, agreed to the following task. Working in small groups, they were asked to identify and specify their core beliefs, related dysfunctional rules for living and behavioural strategies which supported these. They then worked on collaboratively negotiating new core beliefs, new rules for living and behavioural strategies.

In the next part of the teaching project, they agreed to devise and run behavioural experiments to strengthen their new rules. Finally, to maintain a momentum of further, increasingly refined experiments, they agreed to write a monthly update letter which they would give Grant in a sealed envelope. To be sensitive to the risks of post-experiment disclosure, it was agreed that Grant would subject each letter to qualitative data analysis (Duncan-Grant, 2001) and present anonymous themes back to the class (Grant, 2005).

Theoretical rationale

The theoretical rationale behind the project linked together key areas, arguably essential to the educational development of cognitive psychotherapists around case formulation and emerging interventions. These are: creativity; narrative re-storying; the use of cognitive change methods (including behavioural experiments) and self-practice to teach cognitive psychotherapy; the development of skills in compassionate case formulation; widening the therapist's toolbox; encouraging close attention to mismatched cognitions between therapist and client; and helping students manage the beginnings of the novice to expert practitioner trajectory.

Creativity   In keeping with the positive psychological turn in cognitive behavioural psychotherapy (Cheavens et al., 2006; Ingram and Snyder, 2006), Mooney and Padesky (2000) argue that good therapists encourage high levels of creativity (Epstein, 1994), and the related ability of welcoming doubt and uncertainty, through role modelling hope, optimism and curiosity in their work with clients. In this endeavour, Mooney and Padesky (2000) argue that their approach differs from more traditional cognitive psychotherapy in encouraging the client to define both old and new core beliefs, rules and experiments to strengthen and consolidate new ways of living and experiencing themselves:

> **Cognitive therapy through a lens of creativity involves appealing to clients' hopes, wishes, dreams and imagination for how life could be and then helping them define and create that new life vision. The creative process explores possibilities while leaving probabilities in the background. We ask clients to construct a new system of behaviour and thought which they would like to have. By asking the client to reach forward in time to construct a new future we focus on helping the client develop and implement this new way of being rather than spending time deconstructing and revising their past and present. We use a model and methods with clients that can facilitate a paradigm shift ... rather than a retrofit of old ideas. Cognitive therapy methods can then focus on helping the client develop and implement this new way of being. (Mooney and Padesky, 2000: 150)**

Narrative re-storying   In most modalities of psychotherapy, clients are asked to account for their lives and difficulties. It is conceptually useful to view this as a form of storytelling. In creative forms of cognitive behavioural therapy, re-storying is encouraged as clients work towards new possibilities for living, and so can begin to account for themselves in more positive, constructive, adaptational and functional ways (Gilbert and Irons, 2005; Mooney and Padesky, 2000; Padesky, 2003; Pennebaker, 2004).

With a focus on the psychotherapy as a 'journey of the self', creative cognitive behavioural therapy also links to the significance of the self in developmental psychology (McAdams, 1993), social psychology (Bruner, 1990) and the construction of contemporary narrative identity (du Gay et al., 2000; Holstein and Gubrium, 2000).

The use of cognitive change methods (including behavioural experiments) and self-practice to teach cognitive behavioural psychotherapy   The importance of cognitive behavioural psychotherapist teachers using cognitive change methods to teach the approach has been well-highlighted (Bennett-Levy, 2006; Bennett-Levy and Thwaites, 2007; Padesky, 1996). These writers emphasise the importance of self-practice and self-reflection for cognitive behavioural psychotherapists, implicitly and explicitly linking this into attaining skills in cognitive case formulation and cognitive change methods such as behavioural experiments (Bennett-Levy et al., 2004).

However, self-practice linked to change is not without its attendant problems. Synthesising theoretical and empirical work to date around human change processes, Mahoney (2004) argues that humans are fundamentally conservative animals who, for good evolutionary reasons, change as little as possible for as long as possible. So, although change may be desired, change that is experienced as too much or too quick, may result in individuals backing off or withdrawing from it. This has fairly obvious implications for doing cognitive behavioural psychotherapy: gradual change (most common), or quantum leap change (less common) is more likely to occur in a trusting relationship where an individual can explore new ways of being and relating to themselves, and taking risks (Mahoney, 2004).

Compassionate case formulation   Padesky (2003) argues that case formulation becomes compassionate at the point at which cognitive behavioural therapists begin to see that their clients have good reason to behave, think and feel as they do. A client's problems in living become understandable when both the therapist and client map the links between the client's core beliefs, protective rules for living and related behavioural strategies, and the link between all of these and early and key life experiences (see also Grant et al., 2004a). An emerging task is to use this material in helping clients develop greater self-compassion and self-nurturance. This represents an anti-pathologising take on cognitive behavioural therapy, arguably contrasting significantly with diagnostic-led cognitive behavioural approaches (as discussed previously in this text).

In a synthesis of evolutionary, developmental and cognitive theories, and emergent implications for practice, Gilbert (2005, 2007) arguably makes the societal significance for the compassionate psychotherapist more explicit in discussing the importance of striving towards 'compassionate social mentalities', within which information-processing competencies direct goals towards social compassion. In our view, this turn seems to signal an increased sensitivity to the moral basis for practising psychotherapy, arguably previously under-rehearsed within the cognitive behavioural communities.

In order for student cognitive behavioural therapists to develop the patience and knowledge to facilitate and accommodate slow change in their clients, practice in using compassionate case formulation on their own difficulties and goals is important. In our view, quite simply, if you do it you need to experience it, rather than speaking from a position of undeserved privilege or from a 'two sides of the fence' position.

Widening the therapist's toolbox   In apparent sympathy with Mooney and Padesky's (2000) stance on encouraging client creativity, James et al. (2004) argued that in using cognitive change techniques with their clients, therapists should 'widen their toolbox' by working with their clients across as big a range of sensory, cognitive and behavioural modalities as possible. In our view, this can be organised well in the use of behavioural experiments (Bennett-Levy et al., 2004). With an ostensible purpose in helping clients develop new rules for living, experiments, subsuming many cognitive and behavioural strategies, help people work towards new possibilities and goals in their lives.

Encouraging close attention to mismatched cognitions between therapist and client   Self-practice by cognitive behavioural students, particularly around increased awareness of their own core beliefs and rules for living, should in principle be helpful when they find themselves confronted with interpersonal difficulties in the therapeutic relationship (Leahy, 2001, 2007; Miranda and Andersen, 2007; Padesky, 1999; Rudd and Joiner, 1997). In this context, it is important for students to work towards becoming sufficiently self-aware to notice their part in the development of ruptures in the therapeutic alliance and to respond appropriately, in non-defensive and validating ways (Burns and Aeurbach, 1996; Leahy, 2001, 2007; Safran, 1998).

Helping students manage the beginnings of the novice to expert trajectory according to the the Dreyfus scale of competence   The practice competence of cognitive behavioural students at the Universities of Brighton and Derby is measured using the Dreyfus scale of competence within the Cognitive Therapy Scale Revised CTS (R) manual (James et al., 2001). This six point scale is illustrated in Table 5.1 below.

Table 5.1   The Dreyfus scale of competence within the Cognitive Therapy Scale

Competence level	Competence level descriptors
Incompetent	The therapist commits errors and displays poor and unacceptable behaviour, leading to negative therapeutic consequences.
Novice	At this level the therapist displays a rigid adherence to taught rules and is unable to take account of situational factors. He/she is not yet showing any discretionary judgement.
Advanced beginner	The therapist treats all aspects of the task separately and gives equal importance to them. There is evidence of situational perspective and discretionary judgement.
Competent	The therapist is able to see the tasks linked within a conceptual framework. He/she makes plans within this framework and uses standardised and routinised procedures.
Proficient	The therapist sees the patient's problems holistically, prioritises tasks and is able to make quick decisions. The therapist is clearly skilled and able.
Expert	The therapist no longer uses rules, guidelines or maxims. He/she has deep tacit understanding of the issues and is able to use novel problem-solving techniques. The skills are demonstrated even in the face of difficulties (e.g. excessive avoidance).

The Dreyfus competence scale measures students' abilities to respond to clients' needs at any one time in the cognitive learning cycle (James et al., 2001). This cycle conceptualises the elements of case formulation in linking cognitions, emotions, behaviours and arousal. Grant's hope was that self-practice would sensitise students to issues arising in their own cognitive psychotherapy learning cycle and accelerate the pace at which they developed on the Dreyfus scale of competence.

Main themes emerging from students' behavioural experiment stories

Some experiments which were aimed at weakening old rules and testing new ones resulted in pleasant surprises for some students:

> I have learned that if I show my emotions people respond in a very supportive way.

> I have learned from my reflective log that if I persist with this idea... that it is important to me that others do not expect too much of me. However, I have also found that I have beliefs about being strong and capable which dominate from time to time and which I, at the time at least, believe strongly.

> When I have noted that I have slipped into people pleasing, or avoiding saying what I want, I am at times rather hard on myself. I have an inner critic who tends to scold and I begin to feel that I have failed... Maybe I am trying too hard – I could see my growing awareness or watchfulness as a good thing. At least I am no longer unaware. I don't always have to take action.

> In the short time since I wrote (the first story) ... I have had a handful of opportunities to test out my beliefs and fears through behavioural experimentation. I have found that the tendency to avoid remains; that I will still have my performance adversely affected by thoughts of failure...(However) I sense that, by degrees, my confidence has started to grow but that it is fragile and, given a poor performance, it could easily revert to its former state where it was potentially disabling. It is early days, but there is sufficient impetus, generated through reflecting upon the small successes I have had, to persevere.

> What have I learnt? That I become too easily discouraged!... If the principal safety behaviour I use is avoidance, then it is the behaviour I need to drop. So, I need to continue to participate...

The experiment was about testing my old beliefs of 'no good and useless'. During the experiment, the part that surprised me was when I started to feel anxious and had an urge to explain myself and what I was doing... This was actually about wanting others to think I was really good at my job, never putting a foot wrong, and to like me.

...I have avoided following through... I notice that when I consider contacting this particular friend I become anxious with an increase in negative thoughts, some of which are hot. At this point I need to explore with my peers as to why I am having this difficulty. I know it's got something to do with specific distortions, ie mind reading, mental filtering, overgeneralisation etc, but something in me prevents me from making that call which I can't access on my own.

My experiment was to go into the office and ask if someone would do a task I requested, me being in charge. My prediction was that I would either be ignored or they would make up some excuse. To my surprise, they all listened to me and one automatically said she would do it.

As a result of this I learned it is okay not to know how to do certain tasks. Nothing terrible happened as a result. In fact, it prompted other experiments involving risk taking. What have I learned? Firstly, people are much kinder and more forgiving of my mistakes than I am. Secondly, other people make mistakes too.

Ongoing experiments seem to be part of my daily life now. My level of procrastination has diminished. I have increased my level of social and leisure activities slightly.

...I did it and I will be okay to do it again. I still don't like it, but now I have a choice and the fear has been given a whipping... I do now feel a little liberated and need to think about how to move this forward some more.

The survey has made me realise that I am not unusual in the way I feel... I no longer think this rule is a problem because my feelings have been normalised.

...I have made great in-roads in disagreeing with people who I consider to be important...

I brought in a piece of video footage (to class), with the belief that I would receive criticism about developmental issues, which I would mentally filter as a generalisation that I'm always a rubbish therapist. This was completely disconfirmed... decreasing my belief from 60 per cent to 10 per cent.

What students appeared to learn

The above quotes seem to indicate students learnt that certain feelings are normal. The idea that behavioural experimentation can lead to personal liberation, and that experiments can become part of the repertoire of daily life, may also be evident from the above. Surprising, pleasant consequences to experiments, including discoveries about self, such as using avoidance as a safety behaviour, underscored the benefits of risk taking. The fragility of newly developing beliefs about oneself can also be read off from the above. A perhaps overarching learning experience was the discovery of deeply held beliefs and, equally, the emergence of new beliefs about oneself.

Possibilities and re-storying   Students found that they were able to develop a 'possibility focus' and re-story themselves through writing:

If I could develop a new perspective... I would feel less inhibited in (previously) stressful situations... In writing this, it occurs to me that what I might gain from developing new beliefs is a greater freedom to be myself, albeit that 'myself' would be altered.

I would feel freer in myself. I would be more spontaneous when in new company and develop awareness that I do not have to be liked by all people. My major learning would be that rejection happens and I can cope with this.

Writing this has made me realise that my worry about having to do things well has other implications. I am interested in... but... feel that I could not possibly take on any projects... because I do not know much about the area. But, by not doing anything I can not possibly improve. So, I think that is a cue for an experiment.

I re-read my story 'How I would like to be' and discovered an interesting Freudian slip: 'I found myself (at university) in an academic world *inhibited* by lots of bright, articulate students'. I meant to say 'inhabited' but I think my unconscious spoke up!

The above suggests students learning new ways of being their selves, and new possibilities for the journey of the self.

Self-confrontation   Students began to experientially as well as cognitively under-stand how difficult it is to confront and interrogate their own thoughts, feelings and related behaviours:

> **This could quite easily have been a client looking at them-selves and finding it difficult, and I can now understand why that is.**

> **I was surprised to find that I'd actually been experiencing some resistance and suddenly had an insight as to what clients can experience at the point they are facing 'losing' safety behaviours. I felt anxious and fearful at the thought of losing mine...**

Students seemed to find that personal change involved both the personal loss of, and the difficulties involved in confronting personal assumptions held by their (old) thoughts–feelings–behaviour systems. This seemed to help several students build empathy for clients' change endeavours.

Summary

1   Case formulation is said to improve cognitive behavioural practice in several key ways.

2   This argument relates to issues around cognitive behavioural case formula-tion's evidence-base.

3   There are several advantages and disadvantages of heuristic decision making in case formulation development.

4   Equally, there are common therapists' mistakes, and related ways of strengthening confidence in case formulation and its development through triangulation methods.

5   Emerging implications include the role of therapist self-practice.

Activities

1   Keep a reflective diary of your own case formulation construction decisions. Consider these in the light of described heuristic decision making and common ther-apist construction mistakes.

2   Formulate your own rules and related core beliefs. Devise and run experiments to strengthen new rules and core beliefs.

Further reading

Bennett-Levy, J., Butler, G., Fennell, M., Hackmann, A., Mueller, M. and Westbrook, D. (2004) *The Oxford Guide to Behavioural Experiments in Cognitive Therapy.* Oxford: Oxford University Press.
An excellent text on the theory and execution of behavioural experiments.

Gilbert, P. and Leahy, R.L. (eds) (2007) *The Therapeutic Relationship in the Cognitive Behavioural Psychotherapies.* Hove: Routledge.
The chapters in this book will help you consider important formulation and self-development relational issues.

The transdiagnostic turn and models of assessment and case formulation in action

Michael Townend and Alec Grant

Learning objectives

After reading this chapter and completing the activities at the end of it you should be able to:

1   Understand the similarities between traditional and transdiagnostic approaches to formulation.

2   Recognise the limitations of single dimensional models of formulation.

3   Recognise the similarities and differences between generic, disorder-specific and multi-level approaches to formulation.

4   Recognise the advantages and disadvantages of generic, disorder-specific and multi-level approaches to formulation.

5   Recognise the role of diversity and culture on formulation.

6   Understand the historical influences that can be important within formulation concerning onset and developmental factors.

TRADITIONAL APPROACH TO RESEARCH AND PRACTICE

The traditional approach to research and practice in cognitive behavioural psychotherapy is to take a 'disorder focus'. That is, researchers and practitioners have been concerned with the biological, genetic, cognitive, behavioural and affective processes within a specific disorder in order to try to understand what led to the problem appearing in the first place, its process of development over time and how it is currently maintained (Harvey et al., 2004). Disorder-focused work has led to the development of a body of literature that demonstrates the efficacy and effectiveness of cognitive behavioural psychotherapy across a large range of disorders (Harvey et al., 2004; Roth and Fonagy, 1996; Tarrier et al., 1998). This approach has also led to the successful development of a range of cognitive behavioural formulations to account for a sophisticated understanding and specification of disorder-specific cognitions and behaviours for almost all mental health problems (Tarrier, 2006).

However, the traditional disorder approach has the following limitations:

1   Researchers working with a specific disorder often work in isolation from researchers working with other disorders.
2   Disorder-specific research often fails to recognise cognitive, behavioural, emotional, social and biological processes that are common across disorders.
3   Clinicians have been slow to utilise multi-level cognitive theories and frameworks. Multi-level theories can account for a range of processes across disorders and thus they can also be used to underpin formulation.

THE TRANSDIAGNOSTIC APPROACH TO RESEARCH AND PRACTICE

Recently Harvey and colleagues have made a compelling argument for a transdiagnostic approach to research and treatment within cognitive behavioural psychotherapy (Harvey et al., 2004). The essence of this approach is to consider the reasoning, behavioural, attentional, memory and thought processes which are common across disorders and might predispose individuals to develop and maintain problems, or promote remission and recovery. The diagram below illustrates in schematic form the transdiagnostic approach to research and therapy.

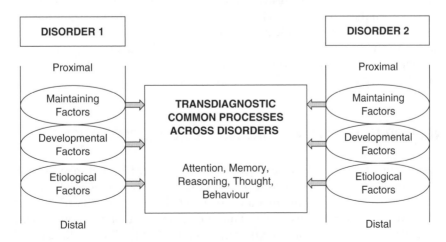

Figure 6.1   The transdiagnostic approach to research and theory

Traditionally, the cognitive behavioural psychotherapist would take a single disorder approach and assess and formulate in terms of a client's maintaining, developmental and aetiological factors. Whilst this remains a valuable and important approach in the context of people with a single psychological problem, it can be difficult for the cognitive behavioural psychotherapist using this approach to adequately consider and account for the interaction between two or more co-morbid problems – seen, for example, in people with depression and obsessive compulsive disorder or depression and personality disorder. A transdiagnostic approach can help to overcome this through the consideration of common processes, such as attention, memory, reasoning, thought and behaviour, across disorders and how they interact or have interacted with each other from the initial development through to current maintaining factors.

Case example of a transdiagnostic formulation

'TERRY'

Terry was a 36-year-old man with a 17-year history of Obsessive Compulsive Disorder (OCD), with contamination fears and rituals and co-morbid major depression. The major depression was recurrent with a first episode when he was 14 years of age, when he had been referred to the local children and adolescent mental health service. Despite his psychological difficulties he had trained as a plumber and was holding down a full-time job. When referred for cognitive behavioural psychotherapy, his OCD had worsened and he was moderately depressed but was still able to work.

The case study for Terry and the formulation shown illustrates the series of processes associated with the maintenance of his OCD and depression. It also shows the relationship between his mood disturbance and his anxiety, as he was depressed about his OCD symptoms and his depression was increasing his anxiety. This approach to formulation also gives the cognitive behavioural psychotherapist the opportunity to consider interactions between the processes associated with the different problems. These include the ease of recall of negative categorical memories, in turn influencing memories related to ritualistic behaviour, and the reduction in activity levels leading to reduced exposure to contamination and either the prevention of habituation or a reduction in experiences that might disconfirm his OCD related beliefs (see Figure 6.2).

SINGLE OR MULTIDIMENSIONAL MODELS OF FORMULATION?

There is an increasing tendency to reject single variable theories of mental health in favour of multidimensional models which propose an interaction of risk factors in the aetiology, development and maintenance of psychological problems (Harvey et al., 2004). A linear, single dimensional explanation of a particular psychopathology, for example depression, might propose that the origins of unhelpful thinking or behaviour can be traced to a single cause. Such single cause models might include chemical

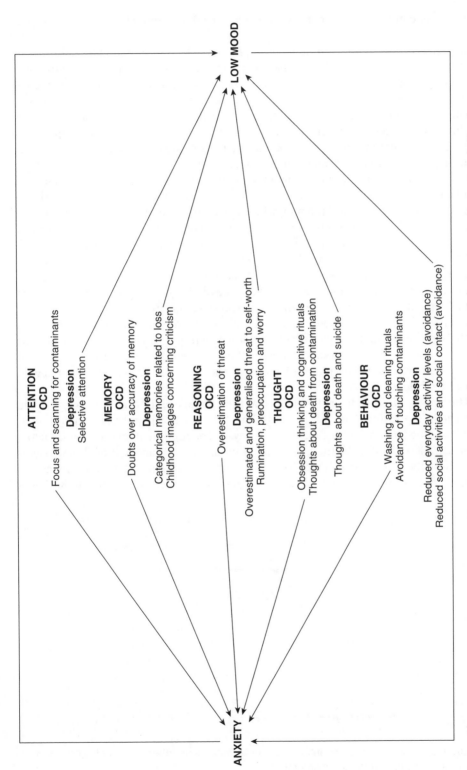

ATTENTION
OCD
Focus and scanning for contaminants
Depression
Selective attention

MEMORY
OCD
Doubts over accuracy of memory
Depression
Categorical memories related to loss
Childhood images concerning criticism

REASONING
OCD
Overestimation of threat
Depression
Overestimated and generalised threat to self-worth
Rumination, preoccupation and worry

THOUGHT
OCD
Obsession thinking and cognitive rituals
Thoughts about death from contamination
Depression
Thoughts about death and suicide

BEHAVIOUR
OCD
Washing and cleaning rituals
Avoidance of touching contaminants
Depression
Reduced everyday activity levels (avoidance)
Reduced social activities and social contact (avoidance)

LOW MOOD

ANXIETY

Figure 6.2 Formulation of the maintenance of Terry's depression and OCD (with each transdiagnostic process capitalised)

imbalance, conditioning or early experiences of family conflict, trauma or adverse life events.

In contrast, a systemic, multidimensional approach to formulation would propose that many factors could influence the production of unhelpful thinking, feelings and behaviour in later life. For example, frameworks for schema, defined as an individual's 'construction and understanding of the world' are in a constant state of change and evolution (Freeman and Martin, 2004: 225). Schemas change through an active and evolutionary process when perceptions and existing cognitive structures are applied to new or novel situations, while new cognitive structures are developed to serve old functions in new situations (Freeman and Martin, 2004).

From this perspective, if individuals are unable to develop new structures or continue to fit old structures to new situations, their construction and understanding of themselves and the world around them may be incongruent and may lead to psychological problems. Similarly, other influences on unhelpful thinking, feelings and behaviour can occur through traumatisation or biological influences such as the ease of conditionability of an individual. Schema development can also be influenced by a broad range of experiences, including cultural and social learning.

Cultural and social learning factors in any formulation cannot therefore be analysed out of context of the individual's unique interpretation of his or her environment. The relationship between behaviour, cognition and the environment has been emphasised in the social learning theory of triadic reciprocal determinism (Bandura, 2004). This theory proposes that behaviour, cognition, other personal factors and the environment all act as interlocking determinants which can affect each other in a bidirectional way, illustrated below.

The context of the individual is defined as their biological state, genetic make up and behaviour, in conjunction with cognitive and emotional responses. The environment itself is defined in terms of social, cultural, physical environment and economic factors (Gilbert, 2004, 2006). We therefore argue that any one component of these systems can effect the other components. Depression in formulation can thus no longer be thought of as simply a product of either biochemistry or social environment. Rather, it

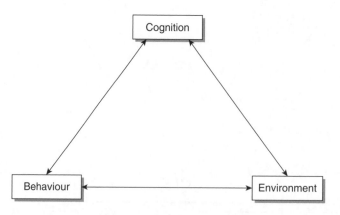

Figure 6.3   Schematic representation of triadic reciprocal determinism between cognition, behaviour and the environment

is viewed as a complex, evolving and, in part, genetically influenced problem, which is expressed when the individual is exposed to a variety of 'risk' variables. Such variables may be environmental, social, metabolic or psychological, depending upon the type of depression or the form that it takes.

These ideas pose a significant challenge for cognitive behavioural psychotherapists attempting to keep abreast of all the research taking place on each of the factors influencing the onset, development and maintenance of even relatively straightforward problems of anxiety or depression. The advantages of using multidimensional models, as demonstrated in the chronic depression with self-attacking chapter (in Part II of this text), through careful assessment and attention to the client's narrative, is that a much better explanatory formulation can be developed compared with sticking rigidly to single factor models. We will now discuss some of the solutions to the difficulties posed by the need to develop complex formulations for complex clinical problems.

FORMULATION IN ACTION

As has been argued previously, a simple rule of thumb when developing formulations with clients is to ensure that they are not so simple that key factors are either missed or so complex that they are overwhelming for both client and therapist – in other words, the formulation must be parsimonious. The formulation needs to be able to account for all the factors at play in maintaining the client's psychological difficulties. What this means in practice is that cognitive behavioural psychotherapists need to be comfortable using a range of different approaches to formulation. Further to the discussion in Chapter 4, we have found it helpful to consider formulation at three levels (but not hierarchically arranged).

This three level framework uses specific theoretical models as the basis for the higher levels, simplified by using clinical heuristics which are based on the main premises of the theories or models. The levels in the framework include multi-level, disorder-specific and generic formulations. We are not suggesting that cognitive behavioural psychotherapists always develop these different levels of formulation with each and every client, but that the different levels may offer a different perspective for both the client and the therapist. What is therefore important is that the most appropriate level for explaining the maintenance (and/or onset and development) of the distress being experienced by the client is used. The form that the formulation takes may also change as therapy progresses, either through the use of different models or through additions to existing models. For example, we have found it useful to sometimes use simpler clinical level formulations with clients, but use multi-level formulations and theory to help to understand some of the more complex ideas such as intellectual and emotional beliefs.

In addition, we have also found it helpful to use more explanatory and multi-level formulations later in therapy to help the client to understand why they have or have not improved with certain interventions, such as cognitive re-appraisal of thoughts, or why they might be experiencing particular types of imagery, or how their schemas may have been formed and maintained and importantly processes of non-cognitive conditioning and automatic experiences of emotion which will be discussed further below and in the health anxiety and depression chapters in Part II of this text.

MULTI-LEVEL FORMULATIONS

Research indicates that emotion is probably influenced by several cognitive and conditioning (associative) processes (Dalgleish, 2004; Harvey et al., 2004). In order to understand these processes, cognitive scientists have developed a number of what are referred to as multi-level or multi-representational theories. Two of the most influential multi-level theories are the Schematic Propositional Associative and Analogical Representational System (SPAARS) (Power and Dalgleish, 1999) and Interacting Cognitive Subsystems (ICS) (Teasdale, 1997; Teasdale and Barnard, 1993). Both these theories were originally developed to help to understand ordinary everyday human experiences, but have since been applied to understanding psychopathology and we have found them very useful as the basis for formulation. The advantage of multi-level theories over other models is in their capacity to account for and explain that emotions can be created in two different ways using different processes. They can also be produced without conscious processing when the associative system is involved (within SPAARS), and the same process is described as an interlock between the propositional and implicational systems using ICS as the theoretical framework (see the health anxiety chapter in Part II of this text for further information regarding this process and a detailed case study example). Further information about SPAARS is also presented below. In addition, we draw readers' attention to an additional multi-level theory that has also been developed for PTSD – dual representational theory (Brewin et al., 1996). This can be used as the basis for formulation in PTSD, particularly when it is important for clients to understand why some aspects of their trauma memories cause them more distress than others, and why they keep re-experiencing their trauma in the form of flashbacks, images and nightmares.

The SPAARS theory consists of four explicit levels of mental representation:

1   The schematic representational level represents abstracted, generic knowledge (as such it is similar to schema theory).
2   Propositional representations represent referential meaning in a narrative form (similar to automatic thoughts).
3   Analogical representational system stores information and memories as auditory, visual, olfactory, gustatory, body state and proprioceptive 'images' and also codes non-verbal referential information to complement the propositional system.
4   Associative representations act by connecting the information in the other representational parts of the system and also code different types of information in memory.

Through the interactions between the above, SPAARS can explain both cognitive representation and process. As suggested above, the importance of this theory for formulation lies in its explanatory value with the generation of emotion through two different routes. These routes are through appraisal where events and interpretations are appraised at the schematic level of meaning with respect to the individual's goals. The second route for the generation of an emotional response is an automatic route through associative representations – which is a very similar notion to conditioning (Dalgleish, 2004). The SPAARS model is shown in Figure 6.4.

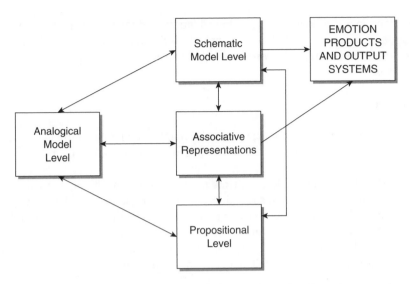

Figure 6.4   A schematic diagram of the schematic, propositional, analogue and associative representational systems (SPAARS). (Power and Dalgleish, 1997: 178; © 1997 Psychology Press. Reproduced with permission)

Research evidence for multi-level theories

There is now an accumulating body of research that supports the clinical observations and the ICS and SPAARS theories that indicate processing can in fact occur at one cognitive level, in the absence of processing at another level. A good example of this can be found in specific phobias. Exposure to the phobic stimuli for people with specific phobias results in intense fear when seeing the feared animal, insect or object despite knowing that it is actually harmless. The fear in this example would be produced associatively in SPAARS and the knowledge propositionally. Similarly, this would occur automatically in ICS through the implicational system without appraisal by the propositional system. This is supported by experimental evidence that seems to show that associative processing can be non-conscious (Ohman and Soares, 1994).

Evaluation

Below are some of the advantages and disadvantages of multi-level theories in the context of the overall development of formulations.

Advantages

1   Multi-level theories such as ICS and SPAARS can explain emotional conflict.
2   There is good evidence that emotions can be produced automatically for which other models frequently fail to account.
3   Multi-level theories offer the clinician an opportunity to consider and incorporate transdiagnostic processes and therefore develop holistic formulations which take into account interactions of different 'disorders' or emotional states within the individual.

An example is that following being raped, an individual may experience co-existing depression, anxiety and PTSD symptoms. These different disorders may interact with each other in the areas of reasoning, behavioural, attention, memory and thought processes.

Disadvantages

1   Multi-level theories are complex and need simplification for client use in formulation.
2   They do not account well for physiological processes without some modification.

A case of ICS being used to underpin formulation in a case of health anxiety can be found in Part II of this text. We have also produced a set of simplified formulation worksheets located at the end of that chapter that can be used for developing multi-level formulations. In practice we have found it useful at times to consider client onset, development and maintaining factors from a multi-level perspective, but use idiosyncratic or generic formulation systems when developing collaborative explanations with clients.

DISORDER-SPECIFIC FORMULATIONS

Cognitive behavioural disorder-specific formulations have been developed for a whole range of disorders such as depression, generalised anxiety, PTSD, phobias, panic, personality disorders, obsessive compulsive disorder, conduct disorders in children, symptoms of psychosis, morbid grief, marital and relationship problems, health anxiety, chronic pain, chronic fatigue and irritable bowel syndrome (See Clark and Fairburn, 2005; Freeman et al., 2004; Grant et al., 2004b; Tarrier, 2006; Tarrier et al., 1998).

In terms of their origins, disorder-specific formulation models can usually be traced back to the original clinical model of Beck and his co-workers (Beck et al., 1979). However, in practice, disorder-specific models are adapted to take account of the specifics of a particular disorder and also, most importantly, the content and form of the cognitions associated with that particular problem. In other words, they follow the premise of the cognitive content specificity hypothesis, that disorders can be separated and understood on the basis of the differences in thought content (Wells, 1997).

Detailed examples of disorder-specific formulations

Social phobia   Social phobia (Clark and Wells, 1995) focuses on the association between negative thoughts and beliefs about social situations and the person's tendency to direct attention inwards. This self-monitoring (behaviour) and accompanied visual images of the self as a social object (thoughts) triggers behavioural reactions which exacerbate the problem by negatively effecting social performance.

To illustrate a disorder-specific formulation, an example of social phobia using the Clark and Wells (1995) model is shown in Figures 6.5 and 6.6 (Gowlett and Townend, 2007).

Research Evidence for a Cognitive Model of Social Phobia   In order to use disorder-specific models well in the practice of case formulation, it is important to understand the specific content of the thoughts and thinking processes. This is exemplified in social

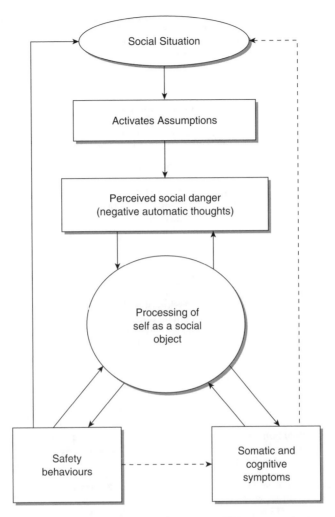

Figure 6.5 Cognitive model of social phobia (reproduced from *Cognitive Therapy of Anxiety Disorders* by A. Wells, 1997: 169; © 1997 John Wiley and Sons Ltd. Reproduced with permission).

phobia, and the model thus indicates areas that need to be assessed in order to inform the formulation.

When using the cognitive model of social phobia formulation, it is important that the therapist recognises the unhelpful processing of the client's 'self as a social object' rather than the processing of other peoples' reactions to the self. This is important as this issue is now thought to be one of the core maintaining features of social anxiety, whereby individuals automatically self-focus during social situations which heightens their awareness of internal cues such as a shaky voice or blushing. This, in turn, confirms their view of themselves as appearing socially inadequate (Harvey et al., 2004).

In developing this perspective of social anxiety, Clark and Wells (1995) argue that it is the manner in which the socially anxious person encounters their feared situations,

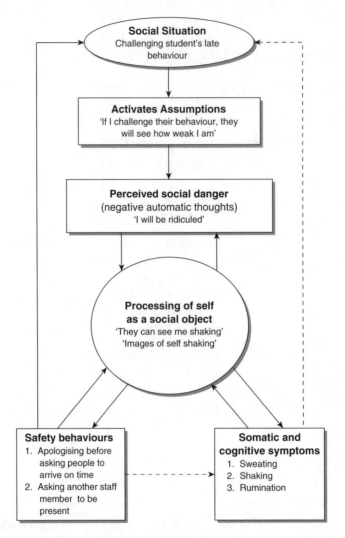

Figure 6.6   The cognitive model of social phobia being applied to an actual case of a socially anxious lecturer.

in terms of the processing priorities, coping behaviours and the nature of normal interpersonal transactions, which conspires to impede reduction in negative beliefs. These behaviours are then responsible for maintaining the problem owing to the development of a closed feedback loop. It is believed that this self-focused attention (SFA), plays a crucial role in the maintenance of social anxiety (Clark and Wells, 1995; Mulkens et al., 1999), as heightened SFA intensifies negative emotional states, physiological responses and also increases unhelpful thinking. This makes social interactions extremely uncomfortable events and also contributes to the socially anxious person's negative self-appraisal (Bogels et al., 1997; Wells et al., 1997).

Clark and Wells (1995) developed a concept of negative self-appraisal, and argued that the persistence of social anxiety may be largely due to the fact that people with the problem seldom encounter situations that are capable of providing unambiguous disconfirmation of their fears. This is in part due to the central feature of social anxiety being a strong desire to convey a favourable impression of one's self to others, accompanied by a marked insecurity in the socially anxious individual that he will successfully carry this off. The person is thus hypervigilant to the possibility that he may be exposed as 'inadequate', and will suffer negative consequences in terms of loss of status, rejection and humiliation by others (Wells, 1997).

Socially anxious people therefore adopt safety behaviours and avoidance in order to prevent what they consider to be a social catastrophe occurring. However, these behaviours only serve to heighten self-focus, prevent disconfirmation, and may directly contaminate the social situation by causing a reduction of objective interpersonal information, and the fact that socially anxious individuals may appear aloof, unfriendly, or lacking social skills (Wells, 1997).

Generalised anxiety   Wells' (1997) model of metacognition, or thoughts about thoughts, in generalised anxiety disorder (GAD), formulates the link between beliefs about worries and the actual experience of worrying. Negative beliefs drive anxiety about worrying and its consequences, while positive beliefs drive preoccupation with the importance of worrying as a means of keeping the individual safe. The disorder-specific cognitive formulation model for GAD is shown in Figure 6.7

According to this model, a main distinguishing feature of GAD is the forms that worry takes and the individual's appraisal of their significance (Wells, 1997; Wells and Carter, 1999). According to Wells (1997) there are two types of worries: Type 1 and Type 2. Type 1 worries refer to worrying *per se*. Type 2 worries, on the other hand, are focused on the significance, and appraisal, of worry. Type 2 worry is essentially 'meta-worry', or worry about worry. According to the cognitive model of GAD, clients can appraise the activity of worrying in both negative and positive ways. Negative appraisals include:

- 'My worries are uncontrollable'
- 'Worrying is harmful'
- 'I might go crazy if I don't stop worrying'
- 'My worries will take over and control me'

Positive beliefs about worrying generally relate to their benefits as a coping strategy, including the importance of worry in preventing bad things from happening (Wells, 1997).

Some examples of positive appraisals of worry are:

- 'Worrying helps me cope'
- 'If I worry about the worst and I can see myself coping then I probably will cope if it happens'
- 'If I worry I can prevent bad things from happening'
- 'If I worry I will always be prepared'

Unfortunately, the use of worry as a coping strategy generates its own problems. It increases sensitivity to threat-related information and generates an elaborate range of negative outcomes and scenarios, each of which is capable of sustaining a worry in its own right.

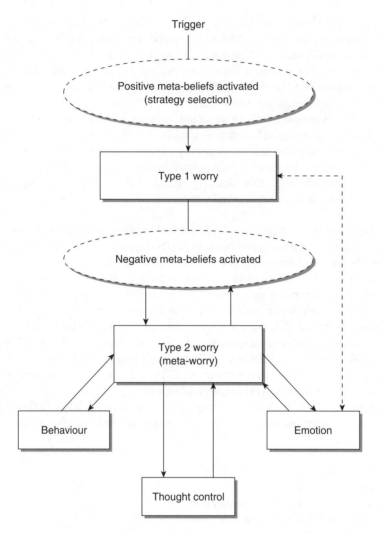

Figure 6.7   Cognitive model of GAD (reproduced from *Cognitive Therapy of Anxiety Disorders* by A Wells, 1997: 204; © 1997 John Wiley and Sons Ltd. Reproduced with permission).

According to Wells (1997), two types of behaviours are also thought to be important in the maintenance of GAD. These are avoidance (including safety behaviours), such as avoidance of social events or unpleasant news, and reassurance seeking. Avoidances may also be of external dangers (Type 1 worry), such as the possibility of drawing attention to the self, resulting in humiliation or shame. Equally, avoidance can also be of the dangers of worry itself (Type 2 worry).

Reassurance seeking is evident in most individuals with GAD and is aimed at interrupting worry cycles or preventing the onset of chronic worry. However, reassurance seeking can lead to conflicting responses across respondents, which is likely to increase the range of stimuli that are worried about. In other situations, reassurance such as having a partner phone at regular intervals to say that she/he is safe, can temporarily prevent worry while equally increasing the propensity for worry if reassurance is not delivered on time.

In this model, the GAD client uses worry as a processing strategy in response to a trigger. Triggers for Type 1 worry vary, such as exposure to negative news, an intruding thought such as an unpleasant image, or exposure to a situation associated with a sense of subjective danger. The selection of worry as a coping strategy stems from the activation of positive beliefs about the use of worry.

Once the GAD client is executing a worry routine, negative beliefs may be readily activated by the early signs of worrying such as the initial intruding thought. Negative beliefs concern the uncontrollability and dangers associated with worrying and stimulate appraisal of worry (meta-worry). The negative appraisal of worry motivates the use of strategies intended to reduce the appraised danger.

The use of thought control is one method of control in GAD and manifests in different ways. Since people have positive and negative beliefs about their worries, worry may be practised within strict limits or in special ways that are intended to exploit the benefits of worrying while, at the same time, avoiding the dangers. Thus worrying becomes a controlled rumination strategy used as a means of generating and rehearsing coping responses. In contrast, strategies may be used to suppress worries.

While the execution of Type 1 worry may be controlled in ways to meet personal goals, a disadvantage of suppression control attempts is that they are likely to increase the occurrence of unwanted thoughts (Clark et al., 1991). The effects of thought control or suppression attempts may be to increase the frequency of worry triggers which, in turn, is likely to strengthen negative beliefs about thoughts such as beliefs about their uncontrollability.

A different perspective might be that worry itself may serve a cognitive avoidance function. Some individuals may use worry or rumination to block-out other types of more distressing thoughts. According to this view, worry represents a form of cognitive-emotional avoidance (Borkovec and Inz, 1990). Both Type 1 and 2 worry are associated with emotional responses. Type 1 worry can lead to initial increments in anxiety and tension. However, with the activation of Type 2 worry, anxiety escalates and emotional symptoms may be interpreted as evidence supporting Type 2 concerns. For example, symptoms of racing mind, dissociation and inability to relax may be viewed as evidence of loss of mental control or going mad.

Research evidence in support of a cognitive model of GAD   The model is supported by the following:

1   Both positive and negative beliefs about worry are positively associated with proneness to pathological worrying (Wells and Papageorgiou, 1998).
2   Individuals meeting criteria for GAD give higher ratings for positive reasons for worrying involving superstition and problem-solving than non-anxious individuals (Borkovec and Roemer, 1995).
3   Patients with GAD report significantly greater negative beliefs about worrying than patients with panic disorder or social phobia (Wells and Carter, 2001).
4   Type 2 worry is a better predictor than Type 1 worry of pathological, GAD-like worry in non-patients (Wells and Carter, 1999).
5   Worrying after exposure to stress is associated with an incubation of intrusive thoughts (Wells and Papageorgiou, 1995), and individual differences in the use of worry to control thoughts is associated with the development of PTSD (Holeva et al., 2001).

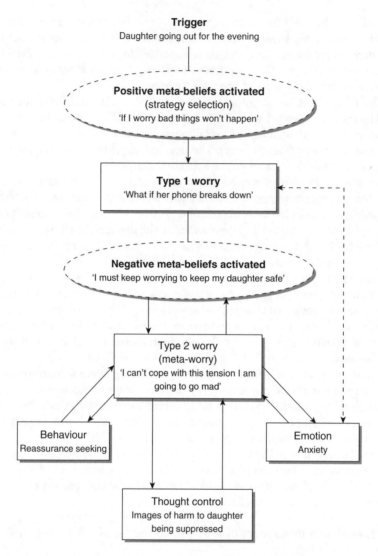

Figure 6.8 A cognitive model of GAD being applied to an actual case

The above data suggests that worrying can contribute to intrusions and are consistent with the idea that it may stimulate negative meta-cognitive beliefs about thinking.

Figure 6.8 shows the cognitive model of GAD being applied to an actual case of a mother worried that harm will come to her daughter on social nights out with her friends.

The examples of social phobia and GAD above illustrate, in depth, with empirical support and using real case examples, specific formulations associated with these two problem areas. As with social phobia and GAD, other disorder-specific models vary in the form and content of the relationship between situations, thoughts, emotions and behaviour. This shifting SETB relationship, as a function of disorder, will now be briefly described for a range of problems seen by cognitive behavioural psychotherapists.

Clark's (1988) model of panic emphasises the link between catastrophic misinterpretations (thoughts), and physiological sensations in the generation of panic attacks. From this perspective, a person might worry that dizziness and a headache are signs of an imminent stroke. Clark also emphasises the link between specific types of behaviour described as 'safety behaviours' and catastrophic interpretations. These safety behaviours serve to prevent disconfirmation of catastrophic thoughts about physical aspects of anxiety as well as other normal physiological sensations.

Formulation models of obsessive compulsive disorder (OCD) emphasise the link between different levels of thinking, or appraisal of thinking, and its link to behaviour and emotion. Salkovskis (1985) points to the role of beliefs about responsibility, suggesting that OCD sufferers believe that unless they take action to avoid a negative intrusive thought coming true they will be responsible, causing great distress (see the case study of OCD in Part II of this text).

In a similar way to OCD, health anxiety models (for example Brown, 2006; Salkovskis, 1989) show how behavioural reactions to beliefs about illness elicit more potential physiological triggers for anxiety (see Part II for a case study of health anxiety).

In auditory hallucinations or voice hearing (Chadwick et al., 1996), the ABC model is used to focus on the person's beliefs about voices. The hallucination is described as a thought experienced by the person as an externally heard voice. What the person tells themselves about this voice determines how they react and feel, which can potentially exacerbate the problem (see also Mills et al., 2004c, 2006 and Part II of this text for a case study of helping someone with this kind of problem).

The Ehlers and Clark (2000) model of post-traumatic stress disorder emphasises the connection between beliefs, emotions and behaviours about the traumatic event as well as beliefs about the normal emotional and psychological responses to these kinds of events. Avoidance and safety behaviours and fragmented memories are highlighted as factors maintaining these negative beliefs (see Part II for a case study of a person with this type of problem).

Fennell's (1998, 2006) model of low self-esteem highlights particular types of thoughts and beliefs, emotions and related behaviour. Beliefs about failing to measure up to standards lead, in the form of vicious circles, to self-critical thoughts, anxious predictions, and negative beliefs about self and concomitant low mood and anxiety (see Part II for a case study of a person suffering from this type of problem).

In all of these examples, the formulation models include links between thoughts, emotions, events, physiological sensations and behaviour. However, there are subtle variations in the types of thoughts, cognitive processes, attention processes, memory forms and types of behaviours at play in the particular problems being described.

Evaluating disorder-specific models

Below are some of the advantages and disadvantages of disorder-specific models within formulation.

Advantages

- Disorder-specific theories and related formulations describe very well many of the features of anxiety and depression.
- They describe the specific cognitive content of the specific problem.

- They frequently describe common processing issues associated with the problem.
- They frequently describe the main behavioural features of the problem.
- They are relatively easily understood by both clients and therapists.

Disadvantages

- They don't always offer the clinician an opportunity to consider and incorporate transdiagnostic processes and therefore develop holistic formulations that take into account interactions of different disorders or emotional states within the individual.
- They do not account well for physiological processes without some modification.
- They don't provide full details of the development of the problem, which may vary greatly between individuals.
- They do not account for emotions that are produced automatically.
- They fail to adequately account for environmental and other contextual factors.

ENVIRONMENTAL INFLUENCES IN FORMULATION

Diversity

When therapists meet their clients for the first time a process occurs whereby individual similarities are assessed, then areas of difference noted as a rapid cognitive/affective process takes place which the client and therapist may have little conscious awareness of. Issues noted might be similarities or differences in age, gender might be another, as might being from the same region of a country, colour or social class or religion. This process is a natural phenomenon and one that cognitive behavioural psychotherapists need to be aware of, as these are differences which need to be bridged if the therapist's own cultural assumptions are not to inaccurately influence thinking, interactions and formulation of client problems.

Cultural and social factors are an important determinant of psychological problems in a number of ways, and need to be accounted for in cognitive behavioural case formulation. They impact on how clients within the psychotherapeutic context express and manifest their difficulties, the style of coping adopted, the family and community supports employed, the willingness of clients to seek therapy and how they might present their problems to their family doctor, primary care professional and ultimately to their therapist. Similarly, the culture of psychological therapy services and mental health services in general also influences diagnosis, treatment and the delivery of services (see Chapter 9 of this text).

Mental health problems are prevalent across all populations, regardless of race or ethnicity (LaTaillade, 2006). There is also no doubt that cultural and social factors contribute to the development of psychological problems, and this contribution is relative to particular problems. We argued earlier that psychological problems are the product of complex interactions between biological, cultural, psychological and social factors. The role of any one of these major factors can be stronger or weaker, depending on the specific problem.

The overall incidence of psychological problems is similar between the larger ethnic groups. What cognitive behavioural psychotherapists therefore need to recognise is that there are a number of high-need sub-groups that have higher incidence and prevalence rates of psychological problems. These sub-groupings of people have often been obscured in larger community surveys (LaTaillade, 2006). Further, there are a number of social difficulties and inequalities which face all ethnic groups, racial minorities and migrant populations. Individuals and groups may be confronted with racism and discrimination which, together with frequent exposure to violence and poverty, can exert a potentially toxic effect on psychological well-being in susceptible individuals.

There is also evidence that some minority groups have a distrust of mental health services, citing clinical bias and stereotyping as significant factors in their mistrust. Such findings, together with other variables such as cultural misunderstandings and communication problems, are all issues that cognitive behavioural psychotherapists must acknowledge and seek to overcome within their practice (see Chapter 9 of this text).

Culture-bound syndromes

A number of specific culture-bound conditions have also been identified and described in the international psychiatric literature. An awareness of these can be important for cognitive behavioural psychotherapists within assessment and formulation when working with particular groups or contexts. Some of these culture-bound syndromes have been listed in the *DSM-IV TR* Glossary (APA, 2000) and in the *ICD-10* Diagnostic Criteria for Research (WHO, 2002). Among the terms listed in both are a number of low mood and anxiety-based reactions which present as physically or psychologically focused problems and reactions. A list of these, adapted from Wolfgang (2001) is shown in Table 6.1 below.

Table 6.1   Culture-bound syndromes: problems and reactions

Culture-bound Syndrome	Language or Region	Name
Fear of genital shrinking	Malay-Indonesian Mandarin Chinese Languages	Koro Suo-yang
Fear of semen leakage	India	Chat or Jiryan
Dissociative reactions to a specific startle stimulus	Malay-Indonesian languages Thailand Phillippines Siberia Rural populations of French-Canadian background in the Northeast of the US	latah Bah-tschi Mali-mali miryachit Jumping
Fear that one's external appearance is offending to others	Japan	Taijin-kyofu
Acute stress depression symptoms	North American indigenous population	Anomie
Vision disturbance when reading	African Students	Brain fag

Culture, religion and ethnicity in the formulation process

In order to be relationally focused and collaborative in a way that respects and is sensitive to difference, it is important that cognitive behavioural psychotherapists are familiar with some of the main tenets of the major religions and societal or community level beliefs and take every opportunity to continue to educate and learn from their clients who are from minority or different backgrounds to their own (Newman, 2007).

These ideas also have major implications for the development of formulations with clients. In relational terms, the therapist demonstrating that they understand or that they are taking the opportunity to learn about the person's heritage or religious beliefs can help to develop the therapeutic relationship (LaTaillade, 2006). Newman (2007) has recently helpfully outlined some of these issues by drawing the cognitive behavioural psychotherapist's attention to the following:

1   The importance and respect for traditional family systems, hierarchical social structures and family member roles in Asian clients. Respect for parents or the head of the household (if not the parent) and the strong influence of shame with consequent reticence in revealing information or engagement in behaviours that might be seen as shaming for the family. This is important in formulation as it is likely to be more helpful to understand this as being dutiful to the family rather than resistance.
2   Black clients (people of African origin), as discussed earlier in this chapter, may be particularly concerned about receiving prejudicial treatment from white therapists or not being offered appropriate therapy. Again this may usefully be incorporated into formulation with particular attention to the therapeutic relationship and other strategies to develop trust. A further issue that can also arise in therapy in our experience is that some clients of mixed race, or in some cases black clients brought up by white parents following adoption, have difficulty identifying with either 'black or white cultures' and report feeling lost, isolated and unsure of their own identity. Again these issues, if present, need to be identified and addressed within formulation.

Religion and its associated beliefs and rituals also need to be understood by the cognitive behavioural psychotherapist if formulation is to be fully reflective of the individual and their needs. It is also important in our view that formulation goes beyond just understanding religious beliefs but that they are incorporated into the formulation when the therapist and client agree jointly that it is relevant and appropriate to do so.

Kumar (2007) in support of the above argues that within Indian cultures standard cognitive behavioural approaches need to be adapted to incorporate a spiritual dimension as a matter of routine. Thus SETB (situation-emotion-thought-behaviour) becomes SETBS (situation-emotion-thought-behaviour–spiritual) or the five aspects model becomes six with the specific addition of the spiritual dimension. Hebblethwaite (2002), in his therapeutic work with people with strong Christian beliefs, argued for adopting standard cognitive models of therapy and formulation by the incorporation of the influence of the Holy Ghost or Will of God into therapy. These approaches demonstrate innovative thinking concerning the structure and content of formulation in particular religious contexts that can be adapted to other religions that may also facilitate connectedness with the client in terms of the therapeutic relationship.

Socioeconomic factors

Poverty has the greatest and most directly measurable effect on rates of psychological need. People in lower income brackets, lower educational status, and certain occupations have a two to threefold increase in their likelihood of developing psychological problems. Racism, discrimination and bullying in the work place are also associated with disorders such as chronic anxiety and depression (LaTaillade, 2006). Again these issues can and should be incorporated into the formulation when the therapist and client agree jointly that it is relevant and appropriate to do so.

INITIAL ONSET AND DEVELOPMENTAL FACTORS IN FORMULATION

It has already been argued that the origin of psychological difficulties cannot be traced back to a single causal agent. Multi-factorial origins might consist of contributions from a number of sources, such as attachment relationships, conditioning, social learning – including cultural and religious influences as outlined above and information all interacting with environmental, genetic and biological factors. This poses a particular problem for cognitive behavioural psychotherapists who, in the process of formulation development, need to tease out these factors and influences in order to understand the individual's experiences which have contributed to the initial onset or origin of the psychological difficulties.

Many of these events will have occurred years previously and in a way in which the individual may not be aware – for example, through poor mother-child bonding following undetected post-natal depression continuing for several years after the child is born. This might lead to later difficulties with relationships and the development of certain communication or behaviour patterns, all of which may influence schema development and ultimately psychological difficulties for the individual in later life.

In short, the initial onset of psychological problems may be difficult to identify and such hypotheses can only be inferred from the information gathered from careful assessment. It is however important that cognitive behavioural psychotherapists make these hypotheses to inform the formulation. Clients also seek to understand the origins of their difficulties and it can be helpful to identify these with the client, although we do routinely stress the tentative and hypothetical nature regarding such origins. We also take great care when doing so, as it can lead to blaming of others for the client's current psychological difficulties. If not handled appropriately, this can lead to resentment developing or clients blaming their parents for their problems in relationship breakdowns.

Like the origins of clients' psychological difficulties, their subsequent development is also subject to multi-factorial influences, including classical and operant conditioning, schema formation, behaviour patterns and biological adaptation. Developmental factors are again important as will be illustrated in the following example:

'FREDDY' FORMULATION

Freddy is 34 years of age, with a diagnosis of borderline personality disorder (BPD). When seen for assessment he had detailed his problems as a problem with controlling his emotions with frequent, intense and unpredictable and at times sudden changes of mood (significant mood swings up and down). Like many other clients with BPD,

(Continued)

(Continued)

Freddy was fully aware of his problem and his apparent 'differences' from others around him. He was desperate to solve these emotional and relational problems, but had been unable to do so despite medication, previous counselling and attempts at internet therapy, book-based self-help and seeking out internet support groups. He described having never being able to form close relationships with others, with a sense of detachment (particularly from his family), and on occasions did not seem to be able to feel the whole range of human emotions in appropriate situations or occasions. He often felt anger or frequently became low and tearful. He felt as if he was full of fear, especially socially, experienced a chronic sense of emptiness and loneliness at other times, and terror of having these experiences most of the time.

Initial onset

From Freddy's history it seemed that several factors and life events had contributed to the development of his BPD. His mother died within six weeks of his birth in a road traffic accident. He was subsequently brought up by his grandmother and father. His father was probably severely depressed throughout most of his childhood. Freddy described his family and wider social environment as critical and uncaring. He would frequently be physically abused by his grandmother who held 'very high expectations of him' which Freddy felt he could never meet no matter how hard he tried. He described his relationship with his father as difficult because of the latter's emotional distance.

His primary negative core belief about himself was: 'I'm unlovable'. Freddy also had the following core beliefs which compounded his sense of being unlovable: 'I'm bad' and 'I'm a failure'. His core beliefs about other people and the world included 'other people can't be trusted, because they will reject me', and 'the world is unsafe, unpredictable and very dangerous'. Conditional assumptions which guided his behaviour in order to prevent Freddy from exposing his painful beliefs and experiences included 'If I work harder at being what others want me to be then people will like me', 'If I am myself then I'll be rejected', and 'If I am out of control (experiencing strong emotions) then this is a sign that I can't cope and that I am mad and no one will be able to or willing to help me'. Paradoxically he also believed that 'If I am in control then I am safe' and 'I should not need to rely on others in any situation'.

In response to his beliefs, Freddy engaged in a variety of compensatory and safety strategies in order to prevent his beliefs being exposed. These included strategies to maintain a sense of control, such as criticising himself continually, self-harm, avoidant strategies such as withdrawing and isolating himself. Freddy also had a long history of seeking excessive reassurance from others (although his social isolation meant that this was now very rare). When in the company of his father he attempted to be special by trying to engage him in intellectual conversations and avoiding talking to him about everyday events. This constituted Freddy seeking approval for his intellectual abilities.

In terms of a more proximal behavioural analysis (see Chapter 2), Freddy hit himself repeatedly in response to perceived disapproval and self-criticism (which was hypothesised to be linked to his belief about being unlovable and therefore being rejected). Antecedents included having a meal with his father at home and being criticised for burning the toast. In that situation Freddy thought 'I'm not good enough', 'nobody cares about me' and 'there is no point to life'. He then felt hurt, angry, rejected, helpless, useless and hopeless. He also experienced tension in his body, particularly in his shoulders, neck and stomach, and hit the table in frustration before returning back to his room where he repeatedly hit himself in the face. The immediate consequence of these actions was a reduction in physical tension, due to experiencing physical rather than emotional pain, and constituted emotional regulation through taking control. The distal consequences were continued use of these safety strategies and reinforcement of Freddy's core beliefs.

Progress in therapy

Freddy has been seen for two years of individual therapy. He also participated with group therapy in the context of a clinical trial for borderline personality disorder (BPD) carried out at a local university department of psychology. By the end of therapy most of his self-harm had stopped, but he still hits himself in private, occasionally when he feels under extreme pressure. Other changes of note included a greater ability to recognise and tolerate emotion without reverting to safety strategies. He had been able to get work as a volunteer, and through this was beginning to sustain interpersonal relationships and was better able to tolerate criticism. This progress was supported by pre- and post-therapy measures and goal achievement.

Therapeutic relationship

The cognitive behavioural conceptual framework presented above provides important information for the therapist in understanding many of the issues and processes with which Freddy presented interpersonally in therapy. Freddy had difficulty establishing trust and believed the therapist would end therapy if the latter discovered what he was really like. The therapist was aware that this might be the case from the formulation, which included the fact that Freddy had never been able to form secure attachments in his relationships. It was therefore highly probable that Freddy might frequently attempt to terminate therapy himself and that he would perceive behaviours of the therapist as rejecting or threatening. These assumptions were borne out within the psychotherapeutic process, particularly in response to situations where strong affect was generated in sessions. These were contained by maintaining a collaboratively agreed session structure, therapy contracting for six sessions at a time, taking a non critical stance and attending to the relationship (in order to help develop a secure attachment base). Importantly for both the therapist and client was the use of the conceptualisation to understand the underlying belief structures which were driving the presenting relationship testing behaviours. This also helped both the client and therapist to cope with the strong emotions and threats presented by the therapeutic process.

Commentary

In the case example of Freddy – a client with severe and chronic interpersonal difficulties who had a diagnosis of BPD – the formulation was influenced by a number of ideas. These included the origins of the problem relating to insecure attachments; genetic familial history of depression; conditioned and social learning due to his father's depression (probably due to a reaction to the loss of his wife); critical family communication and standards over the importance placed on perfection and achievement; and finally the lack of affection and love he received as a child, with physical contact contingent upon him doing things well. His attempts to cope with his social environment over time had become increasingly unhelpful and compounded his problems.

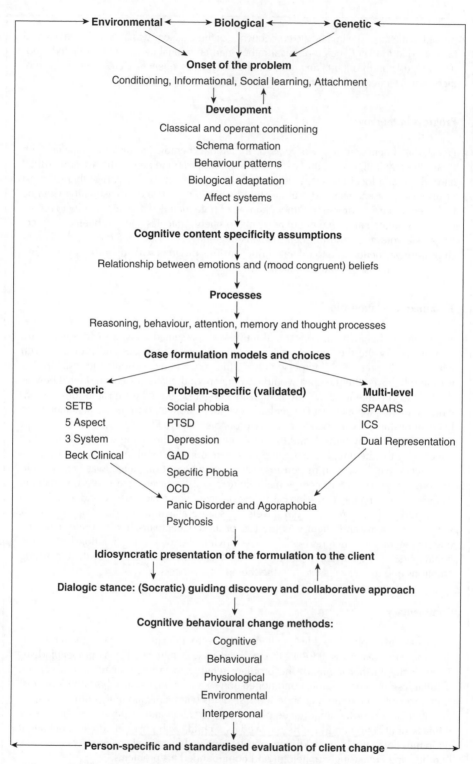

Figure 6.9   Framework of formulation in cognitive behavioural psychotherapy

DRAWING TOGETHER FORMULATION APPROACHES AND ISSUES

In bringing this chapter to an end, we wish to stress that the range of approaches to formulation approaches now available to the cognitive behavioural psychotherapist is a major strength within the field, enabling a flexible approach to understanding client's distress. From this basis, we hope that the concluding diagram opposite will help the reader to understand the ideas presented in this chapter and book regarding the overall approaches that can be taken with formulation – in particularly the complex and interacting onset and maintenance of psychological problems and the different approaches that can be taken to collaborative case formulation.

Summary

1   Traditional approaches to formulation have both strengths and limitations associated with them.

2   Recently transdiagnostic approaches have been developed that consider psychological approaches across disorders.

3   There is a reciprocal relationship between cognition, the environment and behaviour.

4   Formulation can be developed at a generic, disorder-specific and multi-level perspectives and each approach has a number of limitations and strengths associated with them.

5   The cognitive content specificity hypothesis underpins disorder-specific models with many models having been subject to empirical validation.

6   The cultural context of the individual influences psychological problems and the formulation and a number of culture-bound syndromes are also evident.

7   Recognition of onset and development facts is important in formulation.

8   Formulations should be developed in collaboration with the client within a relational context.

Activities

1   Think of two people you are currently trying to help. Formulate their difficulties using a range of different approaches, and do a cost benefit analysis of each approach for you and the client.

2   Identify one suitable individual you are working with. Consider in detail the influence that cultural or socioeconomic factors have played in either the onset and/or development of her/his problems.

Further reading

Bernard, J.M and Goodyear, R.K. (2004) *Fundamentals of Clinical Supervision*, 3rd edn. Boston; Pearson.
This book covers most aspects of supervision to a high scholarly standard. Chapter 5 is excellent for issues of diversity.

Harvey, A., Watkins, E., Mansell, W. and Shafran, R. (2004) *Cognitive Behavioural Processes across Psychological Disorders, a Transdiagnostic Approach to Research and Treatment*. Oxford: Oxford Medical Publications.
This book signals a whole new approach to formulation and research in the field of cognitive behavioural therapy through the exploration of processes across disorders.

Tarrier, N. (2006) *Case Formulation in Cognitive Behaviour Therapy, the Treatment of Challenging and Complex Cases*. Hove: Routledge.
This book applies the principles of case formulation to a range of complex problems in cognitive behavioural psychotherapy. There is also an interesting chapter on formulation applied to the supervision of practice.

Part II
Case Studies

'Ian': A case study of obsessional compulsive disorder

7

Alec Grant

Learning objectives

After reading this chapter and completing the activities at the end of it you should be able to:

1 Make links between case presentation data on the client, the client's narrative, and the theoretical and empirical bases for understanding cognitive behavioural approaches to OCD.

2 Link the client's case formulation to discussions in earlier chapters of this book.

3 Link emerging interventions to the client's case formulation.

IAN: BRIEF BIOGRAPHY

Ian, a 30-year-old man, contacted me for private cognitive psychotherapy following the death of his beloved father, and problems in his relationship with his girlfriend. Key information emerging from the ongoing assessment of his difficulties, during our first few sessions together, included his appraisal of multiple losses and family problems, experienced during his childhood, adolescence and later. Throughout this period, he described his mother – long divorced from his father – as increasingly positioning Ian as the sole source of reassurance and support for the family, including helping his younger brother who couldn't hold down a job for very long.

Immediate triggers for his presenting difficulties included the loss of certainty, support and feeling that life was controllable and safe from having father there when he needed him, and a distressing experience in a shop while buying china (see below). It became increasingly apparent that Ian had been conducting his life and relationships throughout much of his life using implicit rules, specifically that 'decisions/life must be perfect' and 'I must be certain', otherwise the world is 'unsafe'. The understandable behavioural dimension to his problems were, generally, avoiding risk taking and engaging in situations where he wouldn't feel totally in control. At a more specific level, he used checking across multiple domains of his life to prevent bad things from happening.

His day job in mental health advocacy contributed to the attraction of cognitive behavioural psychotherapy for him. Understandably, he chose a therapeutic modality more associated with 'certainty' in the light of its evidence-base. In related terms, a positive transferential relationship developed early on in our work in that he experienced me in 'avuncular' terms as a source of stability, predictability and security. This enabled us to help him increasingly feel safe enough to engage in 'certainty-dropping' and risk-taking experiments, using bibliotherapy as an important dimension to our work.

In his spare time he wrote fiction and was a published author. This led to a collaborative agreement that he would utilise creative writing to 're-story' two of his important losses. This strand of therapy was helpful both for risk-taking generally and for unresolved grief problems.

I worked with him over 18 sessions over the course of a year, and saw him for a three month follow-up appointment and, again, one year after this.

THEORETICAL/EMPIRICAL BASE

From a cognitive perspective, the experience of intrusive thoughts is a universal one (Rachman and de Silva, 1978; Salkovsis and Harrison, 1984). Intrusive thoughts reported by non-clinical populations do not differ from those experienced by people diagnosed with OCD, and include repugnant, unwanted thoughts, images or impulses. What does differ between non-clinical and clinical populations however is the meaning attributed to, or appraisal of, the intrusive thought. People without OCD appraise such intrusions as having no special significance, whereas OCD sufferers have a meta-cognitive appraisal (Wells, 1997) of such thoughts as personally highly relevant and threatening. Salkovskis (1985) argued that responsibility appraisals are of central appraisal, although later work by the Obsessive-Compulsive Cognitions Working Group (OCCWG) highlights the importance of additional appraisal domains relevant to Ian's difficulties. These are: over-importance of thoughts; overestimation of threat; intolerance of uncertainty; and perfectionism (OCCWG, 1997).

The over-importance of thoughts

This appraisal domain can be partly summarised as a form of circular reasoning whereby thoughts are given importance because they are experienced (Freeston et al., 1996; McFall and Wollersheim, 1979; Shafran et al., 1996). A further conceptual dimension to the over-importance domain is thought-action fusion (TAF) (Rachman and Shafran, 1997; Shafran et al., 1996). As the name suggests, thought-action fusion occurs when having the thought and engaging in the action are seen as equivalent (TAF moral dimension) and when having the thought increases the perceived likelihood of the event happening (TAF likelihood dimension).

Over-estimation of threat

The tendency to predict negative consequences is a common cognitive style across the anxiety disorders generally. Foa and Kozak (1986) and Salkovskis (1991) suggest that faulty reasoning is central to threat estimation. Whereas most people assume that, unless proven otherwise, a situation is not dangerous, people with OCD assume danger unless a situation is proven to be demonstrably safe.

Intolerance of uncertainty

It has long been recognised that intolerance of uncertainty is common in individuals suffering from OCD, where the smallest possibility of doubt is considered unacceptable due to feared consequences. According to Whittal et al. (2002), responsibility is the underlying appraisal that may make uncertainty particularly intolerable.

Perfectionism

In OCD, the role of perfectionism is evident in individuals with a need for exactness and the need to know issues fully (Whittal et al., 2002).

All of the above domains are illustrated in Figure 7.1 overleaf, showing a collaboratively developed, diagrammatic case formulation of Ian's difficulties.

Goals

> To check things once only
> To feel more calm generally
> To feel more confident that things will not go wrong in my relationship

Strengths/assets

> Good relationship with girlfriend
> Intelligent
> Curious
> Interested in a pragmatic approach to problems
> Interested in finding out more about OCD
> Already working in mental health field
> Keen on experimentation
> Established writer (novelist), therefore good resource base to use writing as intervention

Measures

> Compulsive Activity Checklist (CAC) (Freund et al., 1987)
> Frost Indecisiveness Scale (FIS) (Frost and Shows, 1993)

Cognitions

Core beliefs

I am culpable, responsible, a failure
Others are more deserving than me
The world is unsafe, imperfect   ←――――――――――――   *confirming truth of core beliefs*

Underlying assumptions (rules)

I must be fully in control of events and decisions in my life
I must be certain about events and decisions in my life   *confirming importance of rules*
If things are not done perfectly, then problems will unravel ←
If I make a mistake, then it will not be rectified
Mistakes must be paid for
If I check things, then I'll prevent bad things from happening

Leading to:
Exaggerated and inflated appraisals of
responsibility, culpability and the need for
certainty in trigger (proximal) situations,
with concomitant feelings of anxiety
and metacognition: 'If I've thought something
it must be important'

Resulting in (problems):
Checking (safety) behaviours
No-risk behaviour (lack of spontaneity)
Reassurance seeking from girlfriend

Figure 7.1   Ian: case formulation

Padua Inventory-Washington State University Revision (PI-WSUR) (Sanavio, 1988)
Thought-Action Fusion Scale (TAF Scale) (Shafran et al., 1996)

Ian's account of his reason for presenting for therapy at this time

I had a crisis in a shop. I'd bought a set of mugs as a reward
for myself for finishing writing a book. I chose the individual mugs carefully to try to minimise the imperfections in
the pottery. However, when I got them home I found a number of 'problems' with the mugs. I took these back to the
shops and tried to change one of the mugs over. The other
mug had the same imperfection, which actually reassured
me, so I kept the original mug. Then I broke one of the
mugs when I was washing it up and went back to the shop

to buy a replacement. On this occasion I checked the mugs and they all seemed to have imperfections. The shop assistant got a few more mugs out of the storeroom for me to look at. I felt unable to make a decision about which imperfection I could best tolerate. The shop assistant looked at me as if I was mad – and I thought 'I can't go on like this. I need to get help'.

Early influences on the development of his problem

Looking back on my childhood I think I had OCD symptoms from an early age... with the benefit of hindsight and therapeutic insights I think many of my life experiences dovetailed with the traits I already had in my personality.

These are the key life experiences I'm thinking of:

• My parents divorced when I was seven because my dad had an affair.
• My parents were very religious (Christian – Presbyterian).
• My uncle committed suicide (at the third attempt).
• My best friend from university died suddenly and unexpectedly.
• My dad died when I was 30.
• My sister had an addiction problem as a teenager.

These are the traits I'm thinking of:

• I worried a lot.
• I had a very vivid imagination.
• I believed in God (and prayed).

Over the years my OCD symptoms took up some of my time and energy but they also brought me some rewards. I was successful academically and creatively as a writer. In both these processes my diligence and tolerance for coping with mentally tough times were rewarded. Over time though, the problems started to greatly outweigh the benefits. Before seeking help I was trying to manage my day to day life to such a high degree that it became unmanageable.

My parent's divorce, uncle's suicide and friend's sudden death were all experiences that caused me deep unhappiness and accentuated the fact I couldn't control life. I felt very alone and thought about these events a lot. The death of the friend in particular seemed to make no sense.

The broader context for the crisis I had in the shop was that it came soon after the death of my dad. This bereavement was an unavoidable sign that life can be brutal and that I can't control it. When he was dying I heard from a relative that my dad had said that he thought he might be being punished. This keyed into the anxieties I'd developed – that mistakes must be paid for and that it's possible to break things beyond repair.

To show why the crisis in the shop was a tipping point for me to seek help I'm going to illustrate why it meant so much to me. The mugs had great significance to me, and this was the problem. They weren't just mugs. They signified my efforts/success in getting to the end of the book. They were a reward. Their imperfections somehow represented bigger problems with the world – that it's imperfect. When I was growing up I saw myself as being on a mission to test life out. I avoided drinking and taking drugs because I wanted to be in control and I wanted to get the most possible from myself. I wanted to develop a coherent narrative for life, which, of course, isn't coherent and isn't shaped like a narrative.

I sought reassurance from my partner and, for a time, this helped me cope, but it eventually started to cause further problems. She found that I was withdrawn, that I was deadened and distant. The reassurance became less reassuring and was given at an increasing cost to our relationship. We were also living in a rented house that she hated. I'd been keen to move there because I found it hard to cope with the noise from the neighbours above in our previous flat. My intolerance for this noise emphasised how stuck in the moment I got and how responsible I felt for things which were beyond my control. At the time I felt I didn't have control, which was terrible because I spent so much time trying to control things. I told my partner that I was going to get help and she was delighted; really, really pleased.

INTERVENTIONS

The interventions below emerged from the context of Ian's developing case formulation. They collaboratively emerged from the agreed assumption that Ian's OCD was maintained by the lack of opportunities or perceived relevance to date of evaluating and considering alternative appraisals. The general aim was to create the opportunities for Ian to test his previously held appraisals and come to his own conclusions, through carefully tailored behavioural experiments.

Using the downward arrow technique

A strategy emerging from our Socratic, guided discovery dialogue early in our work together, downward arrowing allowed Ian to see more clearly the link between his core beliefs, trigger situations, intrusive thoughts and the appraisals he was making of those (see figure 7.2 overleaf).

Probability

I was concerned that I'd left the bathroom window open. I used the probability calculation [see Leahy, 2004] and became calm.

I was anxious that I had left the cooker hood on. I wanted to speak to my girlfriend about it, which was difficult as we were out with guests. I did get to speak to her. Also, I used the probability calculations and became calm.

Fridges and the film *Anything Else*

Sarah (friend's wife) left the fridge open. She noticed it whilst we sat in the lounge. My girlfriend and I went to watch the film *Anything Else*. In the film he closes his fridge and it doesn't stay shut, so he pushes it a second time.
The *Anything Else* evening out:

My girlfriend was late.
It was raining.
We argued about her day at work.
The restaurant was full.
Someone in the cinema was doing the most heinous farts.
It was a really imperfect evening, but I was very pleased we went.

Noise at work

There is a lot of noise outside the work office e.g. a terribly played organ, arguments, drunks. But this is not an impediment to work – this illustrates that the responsibility issues are different at home.

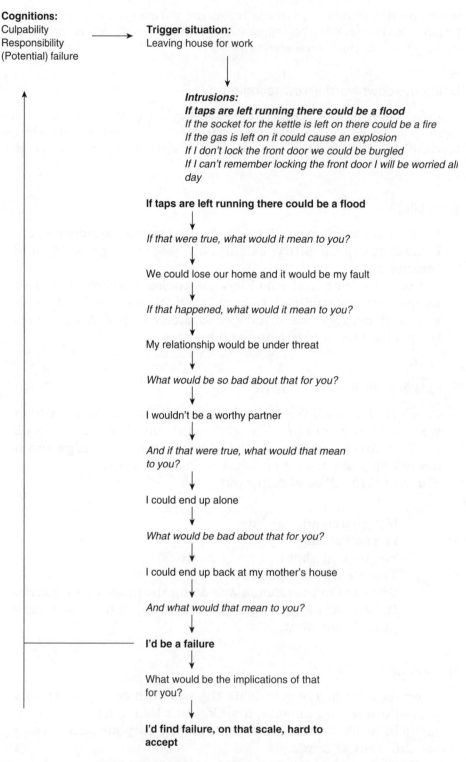

Cognitions:
Culpability
Responsibility
(Potential) failure

Trigger situation:
Leaving house for work

Intrusions:
If taps are left running there could be a flood
If the socket for the kettle is left on there could be a fire
If the gas is left on it could cause an explosion
If I don't lock the front door we could be burgled
If I can't remember locking the front door I will be worried all day

If taps are left running there could be a flood

If that were true, what would it mean to you?

We could lose our home and it would be my fault

If that happened, what would it mean to you?

My relationship would be under threat

What would be so bad about that for you?

I wouldn't be a worthy partner

And if that were true, what would that mean to you?

I could end up alone

What would be bad about that for you?

I could end up back at my mother's house

And what would that mean to you?

I'd be a failure

What would be the implications of that for you?

I'd find failure, on that scale, hard to accept

Figure 7.2   Ian's record of observations of naturally occurring events, August 2004

Getting carried away by anxious thoughts

I went to extremes in my thoughts about:

- 'Musical chairs' on the agenda of a work meeting – *appraisal*: that I'd be moved to a bit of the office I wouldn't like; *result*: nothing. It was about something else entirely.
- Lunch hours possibly becoming half an hour at work – *appraisal*: that there would be conflict; *result*: nothing.
- I had some mis-mailed post for my neighbour – *appraisal*: that they would rent out their house and we'd have bad/noisy neighbours; *result*: nothing.

I've been thinking about the 'need' to be always worried.

Story writing

No Pockets

Some people attribute it to the decline in the popularity of traditional pyjamas, the sort with buttons and a breast pocket. Some cite the fact that we haven't had a bloodletting war on any large scale for generations. Some, more deep thinkers in general, attribute it to the long period of human history pre-pyjamas, coats, jackets and trousers when as many people came and went as are here now. But whichever view you take, it is a hypothesis as good as a fact: *men do not die with pockets*.

I will illustrate this with two case studies:

First, Michael:

The 16th of July 1999 was a sunny day. Michael, 28, saw the sun and decided to go for a jog in Regent's Park, London. Usually his housemate Sue accompanied him on his jogs. On the 16th of July 1999 Sue did not go jogging with Michael; she stayed in to re-arrange the contents of her handbag. Which was good because this way Michael didn't have to take a door key, he could just ring the bell and she'd let him in. It was useful not to have to take a key because he didn't have any pockets.[1]

For a time, like a man in flight, Michael was free. He ran to the park and he ran round it. Then he collapsed, swallowed his tongue and lay very still.

A man with a beard walked through Regent's Park enjoying the sunshine. He noticed Michael lying on the ground. The sun meant that lots of people were lying on the ground and camouflaged his distress.[2] However, we now know[3] that all the other men lying on the ground in Regent's Park on the 16th of July 1999, had pockets.

Nurses, it is a proven fact, tend to be female. In this regard they are in an interesting position: their occupation means they require pockets whilst their gender means they would naturally avoid them. The solution is uniform: the pocket is elevated from the male/trouser position to the base hem of the shirt[4]. (It is worthy of note that this is also the positional solution favoured by the art teacher's/potter's smock.[5]) Later, on the 16th of July 1999, a group of Italian nurses were walking through Regent's Park, hands deep in pockets, heads deep in conversation.

The man with the beard walked back through Regent's Park. Again, he noticed Michael lying on the ground and he noticed that he had not moved a muscle. The bearded man went over to Michael, cautiously, then quickly. He looked around for help and was pleased to see the familiar[6] outline of the nurses' uniform. He shouted and beckoned them over. The nurses spoke Italian.

[1]   As a female Sue does not need pockets to prolong her life. Of course, a male's pockets will occasionally meet her needs, on a night out for example. The obvious comparison for females involves the maintenance of a handbag – although work in this area is in its early stages.

[2]   It is noteworthy that men lying on the ground in parks is often a sign of alcohol or drug-induced distress which repels attention and the kindness of strangers.

[3]   Westmoreland, R.L. (1999). *Lying Down in London's Parks: Horizontality and the Millennium*, 6–19.

[4]   Younger women universally reject the term 'blouse' so I have stuck to this received contemporary usage.

[5]   77 per cent of art teachers are female. For potters this figure reaches a whacking 89 per cent (of whom 14 per cent are art teachers specialising in pottery): Westmoreland, R.L. (1999). *Gender, Occupation and the Millennium*, pp. 543–4.

[6]   Recognition attributable to pocket position.

Secondly, Graham:

> For the first time in a long time, he was awake.
>   He said, 'Get me my trousers, we're getting out of here.'
>   I said, 'You can't get up.'
>   He said, 'Get me my trousers. I want to go to the loo.'
>   I said, 'You can't get up, but you can go to the loo, you've got a catheter.'
>   He said, 'Help me up.'
>   I said, 'You remember what happened the last time I tried to help you up? It didn't work.'
>   He said, 'Look I know I've had a few drinks, but please don't embarrass me.'
>   I said, 'You've got to stay here, Carole will be here to see you soon.'
>   He said, 'I am your father, do what I say.'
>   I said, 'Right. I'm taking control. You're not getting up.'
>   He laughed. I laughed. I took the opportunity to tell him I loved him, but he still wanted his trousers and he started to pull at the catheter.
>   I went to the door of the isolation room and beckoned over a nurse. She got something out of her pocket and put plenty in him and he calmed all the way down. And the moral of the story is that Graham never got his trousers back on again.

Outcome of therapy: Ian's account

I get benefits from the therapy at different points through-out each day. I now feel I have the freedom to do things differently. So, I make toast or use the cooker in the morning for breakfast if I want to, whereas before I would have avoided it to avoid having to turn it off, having to check it and still not being sure. I can iron a shirt before work if I need to and not worry that I've left the iron on. I leave the house once and don't feel compelled to return to check things. At work I only take responsibility for my workload and nothing else. I've read more books. Previously I felt I had to take in every word, now I just read them. I watch less television because so much of it is depressing. I prioritise myself in a way which I never used to. I tell people what I'm thinking much more.

Table 7.1   Behavioural experiments – July–August 2004

Experiment	Appraisal	Result
I wore a loud shirt to John's birthday party	Piss take	**Compliments!**
Didn't check gas taps	It would be on my mind	**All fine**
I wore a loud shirt and jeans to work	Two comments would be made	**Zero comments**
I talked to Terry about Michael	Anxiety	**Terry gave his own examples – we soon talked about something else**
I left the tap running at work	Someone will turn it off within 30 minutes	**I got into a conversation. The tap was off – 40 minutes**
I went out to the local shop from home without making any checks	Fine	**Fine**
I left my work computer on overnight	I thought this would cause me some anxiety	**It wasn't much on my mind – fine**
I was *very* anxious about the sound of wind chimes from next door. Agreed with girlfriend to wait a week and review	This will be intrusive when I'm watching tv. It will effect my friends who were coming to stay in the spare room. I will be stressed. Problems editing	**Very little noise. Good discussion with girlfriend about significance. However, some anxiety, but not justified**
I left the tv on standby during the day	Not a problem – although it would have been in the past	**Not a worry, not a problem**
I didn't deadlock the front door	I thought this will cause me anxiety	**No anxiety**
I watched a delivery driver collect packages from HSBC. He had to unlock and lock the bank.	He won't check the door	**He checked the door handle, twice**

I felt that I'd really cracked it when I found that I was forgetting things and losing things. It was brilliant. One morning I found that I'd left a downstairs window open all night – without consequence. At work I saw a coat hanging up and thought, 'I've got one a bit like that', before realising that it was my coat which I'd forgotten about.

I've taken more risks. At the small end of the scale I've bought brighter and bolder clothes and at the large end of the scale, I've got married. I've become more accepting of uncertainty and

Table 7.2 Summary of emerging interventions and their outcome

Interventions	Outcome
Standardised measure completion.	This helped Ian find out more about his problem by alerting him to things about himself that he hadn't focused on or realised before.
Guided reading (Bennett-Levy et al., 2004; Leahy, 2004; Whittal et al., 2002).	Helped clarify the nature of his difficulties, the scientific basis for the therapy approach and the importance of behavioural experiments.
Gradually dropping safety (checking) behaviours (Salkovskis, 1991, Short et al., 2004).	Ian found out that his feared consequences didn't come true, therefore that his meta-cognition about checking was invalid.
Agreement not to seek reassurance from girlfriend.	He found that he could 'live through' this and that his anxiety about not seeking reassurance gradually diminished.
Diary record of intrusive thoughts and appraisals of these thoughts (Whittal et al., 2002).	This provided material to devise behavioural experiments (Bennett-Levy et al., 2004) to test appraisals and underlying assumptions.
Observation experiments (Bennett-Levy et al., 2004) of events/phenomena that naturally occurred and related to Ian's problems.	These clarified responsibility issues and provided disconfirming evidence (evidence that did not support either the usefulness of Ian's safety behaviours or his beliefs). These experiments also challenged his need to be 'always worried'.
Other behavioural experiments (Bennett-Levy et al., 2004).	Ian found out that if he didn't check a particular thing or area he didn't worry about it all day, as he'd originally predicted. He also discovered that if he carried out 'certainty dropping' experiments things didn't 'unravel' as he originally feared. His beliefs about responsibility greatly reduced.
Probability Estimates (Leahy, 2004)	To his relief, Ian found out that there was a 1 in 1 million chance of bad things happening.
Story writing on father and friend (Leahy, 2004)	By extending risk-taking in introducing humour into these stories, Ian believed he moved further along the grief process by 'restorying' memories.

more alive in each individual moment. I feel like I've woken up and it's lovely.

One year on ...

I'm very pleased that I sought help with my problems. I feel the benefits of therapy almost every day. I've achieved a lot during the past couple of years and the approaches I've learnt

(and the approaches I unlearned) have helped me to manage the uncertainty of these changes. I've got married, had a child, and bought a car – all things that are about risk-taking to a greater or lesser degree. I feel the benefits in small ways too, like not remembering to turn off my mobile phone, or using the cooker in the morning before work to make breakfast. I feel less under threat than I used to.

I recently contacted Alec again. I was experiencing a high level of anxiety about buying a house. I felt unable to cope with this, particularly the complicated decision-making process and the need to feel certain. I felt desperate. It was interesting to observe my reactions though; I didn't revert to any OCD behaviours to manage the anxiety, although I did feel a bit lost without them. This short-term therapeutic intervention was like a refresher-lesson. I knew the approaches that could help me. As I explained before, the final straw that prompted me to seek help a couple of years ago was when I had a crisis about buying mugs. Now my intense emotional response, my anxiety, was triggered by something appropriate. Buying a house is very stressful and inevitably uncertain but I'm going to do it anyway.

Summary

1   The case presentation data on the client, and the client's narrative relates to the theoretical and empirical bases for understanding cognitive behavioural approaches to OCD.

2   This case study chapter also relates to discussions in earlier chapters of this book.

3   Interventions emerged from the client's case formulation and capitalised on his curiosity and pre-existing talents.

Activities

1   Consider a couple of clients on your caseload and how their existing creative talents could be utilised in generic, multi-level or problem-specific formulation-derived interventions.
2   Do an audit of cases of OCD, check that you are routinely assessing for the cognitive themes of: over-importance of thoughts; overestimation of threat; over-inflated responsibility; intolerance of uncertainty; and perfectionism.

Further reading

Clark, D.A. (2004) 'Cognitive-behavioural theory and treatment of obsessive-compulsive disorder: past contributions and current developments', in R.L. Leahy (ed.), *Contemporary Cognitive Therapy. Theory, Research, and Practice.* New York and London: The Guilford Press.
This chapter is an excellent reference point for the empirical and theoretical status of cognitive behavioural therapy for OCD.

Whittal, M.L., Rachman, S. and McLean, P. (2002) 'Psychosocial treatment for OCD. Combining cognitive and behavioural treatments', in G. Simos (ed.), *Cognitive Behaviour Therapy. A Guide for the Practising Clinician.* Hove: Brunner-Routledge.
A good chapter for achieving a better understanding of the cognitive dimension to the OCD experience.

'Alice': A case study of helping a client suffering from 'Borderline Personality Disorder'

8

Alec Grant

Learning objectives

After reading this chapter and completing the activities at the end of it you should be able to:

1 Make links between case presentation data on the client, the client's narrative and the diagnostic basis for understanding BPD.

2 From this basis, understand cognitive and related accounts of the development of the client's difficulties and their maintenance.

3 Link the client's case and situational formulations to discussions in earlier chapters of this book.

4 Understand the relationship between the situational formulation of the relational 'roadblock' and the emerging cognitive intervention which moved us successfully through this.

BORDERLINE PERSONALITY DISORDER

In the last two decades, cognitive therapy has developed theory and techniques, traditionally applied to depression and anxiety disorders, to help clinicians in their work with individuals described as having 'personality disorders' (Beck et al., 1990; Young, 1990; Young et al., 2003). Within this literature, cognitive approaches have been articulated which focus on borderline personality disorder (BPD) (Layden et al., 1993; Mills et al., 2004a; Morse, 2002; Young et al., 2003).

Diagnostically, BPD is classified as a 'cluster B', axis II disorder (APA, 2000). Individuals within this cluster are described as sharing impulsivity, mood instability, antisocial behaviour and disturbed thinking. BPD clients are further sub-categorised in terms of an extended set of criteria including efforts to avoid real or imagined abandonment; unstable and intense interpersonal relationships; identity disturbance; impulsivity; affective instability; and chronic feelings of emptiness (APA, 2000; Mills et al., 2004a).

In contrast to psychiatric diagnosis, psychological accounts of BPD suggest a very different picture to a quasi-medical representation of 'disordered' individuals (see also Chapter 2 this text). This is of people whose emotional and interpersonal difficulties are understandable in the face of their disadvantaged developmental backgrounds (Mills et al., 2004a). For example, BPD clients have difficulty in:

> **Regulating their emotions... reflected in dramatic overreactions and impulsivity, and, while growing up, have repeated experiences of having their emotional reactions discounted by significant others in their life. As a result... they fail to develop emotional regulation skills... (coming) to believe that they are expected to solve... difficulties by themselves without having the personal resources to do this. This leaves them with two extreme options in order to gain self-affirmation: either dramatic outbursts of emotion or avoidance of people and maladaptive ways of emotional and cognitive self-management. (Mills et al., 2004a: 83–4, my brackets)**

In keeping with the view of BPD as a developmental problem, Young (1990; Young et al., 2003) proposes 'early maladaptive schemas' (EMS). Conceptually similar to core beliefs in standard cognitive therapy, Young argues that EMS and related rules for living develop as a result of early toxic experience. In a circular way, EMS and related rules lead to behaviour which reinforces EMS, making them increasingly more rigid and inflexible. BPD individuals may engage in behavioural strategies, information and emotional processing, or avoidance in each domain in ways which confirm the truth of their EMS (schema maintenance). They may equally engage in cognitive and emotional avoidance of EMS (schema avoidance), or adopt cognitive and behavioural styles which seem to be the opposite of what might have been predicted from knowledge of their EMS (schema compensation) (Young, 1990).

Three EMS and related rules are key to the situational case formulation (see Chapter 4) which follows. These are described in Table 8.1 below:

Table 8.1   Three EMS rules

EMS	Related rule for living
Unlovability	If people really get to know me, they will not love me or want to be close to me.
Mistrust	If I don't protect myself, people will take advantage of me and hurt me.
Inadequate self-discipline	Because I can't control or discipline myself, I must be reliant on others.

ALICE: BRIEF BIOGRAPHY

Alice presented as a 28-year-old philosophy undergraduate who had intermitted from her university course on the grounds of psychological difficulties. Prior to her self-referral to me for private cognitive psychotherapy, she smoked excessive amounts of cannabis (skunk) and was depressed and undernourished. Although having a few friends and a boyfriend, and some hobbies such as playing the guitar and piano, she spent most of her time in a flat she shared with an old friend from her home town. He was also depressed, out of work and a habitual cannabis user. Both were very inactive, with Alice staying in bed every day until the early afternoon and spending time with her boyfriend in the evenings.

As a youngster growing up in a one-parent family (with an absent father who had long lost family respect), Alice received continual emotional invalidation from her mother who was also very judgemental and critical of people, giving Alice the constant message that 'every man is out to take advantage of women'. Her mother used to say repeatedly that Alice was cleverer than anyone else, and Alice internalised those messages at an early age, judging her early and subsequent performance accordingly. This seemed to sow the seeds of later, simultaneous schema maintenance, avoidance and compensation, and sometimes resulted in harsh self-criticism and self-defeating behaviour when Alice took the view that it was better not to tackle things in case she performed at second best or below.

Alice was brought up as a Catholic and attended a convent boarding school. Given this background, and her later interest in philosophy, her own personal moral position became a crucial life issue for her as represented in her case formulation.

ALICE'S CASE FORMULATION

Problems
I find it hard to:
be compassionate with myself
experience strong emotions
have my emotions validated

I think and behave in extremes

Core beliefs
I am lazy, worthless,
stupid, miserable, sad,
Pathetic, boring, a
failure

I'm more important than
anyone else
I'm cleverer than
anyone else
I'm special/privileged

Others are better than me; stupid and pointless; not to be trusted

Men are exploitative (out to take sexual advantage of me)

Women are inferior and inefficient (compared with me)

The world is a big mess; really horrible.

Underlying assumptions

(her value compared to others)

If I am seen not to be as clever as others, then I'm worthless

I must be the best

If I'm not the best, then others are better than me

This would mean that my life isn't worthy

This would mean that I'm a failure/not good enough

(her relationship with her emotions)

If I show/have emotions (I'm breaking my own rules), then it means I'm weak

If I feel strong, distressing emotions, then I must do something to get rid of them (smoking pot), (because I believe that I feel stronger emotions than other people)

(her autonomy)

I must be autonomous

If people get close to me it's because they want something; they'll take something away from me

If I stay away from people I'll be safe

If I get too close to people I might kill them

If I can't behave like I want, then I will be cheated and frustrated

If I don't behave like I should, then I might end up like my Dad who is very sad

(her co-dependency)

If I stick with people who are depressed, or avoidant, or with big issues, then I won't feel threatened and I'll be able to fulfil my moral duty of helping people

If I'm completely alone, then there's a danger of me becoming totally reclusive and dwelling on killing myself (as opposed to actually doing it) (so it's helpful to live with a dysfunctional flatmate, based on the rule 'if I'm another body in God's eye's then I've a moral duty to help other bodies')

(her morality)
I should always be humble and self-effacing
(rule for others: people should always be doing worthwhile activity in the eyes of God)
If I'm bored, then I'm not engaged in worthwhile activity
If I'm not engaged in worthwhile activity, then I'm a bad person

(her standards generally)
If you're not really good at something, then there's no point in doing it
If I put my all into things, then I should be the best

(her standards with regard to academic work)
If I don't try, then I won't have to cope with the uncertainty of how well I've done
If it's all going to go wrong, then I shouldn't try in the first place
If I have to work at understanding things, then I'm not clever

Automatic thoughts
Other people have far more serious problems than me. I'm wasting Alec's time
(When people validate my emotions) they are not to be trusted
(When people don't validate my emotions) they are rubbishing my feelings

Therapeutic goals
I want to feel like it's worth being alive *(if this came about, I'd be more active, have more energy and I'd value myself above the opinions others have of me. I would engage in a range of self-valuing behaviours such as meditation, writing to Members of Parliament and generally living in the world in a positive way. I'd be more tolerant of people. I sometimes feel that it's worth being alive when I think about how amazing the world is and how much my life is valued by my cat, my boyfriend, my family and my friends. Also, when I think of things I might want to do that would be important to me it makes me want to live)*

I want to have confidence in my abilities and in my worth as a person *(if I had confidence in my abilities, and self-worth, I would study and write philosophy, consistently and in greater detail. I would also write novels and short stories, and make music a part of my life)*

I want to have the strength and energy to live the kind of life I want and to do the things I want to do *(this includes general living skills like cooking and, when I'm talking with them about their problems, to feel that I'm helping people – if I perceive things as important enough to me I can devote a great deal of energy to them. For example, when I found my philosophy course interesting I worked very hard at it)*

I want to look after myself properly *(if I were doing this, I'd be eating good healthy meals every day, and exercising. I would also feel that having a little body fat was not a problem. I find this easier to do if I also have to look after other people)*

I want to be less afraid of things and people

I want to be self-disciplined *(because of the negative effects it has on my mood and my physical health, I have almost completely stopped drinking alcohol. When it is on offer, despite being tempted, I find it easy to reason to myself not to have it and to bear the social exclusion I feel as a consequence)*

I want to be able to control the effects of my emotion on my behaviour *(recently, since realising that I get angry with my boyfriend because I am troubled by our closeness, I have found it easier to communicate to him that I am angry directly, rather than being short with him or starting arguments)*

Measures

Young Schema Questionnaire (Long Form, Second Edition) (Young, 1990)
BDI II (Beck, 1996)

Situational case formulation

Background relational circumstances   The following represents a situational case formulation in my work with Alice at an important early stage in her therapy. Young

(1990; Young et al., 2003) highlights the relevance of a limited reparenting role for the therapist to provide a therapeutic relationship that counteracts EMS in personality disordered clients generally:

> ...we are advocating...(this)...role... to try to find out what needs of the child did not get met and to try to meet them to a reasonable degree – within the therapy relationship – without violating the boundaries of the therapist-patient relationship... The limited reparenting process can provide one of the most powerful mechanisms for invalidating the patient's schemas. (Young, 1990: 53)

And in BPD specifically:

> As the therapist becomes the (limited) substitute parent, the patient is no longer so dependent on the real parent and is more willing to blame and get angry at the parent. By becoming a stable, nurturing base, the therapist gives the patient the stability to let go of or stand up to a dysfunctional parent... Once patients understand the parent's reasons for mistreating them, they are more able to break the emotional tie between their parent's treatment of them and their self-esteem. They learn that, even though their parent mistreated them, they were worthy of love and respect. (Young et al., 2003: 346)

From the beginning of our work together, it became increasingly apparent that Alice had great difficulty in trusting people. This was perfectly understandable in the context of her developmental history, and I believed at the time that I was working hard to provide the necessary 'limited reparenting' advocated by Young and his colleagues. However, it became equally important to make explicit the automatic thoughts each of us had about the other. This was because the likelihood emerged in my own clinical supervision that the automatic thoughts Alice and I were experiencing about each other represented the mutual evocation of transference representations. These clearly had the potential to impede progress in therapy (Miranda and Andersen, 2007).

Insights on the significance of our thoughts about each other at the time are apparent also from an attachment perspective (Liotti, 2007). Liotti argues that as clients with problematic attachment histories begin to disclose problems and acknowledge difficult feelings, therapists may be perceived as stronger and wiser. In this circumstance, the client's attachment system is likely to be activated, with the client becoming more vulnerable and idealising the therapist who feels increasingly protective towards the client.

Liotti (2007) further argues that clients with complex borderline presentations may oscillate between perceiving their therapist as omnipotent rescuer and malign abuser or persecuter, and switch rapidly from controlling-punitive strategies to sexualising interactions.

I found this part of my therapeutic work with Alice difficult and potentially personally disorienting. However, we managed to discuss our thoughts about each other, contextualise them in her more general formulation (above) and develop a mutually agreed way forward – theory 1/2 – as described below. Over the course of our work together we engaged with several other cognitive behavioural interventions, relevant to and emerging from her developing case formulation. However, my aim in this chapter is to illustrate in simple terms the situational formulation of a potential relational roadblock, likely theoretical issues at play behind this, and the cognitive strategy we used to move the relationship and therapy forward.

Therapist's thought about client
I must help this young woman reach the potential that I see in her.

Client's thoughts about therapist
There's nowhere else in life where people will give me an 'A' for things. Maybe Alec will give me an A, so I must please him. However, I can't really trust him because he's a man.

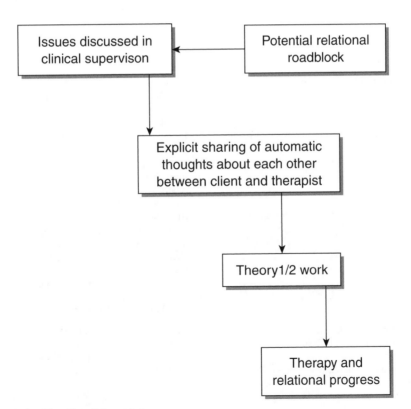

Figure 8.1 Situational formulation

Table 8.2   Theory 1/Theory 2 and supporting evidence

Theory 1 and supporting evidence	Theory 2 and supporting evidence
There's nothing really the matter with me. It's just that Alec hasn't figured this out yet: **Because I've been good at concealing it. Because he's stupid. Because I'm acting really well.** I have faked deafness and blindness when young. I am always trying to give myself serious diagnoses. I have only told you about myself from the perspective of what my problems are. If we had met in a different context it wouldn't seem so big an issue.	*Alec is right. I'm at the most serious and deserving of help end of the continuum.* Suicidal at 8 years of age and currently. Self-mutilation at 16, and still pinch and scratch occasionally. Sexually promiscuous without much enjoyment (particularly when younger).
I am attention seeking.	Cannabis addiction (and large amount of drinking when young). Very little social interaction in current life. High levels of anxiety in social and unfamiliar situations. Bad at taking care of myself. Sometimes idealising myself to delusional extremes and then consequently denigrating myself to excessive negativity. Doing the same with lovers. Paranoid (cannabis?) Low self-esteem. Often angry around others.
What I suspect of others is true People are evil. I am a bad person, therefore others shouldn't be good to me. There are many untrustworthy people around. People are selfish and want to get things from you.	*My suspicions are caused by inaccurate core beliefs about myself, the world and other people* I think I am unworthy of love, sympathy for my inabilities and stupid, boring and annoying. However, I don't believe this of anyone else, because I think that fundamentally no matter how irritating a person might be they are still worthwhile by virtue of being alive. Also, there are people who claim that I am not irritating (although I don't believe them). There is scientific evidence to suggest that people with my symptoms have the kind of core beliefs and rules that I seem to hold, and also evidence that this is the way that the mind is structured
He (Alec) wants to seduce me He is an older man and therefore wants to have sex with me. All men want to have sex with women all the time. I invite it because of the way I behave	*He doesn't have any interest of that kind in me* He hasn't made a pass at me. He never looks at me lasciviously. When he touches me it is never parts of me like waist, bum etc. There hasn't been any flirtation between us (unless I have been giving out signals).

(Continued)

Table 8.2   *(Continued)*

Theory 1 and supporting evidence	Theory 2 and supporting evidence
He (Alec) is doing it for the money. He knows I'm not ill; he can just tell I'm a drama queen It's a fair bit of money (to me). I'm not ill and he's not stupid enough to think I really am, so he must just be laughing at me.	*He is committed to his work and genuinely wishes to help me with my serious difficulties* His fee is standard, if not slightly below average. He has studied and taught psychotherapy for a long time and recognises in me serious problems that are worthy of his effort and attention.
People are always out to get it out of you. No one could really make me feel better, so it has to be a con.	Not everyone in the world wants to rip me off, just like I don't want to do it to other people. (random thought: I couldn't have picked a female counsellor as she would have been (perceived as) incompetent and annoying).
He thinks I'm stupid and boring I am stupid and boring. He looks at me like I'm stupid when I laugh nervously – he doesn't smile (but I don't want to tell him what to do and then suspect him of faking).	*He is genuinely interested in me* He came in despite feeling unwell. He does this job because it interests him, and people with problems like mine and the work that can be done with them interest him too.
	He lets me talk a lot. He asks me questions and really tries to understand my point. He bothers to second guess me when my negative thinking is affecting our interaction.

The chapter will conclude with Alice's account of the outcome of therapy.

Alice's beliefs about herself and her therapist – expressed as theories

My stance during the course of this specific strategy, carried out across three therapy sessions, was to encourage Alice to explore the evidence to support each competing theory in order to come to her own conclusions. After the first set of Theory 1/Theory 2, subsequent sets along with supporting evidence for each theory came unsolicited from Alice, who worked on them between sessions.

OUTCOME OF THERAPY

Alice was engaged in cognitive psychotherapy with me from October 2004 to August 2006, over a total of 25 sessions. At our last session, she reported that she had noticed a number of changes in her experience which suggested that sufficient progress towards achieving her goals had been made to enable her to think about ending therapy. Alice reported these changes as follows:

Less fearful of emotions

I know how to manage my emotions now. I have re-appraised them from 'emotions that are too strong for me to manage and deal with' to 'I have strong emotions, but that's okay'.

I can think clearly now when I have strong emotions. I now realise that when I have strong emotions they don't stay forever, as once feared.

I am better able to appraise emotions, in relation to events, as normal. For example, the presence of my mother is a 'natural' trigger for me to experience strong emotions.

Personal standards

I realise that I will change and develop but will never achieve perfection.
Things can be 'good enough' in my life.

Self-narrative

I use empowering self-talk rather than, as before, 'ill talk' as a commentary and mediator of my life and behaviour. I used to like being 'ill' as this used to give me lots of get-outs for living. I don't want to identify with that ill persona any more.

Risk taking

I am a lot more confident, assertive and determined to be 'up front' with people.

ALICE'S POSTSCRIPT

It was very important to me to be undertaking a therapy with a sound scientific basis which is why I chose CBT. When I went into therapy my impression was that it was the theory and technique that mattered and the therapist would only be someone competent to impart the knowledge to me. I was even under the impression that it could be administered by a software programme and still be as effective.

However when I met Alec, and as I got to know him, I realised how important the personal bond with him was in the effectiveness of therapy. This is because when certain techniques or theory seemed unlikely to me, or its effectiveness doubtful, I would rely on the trust I felt in Alec to give it a fair try. Also, it was important to me early on to feel liked by Alec, and though it may have been down to luck as much as anything we connected and got along well fairly quickly.

Alec often referred to the notion of 'proxy parenting' and while I understood that it was about validating my feelings and experiences in ways that my earlier parenting had failed to, to me this meant that he would step outside of the straightforward therapist role and take the time to make me feel valued, cared about and that I had the space to say anything I liked. Without those efforts from Alec I doubt that I would have trusted him enough to be as open as I have been.

Overall, it was obvious to me that Alec was a compassionate and good person who gave me something to strive towards, and was someone like the person I wanted to be – living by similar values and ideals – who was more than capable of coping with their life and pursuing their goals with confidence. Before that point I had seen people quite straightforwardly as either the good and downtrodden, or the successful and callous. So having known Alec as a person, as much as any of the treatment I went through during therapy, has improved my opinion of myself and other people. I came to see Alec as a friend and teacher with whom I could talk and laugh and generally feel relaxed with, which is a far cry from the business-like detachment I was expecting when I first started therapy. While CBT has produced many differences in the way I think, feel and behave, I think I will always see it as Alec who made the real difference.

Summary

1   There are clear links between case presentation data on the client, the client's narrative and the diagnostic basis for understanding BPD.

2   From this basis, cognitive accounts of the development and maintenance of the client's difficulties can be understood.

3   The client's case situational formulation relates to discussions in earlier chapters of this book.

4   The relationship between the situational formulation and the emerging cognitive intervention moved the therapist and client successfully through the relational 'roadblock'.

Activities

1   Think of one client who you have, or have had, a relational problem with. Construct a situational formulation of this difficulty.

2   Use Theory 1/2 to see if this helps make better sense of retrospective analysis or work through the relational difficulty (current clinical work).

3   Now consider what might need to change about your assessment, relational and formulation practice with future clients.

Further reading

Leahy, R.L. (ed.) (2003) *Roadblocks in Cognitive Behavioural Therapy. Transforming Challenges into Opportunities for Change.* New York and London: The Guilford Press.
An excellent, in-depth source for the relationally oriented cognitive behavioural psychotherapist.

Young, J.E., Klosko, J.S. and Weishaar, M.E. (2003) *Schema Therapy. A Practitioner's Guide.* New York and London: The Guilford Press.
This text will help readers gain a good understanding of early maladaptive schemas and related interventions.

An organisationally focused case study of PTSD

9

Adrian Cockx, Michael Townend and Alec Grant

Learning objectives

After reading this chapter and completing the activities at the end of it you should be able to:

1 Identify organisational factors that impact on the therapeutic alliance in relation to the impact and role of teams in the treatment of a client diagnosed with mental health problems.

2 Reflect upon the therapeutic flexibility and creativity required by therapists in the process of working within teams.

3 Use aspects of creativity within the context of treatment protocols.

4 See the value of compassionately focused organisational formulations in increasing team and client awareness of clients' experiences of their mental health difficulties.

5 Build on work undertaken by other members of the team and professionals who have previously been involved in the care of clients.

A client's journey towards recovery is not always as simple as having the right therapy approach, medication or other treatment options available. There are many factors and opinions involved and sometimes the process can cause additional problems in itself. In this chapter the case of John will be used to explore and illustrate how the impact of healthcare organisations' systems and processes and the related beliefs of mental health workers can impact on the outcome and delivery of therapy.

A collaborative case conceptualisation provides the map that guides the course of therapy, which is influenced by a number of factors and issues. From the perspective of the therapist, both Padesky (1999) and Leahy (2001, 2007) highlight the influence of therapist beliefs using schema theories that can promote and inhibit the therapeutic process. In a complementary way, Safran (1998), Safran and Segal (1996), Safran and Muran (2000) and Stevens et al. (2003) discuss the ways in which the relational problems as they inevitably arise between a therapist and their client can become instrumental in understanding the clients' difficulties, and be the focus for helping the client explore opportunities to address associated schematic, emotive and interpersonal patterns of behaviour.

From a professional politics and research perspective, the question of what is effective in cognitive behavioural practice has been dominated by the power structures within the field and consumers for evidence-based therapy, in turn influencing the proliferation of therapy manuals based on a nomothetic model (see Chapters 1 and 2) and protocols that prescribe the course of therapy or treatment for a specific diagnostic problem. These do not take into account personal meaning or other maintaining factors, or pay attention to the environmental treatment context for the client or the therapeutic relationship (Freiheit et al., 2004; Sholomskas et al., 2005). There is also the added problem that when manuals are available they are very difficult to implement consistently. Persons (1995) identified three main factors that might help to explain the poor uptake of manual-based protocols within clinical practice:

1 Philosophical differences underpinning different psychotherapeutic approaches.
2 Difficulties associated with translating efficacy-based research into practice in non-standard client populations.
3 Shortcomings in both training of students and disseminating results of empirically supported therapies through training centres.

Whilst it can be argued that there may be value in many treatment protocols, there is a point at which they become irrelevant to the client issues being worked with during the therapeutic process. Often, when working with clients presenting with unhelpful relational schemas, a more creative approach is needed. This does not mean that manuals should be abandoned entirely as they can be helpful for novice therapists learning to focus their therapeutic endeavours. They can also offer a good starting point for the experienced therapists working with new client populations.

The cognitive behavioural literature also tends to take an individual focus to clients' difficulties with the apparent exclusion of the contextual organisational effects that healthcare organisations can have on the therapeutic process and interdisciplinary working between diverse professional groups. Most contemporary writers in mental health consider that interprofessional working between therapists can only enhance outcomes for clients and do not consider the negative effects that divergent professional opinions might have on the clients' recovery.

In an attempt to readdress this issue Grant et al. (2004b, 2006), drawing on the work of Morgan (1997), Fineman (1996), Pfeffer (1981) and Goffman (1969), argue that the impact of organisations frequently influences the delivery of care. It is important to recognise that changing established work cultures, and the structural power dynamics inherent within an organisation, is by no means an easy task.

However, equally it can be argued that there is a professional and ethical imperative to adopt a creative approach, which draws upon cognitive behavioural, team working and organisational theories in the construction of a personalised and contextualised formulation that can be used as the basis for collaborative working with the client's individual problems.

In this case study it will be shown how organisationally related beliefs held by a client about his ability to recover impacted on his experience of the service he received and his coping behaviours. The case study will illustrate a contextual organisational cognitive behavioural assessment and formulation process using the 5 aspects approach, the resultant creative cognitive behavioural strategies deployed and the outcome of the therapeutic work that also utilised a problem-specific formulation.

THE STORY OF JOHN'S EXPERIENCES

This case study focuses on one man's journey of recovery through the quagmire of a mental health service. The processes of seeking help and effective therapy are without doubt influenced by the professional quality of mental health workers and their theoretical and professional values. The important influence of organisational decision making and thinking will be considered in respect to the impact they had on John's experience of himself, and how this impeded rather than assisted his recovery. This scenario provides a common challenge for the therapist in respect to the application of a creative contextual approach to therapy.

John's case was first presented to the multidisciplinary team because the main case worker was unsure about how to progress with his case management. John had been making reassurance-seeking phone calls on a regular basis, concerning seemingly mundane daily living activities. This was taking up a great deal of time of the members of staff on duty, thus impacting on their ability to help other clients and organise other requirements involved within their role. During the discussion, the team expressed feelings of exasperation at his neediness and dependence on staff, in conjunction with a lack of progress and stability in his mental health. This was evident in their display of non-verbal behaviours such as shifting in chairs, rolling of eyes, sighs, 'tuts', looking at watches and other similar forms of distracting behaviour.

When pressed, the team's formulation of John's difficulties was expressed in nomothetic terms through the language of diagnosis – in this case 'Dependant Personality Disorder with Disassociation'. The team's working hypothesis was that John was reliant on the team for persistent reassurance and with helping him to cope with significant periods of self-neglect when he also experienced distressing episodes of disassociation.

In view of the above, Cockx suggested that he work with the client, in order to assess, formulate and address some of these presenting behavioural problems. This was met with a mixture of resistance, relief and concern by different team members. Resistance was expressed on the basis of the resources that had been invested in John's care without any noticeable changes, relief that someone else might take on his case work and concern that he might overwhelm Cockx if the latter was not adequately supported. In the past, John had worked with a number of psychologists, community psychiatric nurses, social workers, support workers and occupational therapists.

Time line of care

Five years previously   On examination of the medical records, it became apparent that John had also been seen by another cognitive behavioural psychotherapist five years earlier for post-traumatic stress disorder, following his involvement as a security guard in a bank robbery. The therapist at the time stated that he had followed an evidence-based approach, which involved helping the client relive the trauma and address his related fears through exposure (Foa and Kozak, 1986). Unfortunately, during the exposure work, which included reliving of his trauma, John started to become more distressed and exhibited even more intense symptoms of anxiety. In an attempt to relieve these symptoms he had started to become dependent on his wife, with persistent requests for reassurance concerning his beliefs that he might be going mad. The increase in anxiety led ultimately to a fracture of the therapeutic relationship, and John decided to drop out of therapy as he found it too much to cope with and believed that it was ineffective and simply worsening his problem. The therapist had tried to address this issue of disengagement from therapy at the time, but eventually closed the case on the basis that 'the cognitive behavioural approach does not work for everyone'.

John remained in contact with the mental health service through his consultant psychiatrist and other members of the medical staff. He became increasingly dependent on his wife through relentless reassurance-seeking, and would experience extreme low mood and suicidal thoughts when his need for reassurance was not met. Around this time, he was prescribed anti-depressant medication and support was offered through the involvement of an occupational therapist who, following an assessment, provided a structured daily schedule which included participation at a local day hospital.

As part of the therapeutic package a carer's assessment was also completed and John's wife was offered the opportunity to attend a carer's support group which ran within the local service. Despite this help from the service, John's relationship with his wife started to deteriorate and she decided to leave him, exasperated by his persistent need for reassurance. She had also met someone else through attending the support group and had started a new relationship.

Four years previously   At a team review meeting it was decided that John would require more time to recover but the aim remained for him to return to work, although he was in receipt of disability benefit by this time. The consultant psychiatrist reviewed John's diagnosis in light of his presenting behaviour since he became involved with the mental health services. It was felt that although the trauma was a contributing factor, John was more likely to also be suffering with a dependant personality disorder that had been triggered through events related to the trauma. Due to this change in diagnosis and social circumstances, John started to see a social worker who helped him to apply for Disability Living Allowance. John was described as finding this process difficult as it reflected upon his lack of skills and ability to do tasks which he was more than capable of doing prior to the trauma. Additionally, the introduction of a support worker was added to his care package as a means of aiding him to improve his daily living activities.

Three years previously   Despite the numerous workers involved with his care, John showed little improvement in his mental health status. Whenever he progressed and started to move towards his goals, such as voluntary work or part-time college, the feelings associated with being 'tested' and being a potential 'failure' led to him becoming overwhelmed and anxious, finally resulting in a complete withdrawal from the world. Workers described John as being 'distant', 'not himself' and 'catatonic'. This led to an additional diagnosis of disassociation being added. On several occasions during this period, John's behaviour had become so concerning that the team initiated compulsory admission on the grounds of him becoming a danger to himself through self-neglect. John did not find the hospital admissions to be helpful towards achieving a sustainable long-term recovery.

However, the initial intensive nursing interventions and reassurance given through having the company of staff and fellow patients helped John to get to a point where he was able to look after himself. Complete discharge was finally achieved through his desire to get out of the ward, due to the level of fear and intimidation he experienced from more disturbed patients.

Two years previously   John coped well for a few months but started again to repeat the same cycle of reassurance seeking and dependency. The team recognised this pattern and it was decided that the involvement of a psychologist might make John's experiences and repeated patterns more understandable. The psychologist adopted a psychodynamic approach, due to his experience and training background. Following a review of John's notes, he decided to work on exploration of John's previous relationships and the impact this had on his ability to overcome his mental health problems.

The work with the psychologist helped to identify that John's father had been a strict disciplinarian and had instilled strong beliefs and values in him in regard to what it meant to be a 'man' and related expression of emotions as a sign of weakness. This had been predominantly developed through his own life experiences of being a soldier in relation to the beliefs and values he had adopted in order to survive such a disciplined regimen. On the other hand, John's deceased mother, who had been a deeply religious woman, would seek solace from her church and faith whenever she was faced with any life difficulties. John stated that his father would often be intolerant of her emotional expression calling her a 'silly woman'. When John's mother had died of a terminal illness when he was 15 years old, any expression of his grief – in particular crying – was met with a barrage of verbal abuse from his father. If John was unable to control his emotions, his father would often resort to physical and psychological abuse. In order to cope with these experiences, John had learnt to 'shut down' and endure the pain, becoming disconnected from the experience and unemotional until his father had stopped the abuse.

The psychologist helping John was able to make connections between his past relationships, behaviours and his present problems with emotional regulation. In particular, John became aware of the origins of dysfunctional coping strategies and the triggers that led to the episodes of disassociation. Although he found this connection insightful, he was unable to find any way in which he could apply what he had learnt to his daily life. His sessions with the psychologist came to an abrupt end when the latter left to take up a new role.

John's case was handed over to a trainee clinical psychologist who was asked to continue the therapeutic approach and incorporate some practical solutions within a time frame of only six sessions, due to resource limitations. The trainee clinical psychologist found it difficult to establish a productive therapeutic relationship with John within the time available.

At this time John became increasingly unsure that a trainee would have the capabilities to help him, believing that his problems were too difficult to be addressed by someone not yet qualified. He was also unhappy with, and preoccupied by, the time limited number of sessions he had been allocated. This seemed to further increase his anxiety. John's experience of the abrupt withdrawal of his psychological therapy lead to him becoming distrustful of psychologists, believing that they would reject or use him. Subsequently, current treatment was solely focused on containment and management of symptoms by the psychiatrist involved and other members of the team from time to time for brief periods.

One year previously   At the time the cognitive behavioural psychotherapists became involved, John had a regular care team that comprised of a consultant psychiatrist as the responsible medical officer and a care co-ordinator whose professional background was occupational therapy.

CONTEXTUAL, TEAM AND INDIVIDUAL FORMULATION

In order to illustrate the problems associated with the team's current beliefs and assumptions about John's condition, the case formulation below diagrammatically illustrates the implicit and explicit effect of the team's belief system when the offer was made by the cognitive behavioural psychotherapist to take John on (Grant et al., 2006). This initial formulation sought to achieve a metaphorical understanding and working hypothesis of the vicious cycles that had developed and which had lead to the team members feeling both hopeless and helpless in finding a way to help John overcome his behavioural difficulties (Morgan, 1997).

The formulation in Figure 9.1 was initially developed to help the therapist and team understand their own beliefs and behaviours that might now be contributing to John's own feelings of dependency and lack of adequate help. The next stage involved a full reassessment of John utilising a cognitive behavioural approach.

As discussed previously, and emphasised in this text, the importance of the therapeutic relationship is essential for work with complex cases. The initial contextual team and individual formulation indicated that understanding John's previous experiences of treatment and therapy, and from John's perspective, rejection by some members of the team would make it difficult to develop any form of valuable working alliance. In order to address this relational problem, Cockx met with John informally over a coffee within the mental health centre making it explicit that this was a pre-therapy phase of relationship development for John to decide if he was willing to be reassessed with a view to further therapy.

John agreed to further assessment and, during this, a detailed functional analysis of John's presenting problems was undertaken. This included assessment of his beliefs about himself, his partner and their relationship, and his previous experiences of mental health services, on the basis of all of which he justified his own dependent and reassurance-seeking behaviours. The functional analysis revealed multiple triggering events to reassurance seeking and dissociation and also a number of environmental and interpersonal antecedents, such as his expectations of others (particularly his previous therapists) not being met. Eventually, a full personal and life history was taken as

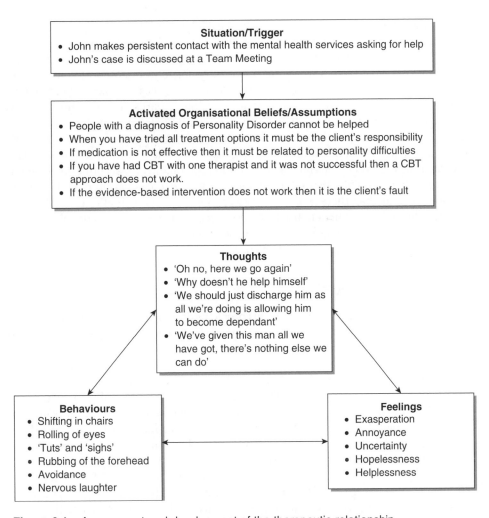

Figure 9.1   Assessment and development of the therapeutic relationship

well as the detailed review of the previous notes and discussion with team members who had long-term knowledge of John's therapy and care.

Importantly, it was apparent that John held beliefs that he would not be able to recover and the mental health service could not help him. In order to address this, Cockx did not seek to defend the previous practices of the team but accepted that things had gone wrong and that professional relationships in the past had not always ended in a way that had been beneficial to John's recovery. Cockx spent time asking John about his time with the mental health services and what he had found helpful and unhelpful. This validated John's feelings of disappointment he had experienced when treatment, therapy and relationships with mental health workers failed to help him previously (Leahy, 2001).

Cockx and John carefully negotiated their relationship, taking care to accept factors that had contributed to problems in the past and which might happen again (Safran and Muran, 2000). This was achieved in particular through reflection on his past relationship with the clinical psychologist who had worked with him. The cognitive theme here was his beliefs and concerns regarding abandonment, what he thought about this and what factors would need to change for John to accept that sometimes people are let down. This opportunity allowed for a list of goals to be formed that related to the therapeutic relationship and John working towards independence. It was accepted that at one time or another Cockx might let John down, and vice versa, by, for example, not being able to honour a prearranged appointment. Potential future possibilities of one being sick or running late were discussed, and a number of possible ways were identified in which one could let the other know, taking into account how it might make the other feel. This ensured that a sense of inclusiveness within the relationship was formed and that there was responsibility for each individual's roles. This was achieved through agreement to use text messages and, if that was not possible, that the team secretary would phone, or John would phone the team secretary and, failing that, that answer machine messages could be used.

Individual case formulation

In order to help John become aware of his problems and the factors that contributed to their formation and continued presence, some of the earlier psychological work he had undertaken with the psychologist was used in the development of an initial formulation. This was particularly helpful in establishing the formation of his core beliefs and gaining a compassionate understanding of how they were maintained through his underlying assumptions and beliefs. Through this process John was able to see how his core beliefs and underlying assumptions had influenced the way in which he saw himself and his ability to recover. By linking formulation elements with his goals, John became more eager to find ways in which he could begin a recovery process through therapy using cognitive behavioural strategies.

It would be usual in cognitive behavioural therapy for those with PTSD to carry out a full and detailed assessment of the original trauma John had experienced. The working hypothesis at this stage with John was that this would be counterproductive as the development of the relationship and containment of his problems were the priority areas. Some of the assessment did gently enquire about how he became involved with the mental health services in order to give him the space and opportunity to talk about the trauma when he felt able. The work with John also created an opportunity for interprofessional working with other members of the team, the first step being to help them understand and contribute their own thoughts on John's formulation through team meetings. Following discussion with John, the formulation was presented to the team. This helped explain the basics of cognitive theory and how this related to the onset and maintenance of John's problems. The team found it helpful to understand the formulation at both the individual level and at the level of their own role in the maintenance of some of John's difficulties. Some team member expressed an interest in working with John and contributed care plans and strategies that might fit with John's goals.

Working with the trauma   Following a six-month period of therapy, John showed great progress towards making a recovery. He had started to become less dependent on

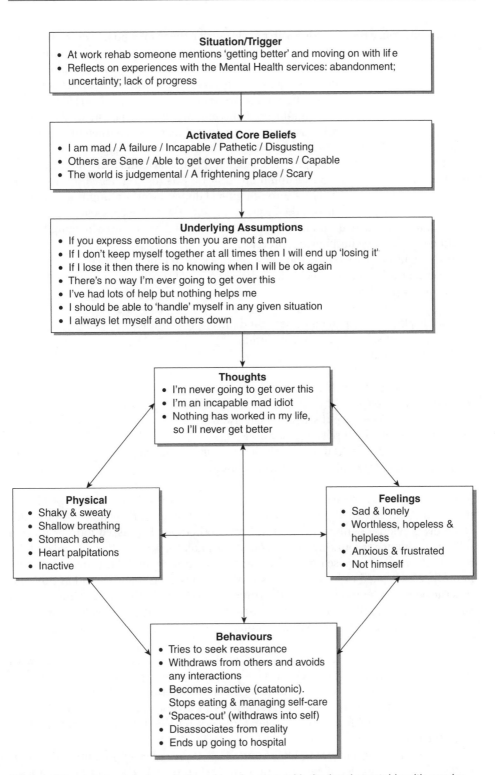

Situation/Trigger
- At work rehab someone mentions 'getting better' and moving on with life
- Reflects on experiences with the Mental Health services: abandonment; uncertainty; lack of progress

Activated Core Beliefs
- I am mad / A failure / Incapable / Pathetic / Disgusting
- Others are Sane / Able to get over their problems / Capable
- The world is judgemental / A frightening place / Scary

Underlying Assumptions
- If you express emotions then you are not a man
- If I don't keep myself together at all times then I will end up 'losing it'
- If I lose it then there is no knowing when I will be ok again
- There's no way I'm ever going to get over this
- I've had lots of help but nothing helps me
- I should be able to 'handle' myself in any given situation
- I always let myself and others down

Thoughts
- I'm never going to get over this
- I'm an incapable mad idiot
- Nothing has worked in my life, so I'll never get better

Physical
- Shaky & sweaty
- Shallow breathing
- Stomach ache
- Heart palpitations
- Inactive

Feelings
- Sad & lonely
- Worthless, hopeless & helpless
- Anxious & frustrated
- Not himself

Behaviours
- Tries to seek reassurance
- Withdraws from others and avoids any interactions
- Becomes inactive (catatonic). Stops eating & managing self-care
- 'Spaces-out' (withdraws into self)
- Disassociates from reality
- Ends up going to hospital

Figure 9.2   John's case formulation of involvement with the local mental health service

others, had formed relationships with people outside the team, and had developed ways in which he could deal with problems through undertaking and testing a number of behavioural experiments and reducing his reassurance seeking and dependency on others. Additionally, the use of thought records had helped him become curious about his automatic thoughts which he noticed were an early step in a chain towards his problematic behaviours. Schema-focused therapy had also helped in weakening old dominant core beliefs and the use of positive data logs helped strengthen more adaptive belief systems (Padesky, 1994).

Despite now appearing to cope much better, John indicated that there was something else that was consistently on his mind but that he was too frightened to talk about. These fears were explored gently through guided discovery over a number of sessions until he was able to talk about the original trauma. He had been avoiding this as he feared that if he opened up and discussed this it would be so overwhelming that he might go mad and be hospitalised forever.

Assessment in PTSD follows the same approach as in other psychological problems, and over time a full cognitive behavioural assessment of the following aspects related to the trauma were elicited:

- Flashbacks, images and nightmares and intrusive memories
- Avoidance of situations or other stimuli
- Safety behaviours
- Physiological arousal
- Emotional effects (e.g. blunting)
- Impact on mood
- Pre-existing beliefs about self, others, world
- Current beliefs about self, others, world
- Any likelihood of re-trauma (e.g. through the assailant being known to the survivor such as a family member with current contact).

John's previous experience of trauma work, based on the Foa and Kozack (1986) model, involved exposure to his fear following his witnessing of a bank robbery. In this work his previous cognitive behavioural psychotherapist had asked John to make a reliving audiotape recounting his version of the bank robbery. He had also taken John back to the bank to expose him to the scene of the trauma and illicit more memories and other associated experiences. This work was based on the assumption that fear was the dominant emotion behind the trauma and the main therapeutic intervention should be exposure (Foa and Kozack, 1986). There was no attempt made to formulate the role of John's core beliefs in this formulation, the focus being purely on the trauma event.

Smucker et al. (2003) have proposed an alternative method of working with PTSD. This is based on studies that show how some patients who have not responded to exposure therapy have associated emotions such as anger, guilt, shame and disgust. This would suggest a working hypothesis that in order to work with the emotion of fear it is necessary to work on the associated emotions that drive the fear response.

The cognitive model of PTSD (Ehlers and Clark, 2000) relevant to John's difficulties is described in simplified diagrammatic form in Figure 9.3. The central hypotheses of this model, which also has the advantage of being able to incorporate associated

Table 9.1   Table of interventions

Problem	Intervention	Outcome
Worried about becoming overwhelmed and losing it when talking about his trauma.	Utilised metaphors of 'tidying the cupboard and rearranging items' in context of reorganising trauma memories. Built on work already done and accomplishments over the last year making reference to: positive data logs, Behavioural Experiments and daily thought records.	Responded well to the use of metaphor and started to create his own to describe emotional problems he experienced. John created a list of accomplishments, how he achieved them and what he did to solve the problem. Kept specific examples in a scrapbook.
	Explored methods of working with trauma using case formulation to focus work on the dominant driving emotion of shame and disgust. Undertook a survey of other examples of trauma work. Read books and watched films of people who were able to overcome their problems and get on with their lives.	A blank case formulation sheet was created for John to complete whenever he was unsure of what was going on for him. He would complete this and discuss in therapy sessions. Novels and 'true-story' films became instrumental in changing John's beliefs that he could not get over his trauma. Read an article about a girl who had overcome a trauma he deemed to be worse than his own. From this he realised that people can get over trauma even if they think that they are disgusting.
Frightened about undertaking any exposure work. Worried I would push him away or reject him as he was such a pathetic person. Also worried that this could lead to an episode of disassociation.	Explained the many steps of exposure from describing the event in the third person, to prolonged exposure including going back to the place it happened and describing what happened in detail. Created specific goals in a hierarchical structure with most feared exposure at the top. In regard to my perceptions of John I agreed I would communicate my feelings about him, at the start of the session, by using evidence to support my beliefs.	Started to use metaphor and third person to talk about the trauma. John's prediction that he would disassociate did not happen. Made a diary of the facts behind the robbery which led to activation of his self-schemas. Reflected on past work drawing on positive data logs before John was able to read the diary out loud again. Disassociation did not happen. John then made a tape of the events that happened in the robbery, including the sensations he experienced. This was placed in the context of his formulation, with emphasis put on any evidence of self-deprecating schemas being activated.
	In respect to fears about disassociation, John utilised case formulation and behavioural experiments. He then incorporated behavioural experiments into his trauma work.	I utilised evidence I collected about John's improvement to dispute the activation of his 'others' schema. I also shared notes from myself and others in the team for him to reflect on his progress.
		John started to show great awareness of the thoughts that were activated prior to previous episodes of disassociation. He would reflect on evidence he had collected to dispute these beliefs.

(Continued)

Table 9.1   *(Continued)*

Problem	Intervention	Outcome
Coming to terms with his childhood abuse	Drew on what was learnt from working through the trauma related to the robbery.	Found that the schematic processes that were developed at early stages in his life were not helping him.
		Gained a compassionate understanding of the development and maintenance of his problems over the years. Strengthened more adaptive schemas through work already undertaken and relevant to his formulation. Behavioural experiments and positive data logs were helpful in this process. Reflections on relationships started to dispute previously held underlying assumptions, and more adaptive rules were created then tested through the development of appropriate behavioural experiments. John started to write about his experiences and found there were others who had similar experiences to his own. He became helpful in helping others which improved his own view of himself.

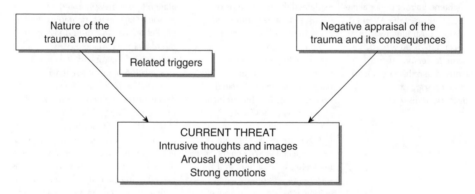

Figure 9.3   The cognitive model of PTSD (Ehlers and Clark, 2000)

emotions such as shame and guilt, are that the individual's unresolved post-traumatic difficulties leaves them with a sense of current threat. Two mechanisms contribute to this threat; these are a negative appraisal of the event and the nature of the trauma memory itself. Intrusive images, nightmares, heightened arousal and fear are then misinterpreted as a sign of current threat, setting up a vicious maintenance cycle. Fragmentation and poor organisation of trauma memory involuntary triggers trauma-related thoughts and images which are poorly elaborated and inadequately integrated with more coherent autobiographical memories.

The table of interventions that follows is linked to the three forms of formulation that proved useful in helping John understand the relational, organisational and individual development and maintenance aspects of his trauma and related mental health problems.

CONCLUSION

This case study has hopefully shown that a client's presenting problems may not be as straightforward as they first seem. It illustrates how the beliefs of those working in organisations can often contribute to client problems or help to maintain them. It also demonstrates some of the ways in which relational problems between staff groups and clients can be utilised as rich opportunities for therapists to address broader formulation issues, and how the therapeutic relationship can provide a safe ground to test healthcare-related beliefs and assumptions held by clients in the context of their goals. Through utilising a case formulation that captured his experiences, John was able to see his problem as more than a diagnosis. The establishment of therapeutic goals, and first undertaking work on the relationship, helped him realise the impact his beliefs were having on himself and helped the team to understand how his problems were being maintained. Once a period of time had elapsed, and more functionally supportive relationships and coping was achieved, John was able to start to effectively address his past trauma.

Summary

1   Formulation can be useful in understanding organisational factors that impact on the therapeutic alliance and therapeutic process.

2   Therapeutic flexibility and creativity is required by cognitive behavioural psychotherapists in the context of interprofessional team working.

3   Generic and diagnosis specific formulation can be useful at different stages of the therapeutic process.

Activities

1   Make note of the language, gestures and other forms of verbal and non-verbal cues team members use when discussing 'problem' clients. When and if appropriate, ask them what has made them respond in such a way and how the experience of discussing this particular client makes them feel as professionals?

2   Once you have collected the information above, attempt to create an organisational case formulation.

3   When you first meet a client who has been involved in the mental health services for a long period of time, find out from them what has been most helpful and unhelpful. Try to explore the strategies utilised by previous mental health workers rather than focusing on psychopharmacological treatment.

Further reading

Grant, A., Mills, J., Mulhern, R. and Short, N. (2004) *Cognitive Behavioural Therapy in Mental Health Care*. London: Sage.
Chapter 5 of this text may help you to consider using cognitive behavioural principles and strategies to enhance team working.

Morgan, G. (1997) *Images of Organization*, 2nd edn. Thousand Oaks, CA: Sage.
This book provides an excellent coverage of the ways in which organisations are socially constructed and influence the social cognition of organisational members.

Case formulation: cognitive behavioural family therapy

10

Adrian Cockx

Learning objectives

After reading this chapter and completing the activities at the end of it you should be able to:

1 Gain an understanding of the application of cognitive case formulation for family therapy.

2 Note how the process of formulation can facilitate the identification, understanding and subsequent adaptation of belief systems and behaviours.

3 Recognise the impact of different beliefs systems within the context of familial dynamics and their subsequent affect on the individual members.

4 Become aware of the significance of the role of 'hope' within the family therapeutic process.

5 See how the Socratic Method within guided discovery can be useful in helping individuals within the family to become more aware of the formation and maintenance of their existing problems.

6 Understand how existing and past family members' behaviours can be utilised to overcome present difficulties.

The origins of cognitive behavioural family therapy (CBFT) are themselves steeped in unique, challenging and diverse approaches. Datilio (2004a), arguably one of the major proponents in the dissemination of this approach, writes about the criticism he was met with by the American Association for Marriage and Family Therapy (AAMFT) when he applied for accreditation in the 1980s. The basis for this was that the AAMFT board felt that the cognitive behavioural approach, in and of itself, was not effective with families. It was suggested he rewrite his case study with one of the more 'acceptable' models of family therapy such as systems theory.

Over the last 20 years, popularity for utilising the cognitive behavioural approach in the treatment of families has increased. However, developmental, attachment, family and systemic strands have been recognised as necessary in the application of therapy (Dummett, 2006). The use of a generic formulation is also essential in incorporating interpersonal factors prevalent in the presentation (Dummett, 2006), although it is arguable as to how much depth is required for this to be effective. Through undertaking such a parsimonious approach, the element of hope can be built into the family unit and potentially help through its application to future problems.

Everyone has views about how a family 'should be' and cognitive theory can be helpful in exploring the beliefs, assumptions and roles that each person brings to a familial relationship. Whenever people and their subsequent belief systems are put together, the majority of shared beliefs that formed the bond are similar and complementary in nature, thus leading to harmony in these areas. However, many relational problems can often be attributed to conflict that exists when beliefs, values and subsequent behaviours clash, provoking an emotional response and a feeling that compromise cannot be sought (Datilio, 2004a). It is at this point that cognitive theory, with its emphasis on different levels of thought and a focus on shared goals, can prove to be helpful to the individuals involved. The process of therapy facilitates the identification, understanding and subsequent adaptation of new belief systems and behaviours, where agreement and compromise can lead to more harmonious relations.

It is important to understand the level of conviction we hold in our belief systems and the investment we have placed in them over the years. On the whole our beliefs work for us and have many different roles that ensure that our sense of self is preserved in a manner that makes us feel secure with others and the world in general. Datilio (2004b: 239) refers to the notion of familial schemas where beliefs amongst familial members serve a purpose to become 'joint schemas'. Changes in familial structure can cause the introduction of new belief systems thus challenging previously held belief systems and forcing change and adaptation. This can prove testing for both client and therapist alike.

The dynamics involved within the therapeutic process of helping families are often challenging for the therapist. Vying for power and an individual's need for recognition within the family unit is often the cause of many disruptions (Cecchin, 1992). This can often lead to therapists finding themselves in difficult situations, which can be interpreted either as overwhelming or as an opportunity to help the family find alternative methods of making sense of what is going on for them. Cecchin (1992) describes how the therapist can use this to their advantage through taking a therapeutic stance of curiosity as an opportunity for the construction of new forms of action and interpretation.

What Cockx was attempting to achieve in the following case study is an illustration of a stance of curiosity through utilising existing skills as those indicated by Padesky's (1993) description of the Socratic method in guided discovery. Within the context of guiding discovery, this process involves the therapeutic qualities of active listening, empathising, summarising and synthesis. The addition of generic formulation models allowed the focus to be placed on the active level of thought relevant to the family's construction and maintenance of their presenting problems. It will also be argued that such an integrative approach, applying cognitive theory and methods to the social construction of perceived realities, can lead to effective empathic practice (Grant et al., 2004b).

OVERVIEW OF PRESENTING PROBLEMS

The 'Smiths' could be described as a modern day nuclear family. John Smith is a 40-year-old professional and his wife Margaret Smith is a divorcee aged 43 with two children from her previous marriage, 10-year-old Shauna and 9-year-old Kieran. A year after Margaret's divorce was finalised, Mr and Mrs Smith had a son they named Eddie who was 3 years old at the time the family entered therapy. Shauna and Kieran's biological father, Michael, remains in contact with them and they visit him and his new wife Patty every other week.

Although there had been problems throughout Margaret and Michael's relationship, they had remained in agreement over how the children should be brought up. This included the choice of schooling, appropriate toys and extra curricular activities, as well as issues pertaining to the children's health and well-being. In order to ensure agreement between themselves and the children on these matters, they would discuss these issues on a regular basis, or as and when the need arose. This pattern had been replicated between John and Margaret although it did not have the same degree of efficacy it had previously between Margaret and Michael, often being a catalyst to family arguments.

Problems started to manifest between John and his step-son Kieran soon after Eddie was born. There were daily arguments between them, especially at meal times when the family would eat together and where any changes to the family members' routine was discussed. Margaret often felt she was unable to say anything that would rectify the situation and John did not think that Kieran was respecting his authority. Shauna kept a low profile, spending a great deal of time out with friends or in her room, listening to music or doing her homework. Whenever an argument developed between John and Kieran, a great deal of emotion was stirred up within the family. Kieran would cry, which John saw as attention-seeking behaviour, and would complain to his biological father Michael thus increasing levels of tension.

During the initial stage of assessment it became apparent that there were several associated physical problems which some of the members of the family complained about. Margaret stated that she often suffered from headaches and sleeplessness, Kieran would complain about stomach aches, and John described a general feeling of tension which would affect his ability to concentrate. Should the family argue, all members stated that it would affect their levels of concentration and they would often feel 'close to tears' over seemingly minor problems which would previously have been brushed off.

At the point of entering cognitive family therapy the Smiths described being at their wits' end. They felt that a great deal of strain was not only being placed on individual family members, but on the marriage. John and Margaret had initially sought couples counselling as a means of resolving their issues. However, following a few sessions the counsellor suggested they try family therapy as the problem appeared to extend further than them as a couple. Shauna initially expressed resistance to family therapy as she did not see the family problems as being 'her issue'. She stated that she was all right and didn't need any help and as far as she was concerned the problem was between John and Kieran.

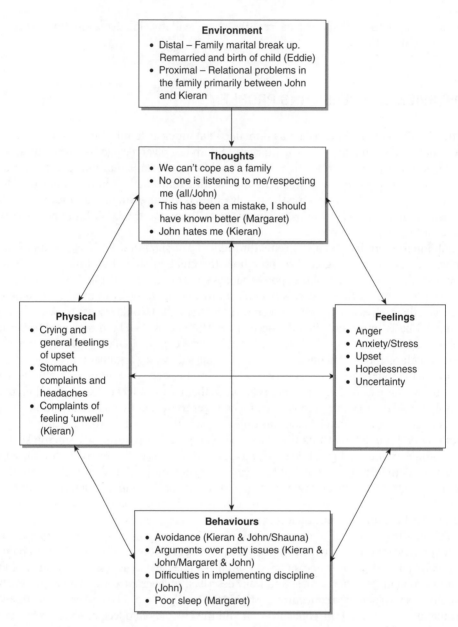

Figure 10.1   Diagrammatic formulation of the whole family (based on Padesky and Mooney, 1990)

ASSESSMENT AND FORMULATION

The family

The first step that was undertaken in the therapeutic process was to provide an overview of therapy and what was expected of all involved. This was placed within the context of the family's presenting problems, as described above. An opportunity was given to help each individual explore their fears, hopes and expectations involved in the process of therapy.

Concerns were initially expressed by John that there would be a great deal of emphasis on the behaviour rather than the emotions that were being experienced throughout the family. This provided the therapist with an ideal opportunity to examine the beliefs John held about cognitive behavioural therapy and how the beliefs that we all hold can lead to the development of assumptions and subsequent associated emotions. This example provided the therapist with a naturally occurring moment that was powerfully utilised as an illustration and introduction into the cognitive model.

The target model (Padesky, 1998) (see Figure 10.2 below) further expanded this understanding to introduce the concepts and roles of core beliefs, underlying assumptions and automatic thoughts. In a change to the original diagram, a dotted line was used between each level of thought to show how there can be movement from one area to another. This illustrates how the different levels of thought relevant to the cognitive model can become more accessible, often seen as cognitive distortions.

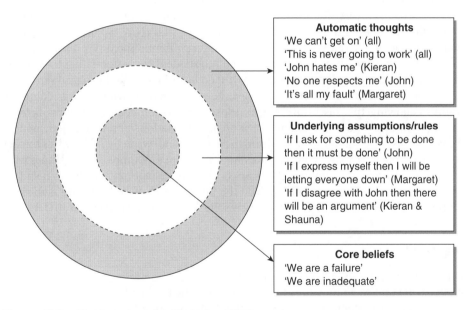

Figure 10.2   The target model (Padesky, 1998)

Recognition was given to the differences that existed between each of the family members with regard to how they saw the problems, and it was suggested that each member have an opportunity to meet individually to air their views. Resistance was met from Shauna at this point, who stated that she did not think she had a problem and that there was nothing she could do to help. Cockx attempted to re-frame this assumption by asking if she wanted to contribute, stating that her views would be invaluable due to the position she currently viewed herself as having within the family. This placed Shauna in a position she otherwise did not recognise: the power she held and her role within the family. Through doing this, Cockx was able to validate her resistance (Leahy, 2001) and engage her in the therapeutic process.

John

John was the first to discuss his interpretation of the circumstances that contributed to the presenting problems. He described a number of negative thoughts and beliefs he held about Kieran and how he felt that Kieran's behaviour was attention seeking. An example of this was his assumption that Kieran was always attempting to gain approval and affection from Margaret. After careful empathic Socratic questioning by the therapist (Padesky, 1993), John was able to recognise how these thoughts often led to him making condescending remarks about Kieran, and the predominant associated emotional state in which he found himself prior to making these comments.

In respect to Shauna, John experienced her as an independent young girl who appeared only to be interested in pursuing her own interests. At times when a family argument erupted, he described how she would often take the side of her brother Kieran, along with Margaret, but he did not feel he was able to confront her as he himself felt victimised by all three when this happened.

John was concerned about his relationship with Margaret as the tensions with Kieran affected any expressions of intimacy. The costs and benefits of addressing the familial problems were discussed and praise was given for John's determination and motivation to address these. He was also able to see that there would be a secondary gain, in respect to increased intimacy with Margaret, should the problems be resolved.

John also expressed how he found it difficult to suddenly be a step-father to two older children. He mentioned that it was easier with Eddie as he was his biological son but, as far as Kieran and Shauna were concerned, he never knew if what he was doing was 'right'. Following this disclosure, Cockx spoke compassionately about links between thoughts, feelings and behaviour and their impact on relationships. In addition, assumptions were discussed about what we deem to be 'right' and 'wrong' and how this impacts on our relationships. Using some of the examples of John's assumptions, and times when he had felt stressed and shouted at Kieran, Cockx was collaboratively able to help John explore what was going on. This enabled the introduction of collaborative empiricism within the context of the therapeutic process (Beck et al., 1979), see Figure 10.3.

Margaret

During Margaret's individual session, she was emotionally expressive throughout, often crying and weeping whilst telling her story. She blamed herself for all the family problems and was at a loss as to why the family did not function as well as it had in the past. Margaret was concerned that her current marriage would end in divorce due to these problems and felt torn between her love for her son and new husband. She identified the primary family problem as being the relationship between John and Kieran and her concerns for her future relationship with John.

Margaret began to recount how John and Kieran had had a good relationship before Eddie was born and how they would often spend quality time together engaged in constructive activities, such as washing the cars and gardening. Since Eddie's abilities had developed with age, John tended to primarily involve him in any activities he was undertaking. Margaret had felt this change in John's behaviour to be natural as Eddie was 'his' child and had therefore not questioned this. This was based on her assumption that it was important that John and Eddie develop a father–son relationship as Kieran had done with his biological father.

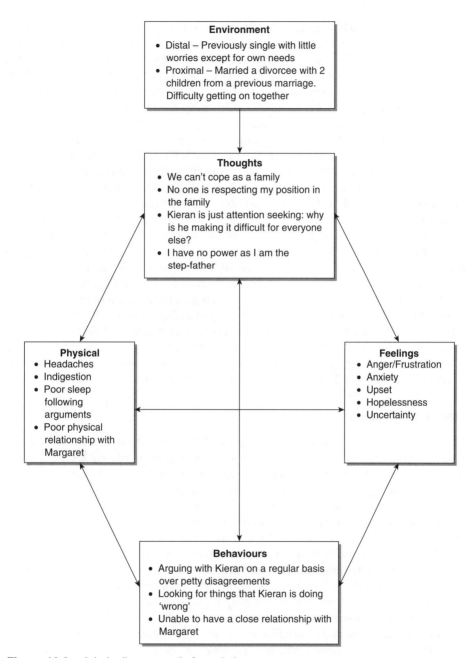

Figure 10.3 John's diagrammatic formulation

This account led Cockx to gently explore the role of assumptions. From this, Margaret was able to recognise that although her assumptions had some credibility, there was room to create a degree of accommodation. A discussion around how assumptions lead to the development of rules allowed the therapist and Margaret to understand that flexibility could be introduced into her rules about the importance of Eddie and John's relationship.

The exploration of what Margaret had meant about John and Eddie previously having a 'good' relationship, led to the expression of her guilt and shame over the divorce and the subsequent affect this had on Kieran and Shauna. Whilst Margaret was explaining this she would often express cognitive distortions, such as 'if only I had ...', 'it's all my fault because ...' and 'I should have ...' Through gentle Socratic questioning (Padesky, 1993), and keeping her goals in mind, Cockx was able to empathically deconstruct Margaret's negative thoughts around these assumptions. A diagrammatic formulation using a white board, with sections for thoughts, feelings and behaviours, was drawn up. Cockx was then able to help her to make the connections, through summarising her statements along with her presenting affect, thus solidifying the connections.

Once a conceptualisation of the problem had been illustrated and related to her negative automatic thoughts, Margaret was able to become aware of how this pattern caused a vicious cycle, which she identified as contributing to her overall feelings of hopelessness. Through the persistent use of the question 'What do you want to do about this problem?', Cockx was able to help Margaret return to her goals and the goals of the family, thus helping her to break the negative cycle of hopelessness.

Although the identification of goals and its shared outcomes with other family members was partially effective in raising Margaret's hopes, the addition of a previous functional relationship between John and Kieran provided a point at which Cockx could potentially deconstruct what was going on at that time, in order to build on hope that a solution can be attained. Through sharing this information with Margaret, the installation of hope was paramount in changing her outlook of not only the therapeutic process but of herself (Cheavens et al., 2006), see Figure 10.4.

Kieran and Shauna

As mentioned earlier, Shauna had initially stated that she did not want to get involved with family therapy as she felt that the problem was primarily between John and Kieran. The therapist had told her that her opinion and perception of how she saw the events that led up to family arguments would be invaluable. As Kieran found the process of meeting the therapist difficult, the support of Shauna's presence was felt to be a method of addressing this and also provided an opportunity for Shauna's perception of the situation to be aired. When asked about this, Kieran too had felt that Shauna would be able to add things he might have forgotten as well as providing some support.

Cockx started with asking how they saw the current problems within the family home and how it affected them. Kieran and Shauna both stated that the arguments between John and Kieran were causing a 'bad' feeling in the home and that this affected them both. By asking more concrete questions about what led up to this feeling starting, and the associated behaviours that would lead to arguments, Cockx was able to elicit specific examples that could be formulated. Through adopting an approach of interest and compassion for their problem, Cockx was able to help them feel relaxed about the process. An example of how this was achieved was by the therapist initially not taking any notes, thus allowing them to see and feel that they were being listened to.

Kieran and Shauna told Cockx of an event that happened on a regular basis where they would often watch television on their return from school. When John arrived home they would have to turn the television off and 'look busy', as on several occasions he had aired his dissatisfaction with them watching television which had led to an argument. His basis for this disagreement was that he believed they should be doing their homework or helping their Mother with household chores. Both Kieran and

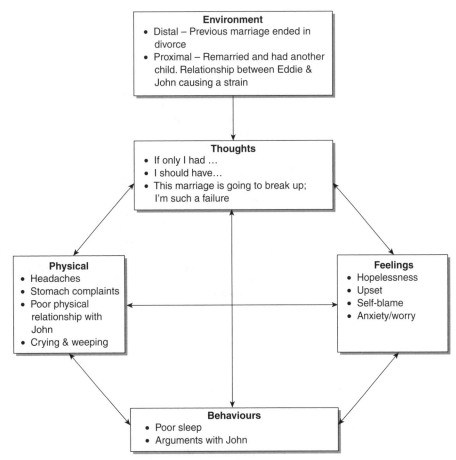

Figure 10.4   Margaret's diagrammatic formulation

Shauna felt this to be unfair as most of their friends were able to watch television. When Kieran said this to John, an argument ensued. Kieran stated that whenever he had argued with John he did not feel that his point of view was ever taken into account. He mentioned that he did not feel that John listened to him and was only interested in asserting his side of the argument. On further exploration, it became apparent that this was how Kieran and Shauna generally felt about their relationship with John.

Cockx asked them if they would mind if he tried to make sense of this problem by drawing a diagram on the white board in his office. In order to demonstrate the function of this action, Cockx helped them to focus on global examples of how differences in beliefs can lead to conflict. This was based on Kieran's example of how boys at school would argue over who was the best football team in the country. This was then placed in context with the ABC model (Ellis, 1962) and both children were able to see that the 'beliefs' each individual held were instrumental in causing an argument. Cockx was then able to explore with them what kind of beliefs would need to be adopted in order to ensure that an argument did not follow. This enabled both Kieran and Shauna to understand how there needs to be flexibility in people's beliefs in order to have a desired outcome that suited both of them.

Table 10.1   Table of interventions

Family member	Presenting problem	Intervention	Outcome
All	*Automatic thoughts –* We can't cope as a family. This is never going to work. No one respects anyone else.	Family engaged in weekly outings which were increased over time in duration. They suggested they record their days out through taking photographs and making scrap books. This would be discussed in therapy sessions.	Family started to bond more spending time together and individually. Kieran, Shauna and Eddie started to draw pictures recounting their times together. Noticeably the drawings depicted smiles.
All	*Rules and assumptions –* If I don't assertive myself then no one will listen.	The creation of appropriate times for the family to discuss what they individually and collectively wanted. Should too much emotion be expressed, then they would agree to postpone for a short period of time until the emotional expression had stopped.	Initially predictions that they would argue and then not make collective agreements were proven wrong. The intervention of taking timeout was so successful they used it in other areas of their lives when they felt similarly activated.
All	*Core beliefs –* We are a failure. We are inadequate. Other families are able to cope and get on. The world expects familial harmony otherwise the children grow up with dysfunctional behaviours.	Although identified, work was not directly undertaken on collective core beliefs and familial schema patterns. (The rationale for this was based on the presenting problems being more related to rules and assumptions and associated automatic thoughts.)	Initial baseline scores measuring the conviction in these beliefs weakened over the course of therapy. There was noticeably less emotional expression whenever they did have a recurrence of these beliefs, as they were more able to reflect on the progress they had made for themselves.
John	*Automatic thoughts –* No one is listening to me/respecting me.	Observed and recorded the times he spoke and the responses from others in the family.	Noticed that on the whole he was listened to, and Kieran contributed to some of his conversations by asking questions.
John	*Rules and assumptions –* I have no power as a step-father. If you are a step-parent, then you have no power in the family.	Undertook a survey amongst work colleagues and friends.	Found others had difficulties too. There were also some responses where people stated that their step-parent was of a greater positive influence on them than their biological parent, giving John hope.
John and Kieran	*Assumption –* We don't get on therefore there's no point in trying.	Planned weekly time together which increased over the course of therapy. This time was recorded through the use of photographs and engaging in a constructive activity (model making).	John became more involved with Kieran's interests and then introduced him to activities he enjoyed as a young boy. This improved their relationship and weakened the assumption that they did not get on.

(Continued)

Table 10.1   *(Continued)*

Family member	Presenting problem	Intervention	Outcome
John and Margaret	*Assumption* – We are going to fall apart. We are not strong enough.	Decided on an agreed time to reflect on the process of therapy and ways in which this could be measured – for example, John and Kieran getting on better.	Created time for each other by going out on their own. John shared positive memories of the time he spent with Kieran which increased Margaret's hope that they would become stronger as a family unit.
Margaret	*Automatic thoughts* – Content around: If only … and I should have …	Formulated vicious cycles and utilised Dysfunctional Thought Records (DTRs) to challenge negative thoughts.	Reflected on times together when the family did get on and became more proactive in suggesting family days out. Utilised DTRs to provide the evidence.
Margaret	*Assumption* – Biologically inherited relationships are more important than step-parent relationships	Collected evidence through a survey of what it meant to have relationships within families.	Became aware that there are some people who see that a step-parent was a better influence on them than a biological parent. This belief was reinforced by someone she admired having had this experience.
Shauna and Kieran	*Assumption* – There's nothing I can do to change this situation.	Shauna and Kieran would ask if they could share their opinion at family meetings.	Both were surprised by John and Margaret wanting to hear what they had to say. Became more involved in family meetings and made suggestions for days out.
Kieran and Shauna	*Assumption* – John doesn't care about us, he won't let us do anything we want to do such as watch television after school. All he wants us to do is chores.	At a family meeting time they all agreed that when Kieran and Shauna had finished their homework and had shown it to either Margaret or John they could watch television for an agreed time. They agreed that if they had not done their homework they would not have any television the next day. The family drew up a chart with all the household chores and each member agreed to complete a number of these chores. If they did not then they would be forfeited.	By stating that responsibility was a familial obligation, John and Margaret did their part of the chores too and recorded it on the chart. They were also subject to similar forfeits. This helped Kieran and Shauna to recognise the value of working together. As forfeits were agreed collectively, responsibility was placed on the individual.

CONCLUSION: INTERVENTIONS

Through creating a comprehensive case formulation, and the time spent on assessing the unhelpful thoughts, behaviours and affect, the family were given a conceptualisation of their problem they could understand and relate to. The role of 'beliefs' and associated affect led to a shared understanding that it was this area which the family would benefit from addressing. A shared familial goal was identified as being 'we would like to get on better without arguing'. The identification of anger and anxiety as the key emotional triggers enabled the therapist to place the primary focus of therapy on the individual and shared assumptions and rules.

Through collaboratively formed behavioural experiments, new rules were tested and reinforced, thus changing presenting behavioural problems. Success was attained by strengthening the new rules and repeating the behavioural experiments through applying the same rules to different situations. The family was also able to recognise changes in affect, that arguments in the home reduced, and that problem solving replaced previous patterns of self-blame. Once each family member was able to apply these new rules spontaneously in naturally occurring moments, therapy became focused on relapse prevention strategies. These included not speaking when too much emotion was present and creating 'talking times' to discuss problems in a more calm and rational manner.

Summary

1   Cognitive family-based case formulation is useful in helping distressed families.

2   The process of formulation can facilitate the identification, understanding and subsequent adaptation of family belief systems and behaviours.

3   Hope is a crucial variable in the process of family recovery.

4   The Socratic method, utilising guided discovery, can be useful in helping individuals within the family to become more aware of the formation and maintenance of their existing problems.

2   Existing and past family members' behaviours can be used as examples to help overcome present difficulties.

Activities

1   Try to construct a family formulation of your own family, to include both shared and discordant beliefs and rules.

2   Review some cases on your caseload where family factors may have influenced outcome. Consider the implications for future assessment and formulation practice.

Further reading

Beck, A.T. (1989) *Love is Never Enough.* New York: Harper Collins.
This is an excellent text in elucidating the role of beliefs in relation to marital harmony and disharmony.

Datilio, F.M. (2004) 'Family therapy', in R.L. Leahy (ed.), *Roadblocks in Cognitive-Behavioral Therapy: Transforming Challenges into Opportunities for Change.* New York: Guilford Press.
A great critical analysis and practice guide of cognitive behavioural family therapy from one of the leaders in the field.

Broadening the cognitive behavioural formulation for low self-esteem: helping 'Claire' with her damaged and broken self

11

Jem Mills

Learning objectives

After reading this chapter and completing the activities at the end of it you should be able to:

1 Have a basic understanding of Fennell's low self-esteem model and the specific ways in which this model can be broadened in the light of contemporary cognitive behavioural, and related, theoretical-conceptual material.

2 Understand the role of empty chair work in the development of compassionate case formulation.

Low self-esteem has emerged in recent years across the cognitive behavioural literature in association with a wide variety of diagnostic disorders. It is consistently linked with problems such as depression, social anxiety, obsessive compulsive disorder, bipolar disorder and psychosis. This transdiagnostic nature of the low self-esteem construct offers an opportunity to draw together a number of models and in doing so broaden the dialogue around cognitive behavioural case formulation.

FENNELL'S MODEL OF LOW SELF-ESTEEM

Fennell's (2006) model is the first, non-diagnostic led, cognitive behavioural formulation model to encapsulate the relationship between a range of cognitive, behavioural and emotional aspects of low self-esteem. She presents the notion of a 'bottom line' as being at the heart of the problem. Equivalent to a self-related core belief, this is a tacitly held, negative self-evaluative sense of self arising from early life experiences. Thus a person growing up in an invalidating environment is likely to encode that experience within a belief such as 'I'm worthless'. The bottom line then shapes the person's interaction with the world by influencing the way that sensory information is processed through attention and organised in memory (Fennell, 1998). Put simply, once people believe they are worthless they then tend to act and engage with the world in a way that maintains and strengthens that belief.

Fennell (2006) goes on to show how a person with low self-esteem develops protective standards, or rules for living, which serve to reduce the activation of the bottom line and hide it from others. For example, a person with the belief 'I'm worthless' might develop a perfectionist rule 'If I do everything perfectly people won't discover I'm worthless'. In the same way that safety behaviours prevent disconfirmation of catastrophic misinterpretations in panic disorder, a behavioural strategy of perfectionism serves to prevent disconfirmation of the belief 'I'm worthless' by never allowing the person to discover whether their ordinary efforts are good enough. Ironically, people with this combination of beliefs and associated drive often achieve higher than average degrees of success in their endeavours, which they discount due to the effects on attention and reasoning of the worthlessness belief.

These standards or rules for living formulated by Fennell (2006) go some way towards explaining the range of emotional problems experienced by people suffering with low self-esteem. She describes how failing to meet the standard leads to self-critical thinking and depression and how facing just the possibility of failure leads to anxious predictions and physical sensations, and unhelpful responses. For instance, a person with the worthlessness/perfectionism dynamic described above would, on the way to an important interview, have worrying thoughts about the consequences of failure, anxious feelings and a number of self-defeating behaviours. If she discovered later that she had indeed failed the interview she would become self-critical and depressed. Fennell's notion of standards that might be broken or threatened neatly explains the oscillation between anxiety and depression so often experienced by people with low self-esteem. However, despite its heavy influence on our practice, relative accessibility and obvious popularity with users of the self-help manual developed from the model, Fennel's (2006) approach is limited in its ability to accommodate other emotional problems associated with low self-esteem such as anger, guilt and shame.

Another drawback is the model's reliance on a unitary notion of identity traditionally accepted in Beckian cognitive psychotherapy. The idea that the sense of self is centred on a single or small number of, often word-based, beliefs or a 'bottom line' is questionable. In the light of Teasdale and Barnard's (1993) ICS model, Gilbert's (1989) bio-psychological model, Chadwick's (2006) drawing on Buddhist theories regarding the self, and our own leanings towards social constructionism (Burr, 1995; Gergen, 1999; Grant et al., 2006; Poole and Grant, 2005), we view the self as an ever changing, evolving and socially negotiated process.

THE MIND-IN-PLACE AND LOW SELF-ESTEEM

In Chapter 6 of this text, Michael Townend describes how, drawing on cognitive neuroscience, Teasdale and Barnard (1993) have developed the Interacting Cognitive Subsystems (ICS) model. People experience their identity in many different ways, clichés such as 'he has different sides to him' or 'I feel like a new person' demonstrating how embedded this phenomena is in everyday language. The ICS model explains this from a cognitive science perspective describing how we have many different available mind states, each with its own way of processing current and past information. These mind states interact with each other as well as the world at large and can become negative and self-perpetuating, thus giving the appearance of being static.

Some people with extremely low self-esteem are able to perform well in some areas of life, dealing with criticism and failure adaptively. For instance, I helped a man with obsessive compulsive disorder, body dysmorphic disorder, depression and extreme social anxiety. The man had very low self-esteem and was very sensitive to rejection. However he was a keen rugby player, was assertive with his team mates and dealt with aggression on the pitch easily. He was also a keen musician and enjoyed playing solos in front of an audience.

The traditional Beckian perspective on this man's experience might formulate that the situations in which low self-esteem appears to be absent are merely times when compensatory assumptions, rules for living, or standards are in place serving their function of keeping the negative core beliefs at bay. However, in our view, some of our clients' descriptions of how they fully experience themselves as different people in these different situations goes beyond this explanation. From a different paradigm position, a complementary point is made in postmodern and post-structural work on the multiple, dynamic and interactive nature of subjectivity:

> **Instead of seeing the self and identity as an inner psychological essence possessed by individuals... discursive psychology argues that identities or 'subject positions' are brought into being through discourse. Different ways of talking invoke different subject positions for speakers, such as 'mother', 'daughter', 'lover', 'professional woman', 'friend', etc., so that specific patters of talk are recognizable for the work they do in discursively constituting identity... Unlike the traditional notion of a stable, cognitive self, discursive psychology emphasizes the shifting and multiple identities that speakers actively construct in talk (some of which may even be contradictory) to accomplish a range of interactional goals. Discourse is constitutive of identity... people can be positioned by particular ways of talking, but at the same time people can make active choices about the identities they mobilize in particular settings. (Augoustinos et al., 2006: 57)**

Teasdale (1997) borrows the term 'mind-in-place' from Ornstein (1992) to describe how we have different configurations of cognitive sub-systems that come 'on-line' when particular cues are recognised. Each configuration is said to operate as if it has its own historical development, set of memories and associated attention patterns. Teasdale particularly highlights the difference between a propositional level of cognition and an implicational level, both of which feature in each 'mind-in-place'. Self-defeating patterns at the propositional level of cognition can be accessed using traditional evidential review styles of cognitive behavioural interventions such as thought records, guided discovery and some behavioural experiments. However, the implicational level of cognition (the sort that gives us a 'gut feeling' about things) can only be engaged through experiential intervention methods such as meditation, empty chair work and role play (see, for example, Lee, 2005). Teasdale and Barnard explain the rise of these cognitive behavioural approaches:

> From the ICS perspective, it comes as no surprise that major recent importations into cognitive therapy have come from experientially oriented approaches such as Gestalt therapy. Like ICS, these approaches recognise the importance of holistic levels of representation, the role of body-state and of the wider semantic context. ICS provides a framework within which the effectiveness of experiential therapy techniques, for which there is little justification in the clinical cognitive model, can be understood. (Teasdale and Barnard, 1993: 242)

EVOLUTION AND LOW SELF-ESTEEM

Gilbert (1989, 2005, 2007) presents a bio-psychological formulation in which 'low self-esteem in effect renders the individual as a subordinate' (1989: 49). He describes various inherited neurological systems concerned with dealing with threat and social cohesion in mammals which become linked to the individual's identity.

> Subordinates tend to occupy the peripheral positions of the group and are especially predisposed to exhibiting submissive displays. Furthermore because subordinates are so located and because predators tend to select peripheral animals, both the non-social defence system routines (fight, flight, freeze and faint) and the social defence system routines (submission, reverted escape) may be sensitised or attuned by holding a subordinate position. In other words the defence behaviours need to be continuously 'at the ready' to facilitate rapid escape and

> injury avoidance. **The tense postures and anxious vigilance of subordinates suggest they are in a state of braced readiness; a state of high but un-discharged arousal. This may explain various sleep disorders especially in depression because predators are especially active during the twilight hours.** (Gilbert, 1989: 47)

Human beings share these systems with other mammals and are located in the oldest part of the brain; what is often referred to as the reptilian brain. The systems are cognitively unsophisticated, often manifesting in the all or nothing thinking styles common in low self-esteem. Gilbert's hypothesis sits well with Teasdale's model. It might be argued that in people experiencing low self-esteem, one configuration of cognitive sub-systems or 'mind-in-place' forms a link between the person's identity and the subordination and defence systems described by Gilbert (1989).

MANY SELVES: THE DIALOGUE BETWEEN MULTIPLE SELVES AND LOW SELF-ESTEEM

Many psychotherapy systems and theories of identity contain the notion that we have multiple selves which relate to each other in different ways, as if forming inner social relationships, and that these selves constitute different ways of processing information and engaging with the world (Gilbert and Irons, 2005).

Bentall (2004) for instance relates self-discrepancy theory to low self-esteem in depression and psychosis. This approach puts the discrepancies between a perceived self (how we think we are) and an ideal self (how we think we ought to be) at the heart of low self-esteem. This also applies to how we think others view us, for instance how I think a parent/partner/boss views me versus how I think they would like me to be.

Safran (1998) draws on interpersonal theory to demonstrate how negative representations of the self and others set up self-fulfilling cycles in the person's attention patterns and interpersonal behaviour.

Gilbert (1989, 2005, 2007) presents social mentality theory suggesting that certain programmed displays of behaviour are designed to produce certain responses in others and the individual. A simple example is that of an individual who feels vulnerable displaying aggressive behaviour designed to intimidate the other and to make himself feel safe in the process. These interpersonal systems become internalised and acted out between different constructions of the self. Hence a person with low self-esteem can generate inner aggression (for instance in the form of self-criticism) when feeling vulnerable or threatened as a way of generating feelings of safety. The unhelpful consequence is that in the process this 'self-dominance' maintains the subordination system described above (Gilbert and Irons, 2005).

In summary, useful concepts in formulating low self-esteem include the notion that we have multiple, ever changing constructions of identity which in turn have different ways of processing information, using language, relating to others and relating to our inner selves. The task in helping someone to understand and overcome low self-esteem is to identify the self-defeating ways in which these selves interact. It can be helpful to plot the historical development of these selves as they are often internalised relationships from the past. Important aspects of these selves are encoded at an implicational level, rendering them more of a felt sense of low self-esteem rather than a clearly articulated set of beliefs. These aspects are amenable to experiential based interventions which include, for instance, a focus on the body-state aspect of the meaning.

CLAIRE'S FELT SENSE OF BEING BROKEN

Claire is a 38-year-old mother of three with a history of low self-esteem manifesting in several episodes of anxiety and depression, including post-natal depression following the birth of her daughter. She was referred for individual cognitive behavioural therapy, following an eight-week group cognitive behavioural programme at the hospital where she had recently been admitted for a depressive episode. She had a great sense of shame surrounding her difficulties, but to the friends and family who were unaware of her problems she came across as strong, supportive, coping and successful.

Claire rose quickly to executive management level in a major retail firm before having children and described herself as a different, highly assertive person in the work environment. The following excerpt from her therapy journal summarises the personal history relevant to the formulations we used and exemplifies the activation of what might be called her 'broken mind'. Her descriptions also illustrate some of the defence systems Gilbert (1989) describes and demonstrate some of the memory and imagery systems associated with her sense of being broken:

> I wake up, it's 4 am. The thought enters my mind 'Oh, it's today. What am I going to have to face?' Then I start ticking off all the things I have to face and with each one I ask myself, how will I cope with that? What if I can't? What if I get anxious? What do I need to do in order to get myself through it? My mind fills with these possibilities and the anxiety starts to rise. I get this sinking nauseous feeling in my stomach and then the feeling of being broken and damaged washes over me again. I feel so vulnerable. I don't understand why I am in this situation again. It feels like I am back at square one. If I can't control myself, I am failing. All the things I have learned seem to be lost to me now. I feel so powerless.
>
> As the anxiety and feeling of being broken washes over me, the familiar image enters my mind. There I am stood at the sink retching at 4 o'clock in the morning, feeling so desperate, helpless and anxious. I can't go back to that place, I tell myself. It feels so dark and powerless. It reminds me of a memory of being a teenager. Being alone in my bedroom,

feeling helpless, powerless, anxious and dark. All the awful things were happening in my parents' relationship that they individually confided in me. I was just a teenage girl, not meant to be their go-between and somehow, I got lost in all that. But it would not do in our family to have this secret despair on show. We weren't allowed to show our vulnerability and so I learnt to bottle it up and, in the end, lost touch with myself in the process. It was the only way I knew how to cope and I had to cope. Now this image is in my mind of a year ago when the depression finally overcame me. At that point retching into the kitchen sink at 4 o'clock in the morning was the point at which I knew I could go no further. Something had to change. Here I am now one year later, 4 o'clock in the morning, feeling anxious with this memory in my mind, thinking to myself 'it's happening again'.

I have to cope somehow, so my mind scans the day ahead, looking for obstacles, things that might go wrong, things I can do to lessen the stress, and already, at 10 past 4, I feel lost. My mind is full of all the things I imagine I can't do. The panic rises, nothing seems to work, the meditation, telling myself it will pass. I know there is another way of looking at the situation but I just can't see it. All that seems real to me right now is that I feel broken, damaged forever. Here we are, one year on, and this is proof that I am never going to get over this. My worse fear, I am going to be a long-term mental health patient. I really am broken.

Claire described her sense of being broken as much more of a feeling washing over her than a form of words entering her mind. We explored the physical feelings, body posture and interpersonal behaviour associated with it. She described a range of experiences and behaviours commensurate with the subordination system described by Gilbert (1989) above. We engaged in a standard cognitive behavioural assessment process, giving linguistic labels to these experiences but agreeing to bear in mind that they were more like feelings. The process of articulating them this way was useful to Claire in understanding how her problems were maintained, but evidential review methods such as verbal reattribution and thought records had been ineffective for her during group cognitive behavioural therapy.

Claire's old core beliefs

I am broken and damaged 90 per cent – I am unlovable

Her old assumptions

If I play small, I won't get depressed
If I avoid trying to cope with large challenges, I won't get depressed

If I am open about my vulnerabilities, people won't like me
If I let people get close, they will leave me
If people leave me, I am a failure
If I share my feelings with people, they will think I am mad

Her safety behaviours

Always taking anti-depressants
Avoiding challenges however small
Being really busy
Being unassertive in family relationships
Scanning the day for things I might not cope with
Distraction

Her alternative core belief

I am complete

Her alternative assumptions

If I express my vulnerabilities in a matter of fact way, others will receive them like
that and I will feel more normal

Her key 'I am a complete person' activities

Being proactive
Exercising
Nurturing myself
Keeping space in the day for me
Meditating
Talking to people openly about how I am feeling

Her goals

1   To make regular time for myself to do things I enjoy
2   Organising the family in a relaxed paced way
3   To spend time mindfully aware of my emotions rather than use distraction and busyness
4   To be able to work in a career I have chosen
5   To express my thoughts and feelings in relationships in a calm, open and accepting manner
6   To free myself from responsibility for other peoples' emotions

Empty chair work script to 14-year-old version of self (see also Gilbert and Irons, 2005)

Claire identified her isolation during teenage years, her parent's relationship issues and
the family script around not expressing distress, as distal influences on her vulnerability
and her felt sense of being broken. She had spent many hours desperately unhappy alone
in her bedroom as a teenager. Both of her parents used her as a confidante and mediator
during the long breakdown in their marriage. She recognised that as an adult she had a
negative attitude towards this vulnerable side of herself and used the empty chair technique to explore the inner dialogue she had with it. She realised that she had had these
feelings as a teenager and explored the devastating effects of her criticism on this side of

herself. This involved talking to her broken self and then imagining hearing those words as a vulnerable, depressed teenager. She identified a common inner criticism:

- You're horrible
- You're ill
- You're depressed
- You're needy
- You should be able to feel better
- I am ashamed of you
- I can't tell people about you
- You are holding me back

She then identified a more compassionate way of talking to this vulnerable teenager:

- This will pass
- You can get better
- It will happen
- You can be more open about the relationships you have
- You're okay

Claire used this alternative dialogue as the basis of a compassionate letter to herself which she would read when her sense of being broken was activated. This letter would prompt her to re-engage with the interventions listed below.

Formulation of recurrent low moods and summary of experiential interventions

Claire's feeling that she was damaged or broken led her to adopt an attitude of needing to fix herself. We formulated that finding a list of techniques in order to fix herself was actually contributing to the sense that she was broken. She acknowledged that accepting the part of herself that felt vulnerable and in pain was difficult for her.

She also had the belief that if she couldn't cope, or became depressed or anxious, this would confirm her sense of being broken and damaged. In a sense, she had been traumatised by the fact that her mood had got so low she ended up being admitted to a mental health unit.

Consequently, she was very sensitive to the possibility of relapse. This set up a kind of scanning, monitoring attention, pattern which led her to be very sensitive to certain events and anniversaries in her previous decline. For instance, Christmas and summer holidays continued to be painful reminders of how she had originally become depressed and so she would often anxiously anticipate their arrival. Her husband going away on business had the same effect as did being alone with her children, especially if they could see she was upset. Holidays and social events also had the same effect.

As she anticipated these events, her mind would fill with worries about not coping which, in turn, would trigger anxiety. This activated her belief 'I should be able to stop this and if I can't there is no life for me'. This would increase the anxiety and lower her mood and thus confirm her suspicion that she was 'off track'. The more off track she felt she became, the more convinced she was that she *was* relapsing, thereby confirming her sense of being broken and damaged even more.

Claire's challenge was to let go of the idea of being fixed and to accept herself in her entirety, including her vulnerability. She summarised this as 'feeling like a complete person'. Experiential interventions included the following:

- Communicating authentically with people including discussing her depression with trusted people.
- Nurturing her own needs on a daily basis.
- Adjusting her body posture to a 'complete person' style, that is non-subordinate.
- Having regular in session role play based dialogue with her 'broken side'.
- Developing self-compassion through meditation and imagery work.
- Grounding all these in what Claire saw as an 'I'm complete as I am' lifestyle.

This approach would often lead to her feeling more centred or grounded or at ease with herself, and she would have to guard against the sense that she was fixed and that her feelings of anxiety and depression would never again return.

She felt she shouldn't hold on too tightly to this centred state but just to allow it to pass as everything else passes, something she is still practising. In that sense she identified with a line from her favourite William Blake poem:

> **He who binds to himself a joy**
>
> **Does the winged life destroy;**
>
> **But he who kisses the joy as it flies**
>
> **Lives in eternity's sun rise.**

Summary

1 Fennell's low self-esteem model, combined with contemporary cognitive behavioural, and related, theoretical-conceptual material, was helpful in repairing Claire's sense of herself as damaged and broken.

2 Empty chair work helped her develop more of a compassionate sense of herself.

Activities

1 In the context of the preceding discussion, consider the extent to which you are one or many selves.

2 Work through Fennell's (2006) programme yourself as an exercise in self and reflective practice.

Further reading

Fennell, M. (1998) 'Low self esteem', in N. Tarrier, A. Wells and G. Haddock (eds), *Treating Complex Cases The Cognitive Behavioural Therapy Approach*. Chichester: Wiley.
A good synthesis of Melanie Fennell's ideas for working with low self-esteem.

Gilbert, P. and Irons, J. (2005) 'Focussed therapies and compassionate mind training for shame and self-attacking', in P. Gilbert (ed.) *Compassion, Conceptualisation, Research and Use in Psychotherapy*. London: Routledge.
This excellent chapter will help you understand empty chair work more thoroughly, in the context of compassion-focused therapy.

Wade Eppeley and the liquid faced masks. A cognitive behavioural case formulation for distressing psychosis

12

Jem Mills

Learning objectives

After reading this chapter and completing the activities at the end of it you should be able to:

1 Understand the role of the ABC model in assessing, formulating and helping individuals who hear voices and have false beliefs.

2 Understand the link between this model and emergent behavioural experiments.

'Diagnosis, treatment, patients, symptoms, dose effects ... ...'. Why are the pages of the cognitive behavioural literature littered with medical language? This question is particularly pertinent to the literature surrounding cognitive behavioural therapy for schizophrenia, if it is accepted that the medical model of schizophrenia lacks scientific credibility as well as clinical utility (Bentall, 2004). We eschew the use of medical discourse in cognitive behavioural psychotherapy. Whilst it is sometimes a struggle to describe our work to mental health colleagues without it, we believe that it is a worthwhile struggle.

The value of an individualised conceptualisation based on a simple ABC model is discussed here in relation to a young man experiencing distressing hallucinations, paranoia, anxiety and depression. My willingness to critique the schizophrenia concept and to base our discussions on a variety of psychological and spiritual models helped to build a strong therapeutic alliance. This alliance was essential during the planning and undertaking of interventions which he sometimes found difficult.

This summary of the first 30 sessions of cognitive behavioural therapy highlights the benefits of focusing on the person's distress as the main guide to identifying goals and interventions in the face of complex difficulties. In this example, the young man reported a number of problems in his first session including visual hallucinations, voices, paranoia, visual disturbances, panic attacks, depression, hopelessness, suicidal feelings, very disturbed sleep, nightmares, boredom, social isolation, urges to use illicit drugs and periods of extreme anger.

WADE EPPELEY AND THE LIQUID FACED MASKS

Wade Eppeley (pseudonym chosen by the client) is a 19-year-old man who has been experiencing voices, paranoia, visual hallucinations and visual disturbances since a period of heavy drug use between the ages of 14 and 16. He is very creative, working in various media to convey his experiences to others. He has produced digital sound art, visual art and dance music in an attempt to portray his complex, sometimes terrifying internal world.

He is terrified of being diagnosed as a 'schizophrenic'. He believes that if this happened he would have no control over his problems and that the resultant depression would trigger hopelessness and suicide. However, Wade is also desperate for an explanation of his experiences. He feels very alone in his suffering and has spent many hours searching the internet for people who share his predicament.

He grew up with his Mother and maternal grandparents following his parents' divorce when he was very young. Wade was a very bright student with an IQ of over 140 and described himself as 'a good little teacher's pet' prior to the events of his teenage years. He had a difficult experience of the transition into young adulthood, describing feeling suddenly very bored with school and disillusioned with his academic path. He and his friends got into experimenting with strong cannabis, and then magic mushrooms and other hallucinagens. Around that time he began having more serious romantic relationships and one in particular ended badly when his girlfriend left him for his best friend. His drug use escalated and he started hearing the voices of his friend and ex-girlfriend plotting to kill him.

By the time Wade was referred for cognitive behavioural therapy, he had been oscillating between a hermetic lifestyle and over-ambitious attempts to get back into college for two years. His family were very concerned about his history of self-isolation leading to paranoia and violent urges towards his ex-girlfriend and his mother. He found that anti-psychotic medication reduced his voices and paranoid thoughts somewhat. He was also taking prescribed antidepressants, anxiolytics and hypnotics. However, he was left with debilitating powerful visual disturbances, hallucinations, bouts of severe depression, low self-esteem and anxiety. Standardised measures supported this picture (see the Outcomes section below).

The cognitive behavioural model for voices and paranoia emphasises the need for collaboration and a strong therapeutic alliance (Chadwick, 2006; Chadwick et al., 1996; Fowler et al., 1995; Mills, 2006). Distress is the prime focus and these three considerations (collaboration, alliance and the person's distress) guide the assessment and formulation process. Chadwick (2006: 25) uses the notion of 'radical collaboration' to emphasise the process of allowing clients to set their own pace for therapy. The therapist acts as a supportive, accepting facilitator tentatively guiding the client's exploration of the problem and possible goals.

Wade identified two main areas as sources of his current distress: fear of being around people in public and concern around his diagnosis. What follows is a summary of the goals and associated interventions which were based on the ABC formulations below. The process of assessment, formulation, goal setting, intervention and reflection is fluid and cyclical. The stages blend together and inform each other; hence the summary below does not represent a linear progression of therapeutic stages. The therapy plan often changed to deal with the ebb and flow of Wade's experience such as increases in his feelings of hopelessness and suicide. The formulations and goals transformed over time, sometimes changing focus completely for a while. Wade initially wanted to address his anxiety in public places as his goal was to return to college within six weeks. It was acknowledged that this goal put a lot of pressure on him, but equally that he found his music technology course central to his ambition to convey his inner experience and we agreed that we would work towards this aim.

THE ABC MODEL

The ABC model highlights a central feature of cognitive behavioural psychotherapy – that meaning mediates our experience of events. In psychosis, the strange experience itself, which is the voice or visual hallucination, is presented as the activating event (A). The belief (B) is the meanings associated with that event. These can be expressed as thoughts or underlying assumptions as well as 'implicational' level meaning (Teasdale and Barnard, 1993), such as a felt intuitive sense. The consequence (C) is the range of emotional, physiological, behavioural and cognitive reactions arising from specific meaning attributed to the event. So-called 'vicious cycles' are created when the consequences become activating events themselves. Hence Wade feared public places believing he might lose control. His resultant anxiety seemed to confirm this which made him even more anxious.

Consequences often serve to prevent disconfirmation of unhelpful beliefs. For instance, Wade believed that the 'mask' characters he saw could never have derived from his own mind and so he never reflected on possible links with own experiences. When exploring this issue further he remembered two key links with his past experience. The faceless figures resembled characters from a favourite comic book he had read years ago. Also his belief that they were from the future trying to warn him about something terrible he might do resembled a plot line from the film 'Back to the Future', again a favourite from his younger years. This helped a great deal in forming more helpful explanations of his experiences.

These ABC formulations guided the process of setting up Wade's ongoing series of behavioural experiments. Guidance on collaboratively constructing behavioural experiments can be found in depth elsewhere (Bennett-Levy et al., 2004; Chadwick, 2006; Grant et al., 2004b). In Wade's case, two characteristics of the process were particularly crucial and worth noting.

Table 12.1   Various ABC formulations made over the course of therapy showing underlying themes of fear of loss of control, meaninglessness and alienation.

Activating Event	Belief	Consequence
Being around people in public places	I might vomit, lose control	Anxiety, nausea (seeming to confirm belief), avoidance (preventing disconfirmation).
Seeing 'Masks' – faceless figures – with goo flowing from a hole where the face should be.	These are beings from the future trying to warn me about something terrible I'm going to do	Concentrate on the experience trying to hear the message. Reflecting on what terrible things he might do, such as suicide or stabbing someone. Avoidance of alternative explanations.
Experiencing boredom	Unless I'm having intensely meaningful experiences my life is meaningless. If I try to tolerate boredom I'll get depressed and suicidal	Trying to produce intensively meaningful art encapsulating his inner experiences perfectly. Increased disconnection from everyday life making it seem more mundane, meaningless and boring. Increased perfectionism around artwork and music. Avoidance of social contact with friends. Urge to take recreational drugs.
Voices and visual hallucinations	If I can convey these experiences creatively to others they will reduce	Focus on the experiences reflecting deeply on their meaning. Perfectionism around artwork and music. Sense of disappointment and failure when unable to perfectly capture ineffable experiences.
Visions and voices	I'm a demon. I'm not of this world. I belong in a different place.	Focus on horror films, Gothic and 'Dark' adult comics. Avoid trying to connect with everyday life. Focus on inner world until it becomes more vivid than external reality.

Validation

Wade found my interest and acceptance of his experiences very validating. He had found previous mental health professionals very kind but unwilling to explore his ideas in any depth. In particular, he reported that his consultant psychiatrist avoided answering his requests for an in-depth discussion about diagnosis. Instead he would focus on managing Wade's problems with lifestyle changes and medication.

Wade and I worked together to generate an in-depth shared understanding of his experiences. This allowed him to explore the edges of his understanding and helped him to feel more confident about questioning some of his own assumptions about himself and his experience. This involved actively listening to his descriptions of visions, voices and paranoia. I would feedback my understanding and ask for his evaluation of it, summarising my understanding of how he had reached certain conclusions and making explicit the internal logic of his thinking. This process, and my openness to his views, helped him to develop trust in our relationship as well as giving us the information we needed for our formulations.

Discussing the benefits and evidence for alternative beliefs

After recognising his conclusions about his experiences and formulating their consequences, we were able to see some of the damaging effects of his reactions. Generally these reactions constituted some form of isolation coupled with an over-preoccupation with his internal world. Wade realised that, whilst the creative drama of his internal world was a welcome and seductive distraction from the mundane nature of his life, over-preoccupation had its own dangers in the form of losing touch with reality and ultimately suicidal depression. This realisation led naturally to the process of him considering alternative perspectives and associated new responses.

Wade is an intelligent young man who enjoys thinking deeply and we utilised this by discussing research evidence and philosophical perspectives on his problems. This would include a range of discussions from psychological studies of paranoia to Buddhist notions of the self. These discussions helped him to question his assumptions and gave him the confidence to test them out. After a while this style of enquiry became more natural to him and he began to use it independently. For instance, he decided to explore his belief that his upsetting visual disturbances were unique by making contact with some of his old friends with whom he had shared drug-taking experiences. He discovered that two of his old friends had ongoing problems which were very similar. One of them had almost identical visual disturbances but was far more distressed by them.

OUTCOMES

Wade's cognitive behavioural therapy continues, focusing particularly on his underlying low self-esteem. The standardised measures show some reduction in depression and hopelessness and some increase in self-esteem. The anxiety inventory shows the greatest reduction (see Table 12.2).

With regard to the work described in Table 12.2, he has made several important gains. He has achieved all of the goals he set himself. The main outcome is a reduction in his levels of anxiety which in turn has decreased the frequency of his visual hallucinations. He is socially much more active and although he still experiences nausea he is confident that he will not vomit uncontrollably. He has an explanation of his experiences that he is happy with for now. He believes he has increased his susceptibility to psychosis through a period of heavy drug use during his early teens. This leaves him with an unclear dividing line between his imagination and his perception of reality. He understands that over-preoccupation with his internal experience blurs this dividing line even more, although he still is sometimes tempted to retreat into his imaginary world.

He believes that some of his visual disturbances are the result of biological changes in his brain due to excessive drug use and is waiting neurological investigation into this.

He is experimenting with different forms of digital art and is much less perfectionist about projects he undertakes. He still dislikes mundane aspects of life and feelings of boredom but he believes he can tolerate them, and he is willing to do so, particularly when he can see benefits for himself.

Table 12.2   Testing beliefs

Cause of distress and underlying beliefs to be tested	Goals	Interventions
Inability to return to college due to fear of being around people in public ↓	To return to college in six weeks ↓	Research and discussion on anxiety to identify the causes of nausea and the likelihood of vomiting A series of behavioural experiments: 1) Walking in public areas near to home to test beliefs about vomiting
Fear of escalating voices and visions	Defer college course for a year and build up social life	2) Swallowing five times in a row to test beliefs about choking
Belief: I might vomit, lose control	To go into town and meet friends	3) Bringing on voices and reading aloud to test beliefs about control over voices
	To meet up with friends socially at least three times per month	4) 'Going with' visual experiences rather than trying to fight them off or understand them Guided discovery, looking for evidence that voices and visions were based on his own experience Mindfulness meditation to practise developing a 'let it be' relationship with inner experience Lifestyle changes based on stress vulnerability model, such as: caffeine reduction; socialising with trusted friends, talking more openly with family, sleeping more regularly, developing a balance of activities rather than spending long hours on the computer, eating a healthier diet and stopping cannabis use

(Continued)

Table 12.2   *(Continued)*

Cause of distress and underlying beliefs to be tested	Goals	Interventions
Fears around attracting a diagnosis of schizophrenia	Have an explanation of experiences that generates hope for change	Discuss continuum models of psychosis based on stress and vulnerability model and normalising rationale Request a second opinion and change consultant psychiatrist
Having no explanation of his problems		
Belief: I'm a demon. I'm not of this world. I belong in a different place		Discuss experiences with friends who took drugs at same time
Having no sense of meaning to life pursuing intensely meaningful experiences through creative activities and avoiding anything mundane	Increasing personal sense of meaning to life (Measured on 0–100 per cent scale)	Look for interest in parts of life classed as mundane and boring
Beliefs: Unless I'm having intensely meaningful experiences my life is meaningless		Creating continuums of meaningfulness and exploring more activities on this basis
If I try to tolerate boredom I'll get depressed and suicidal		Testing his tolerance of 20 minutes of mundane television
If I can perfectly convey my experiences through art they will reduce		Lowering personal standards around art work
		Purposely trying to produce 'cheesy' music

CONCLUSION

The work described here represents a first phase of cognitive behavioural psychotherapy, and in terms of the foundation it provided for later sessions two factors emerged as being important. First, the approach facilitated the development of a strong therapeutic relationship. This included moving away from a medical model of his experiences which was very engaging for Wade. The disease concept of schizophrenia was irrelevant to our formulation of his problems even though we incorporated a biological understanding of his visual disturbances. The focus on his distress and interest in the complexity of his internal world was experienced as compassionate and validating.

The ABC model was very helpful in directing our focus on the beliefs associated with his distress and it guided our behavioural experiments well. The consequent reduction

Table 12.3   Evaluation

Measure	Pre-therapy Score	Scores post interventions described here
Rosenberg Self-Esteem Scale (Rosenberg, 1989). A 10 item self-report scale measuring agreement with positive and negative self-beliefs. Scoring range 0–30 (30 indicating the highest self-esteem)	0	10
Beck Depression Inventory (Beck, 1996). A 21 item measure of various aspects of depression with a maximum score of 63	47	28
Beck Hopelessness scale (Beck et al., 1974). A 20 item scale where respondents rate statements about the future as true or false. A maximum score of 20 indicates extreme hopelessness	17	7
Beck Anxiety Inventory (Beck et al., 1988). A 21 item measure of anxiety features. Maximum score 63	35	8

in his anxiety had other beneficial effects on therapy. He became more sociable which gave us more opportunity to explore and test beliefs about his self-esteem. He generally became more confident about the therapy process and the idea of testing his beliefs. He had less cause to control his anxiety through long periods of distraction and isolation. He was also able to begin reducing some of his medication which helped him to engage more fully with life in general.

Summary

1 The ABC model is extremely useful in helping individuals who hear voices and have false beliefs.

2 The use of this model can lead to equally helpful behavioural experiments.

Activities

1 If you are working with a client with 'psychotic' difficulties, attempt to formulate her/his difficulties using an ABC formulation.

2 Now consider the potential or actual usefulness of the behavioural experiments that emerge from this formulation.

Further reading

Chadwick, P. (2006) *Person Based Cognitive Therapy for Distressing Psychosis.* Chichester: John Wiley & Sons.
This extremely compassionate and well-written book will help you appreciate the great potential in using behavioural experiments with these populations.

Health anxiety:
a case study

13

Michael Townend

Learning objectives

After reading this chapter and completing the activities at the end of it you should be able to:

1 Appreciate the epidemiological significance of health anxiety in primary and secondary care populations.

2 Recognise the important advantages that interacting cognitive subsystems as a framework offers over Beckian clinical models of cognitive behavioural therapy.

3 Understand the importance of a client's history and background in the onset and formation of health anxiety.

4 Understand and appreciate the key elements of assessment and formulation as it applies to health anxiety.

5 Recognise the importance of linking formulation to empirically validated interventions.

THEORETICAL AND RESEARCH BASE

It is very common for people to seek medical consultation on a recurrent basis for problems which, in spite of considerable investigation, do not have any organic bases. These problems are referred to either as medically unexplained symptoms or functional somatic symptoms (Brown, 2006). People with functional symptoms are a heterogeneous group of clients with problems such as chronic fatigue syndrome, somatisation disorders, hypochondriasis or health anxiety and body dysmorphic disorder (APA, 2000; WHO, 2006). It has been estimated that as many as 25–50 per cent of all consultations in primary care or new outpatients might fall within this group (Bass, 1990; Kitchiner and Short, 2004). People with these problems are significantly distressed by their symptoms, have high rates of co-existing psychiatric problems and tend to use a large amount of healthcare resources. However, they remain frustrated by a medical system that only tells them what they don't have while failing to provide a satisfactory account for their very real symptoms and consequence distress.

This chapter will focus on a case study of a middle-aged woman with health anxiety, diagnostically referred to as 'hypochondriasis' (APA, 2000). It will illustrate important assessment, engagement, formulation and therapy issues. The person was seen within the context of a secondary care specialist cancer and psychological therapy service.

The formulation model that underpinned the approach was based on ICS (Interacting Cognitive Subsystems) (Teasdale and Barnard, 1993). ICS offers a framework that can provide an integrated explanation of the interaction of automatic and conscious thoughts, emotions and behaviours, and also the disjuncture of thought, emotions and physiological responses found in some psychological problems.

ICS theory differs in an important way from Beck's model of emotional disorders (Beck et al., 1979), in that, importantly, it specifies two qualitatively different levels of meaning. These levels of meaning play distinct roles in the production, maintenance and modification of emotion, clarifying the distinction between 'cold' or intellectual beliefs (propositional meaning) and 'hot' or emotional beliefs (implicational meaning).

ICS theory suggests input subsystems into the 'central engine' of the model. These subsystems are proprioceptive (feeling sense), imagery (visual images), visual (what the person can see in the environment), acoustic (what the person can hear), peripheral, articulatory (movement) and morphonolexical (what is said to the person). These subsystems feed into the two main systems that are responsible for the management of meaning – the propositional system (moment by moment verbal meaning) and the schematic or implicational meaning system. The central engine of the theory is thus the interplay between the propositional and implicational levels of meaning. The diagrams below provide an overview of the architecture of ICS theory.

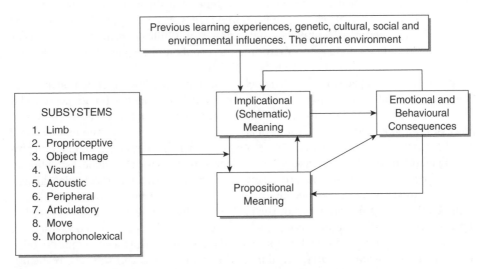

Figure 13.1   Simplified model of the interacting subsystems theory

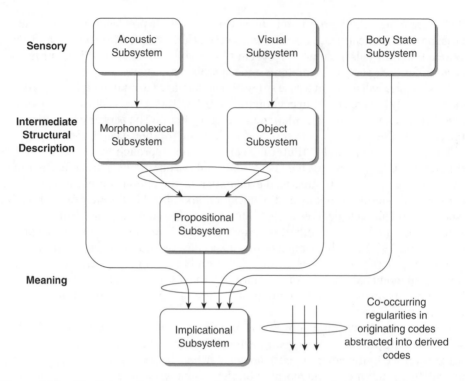

Figure 13.2 The Interacting Cognitive Subsystems framework (reproduced from Teasdale and Barnard, 1993: 53; © Lawrence Erlbaum Associates)

According to ICS, the propositional level is not directly linked to the generation of emotion but is characterised by a memory system of verbal non-emotional representations of meaning. In ICS formulations, emotion is generated through the activation of a generic and holistic affect-related implicational beliefs system, again stored within its own memory structure. The implicational system stores holistic meanings, patterns of direct sensory inputs, details of environmental events and responses derived from a wide variety of inputs (Gumley and Power, 2000).

The explanatory capacity in the ICS model enables both targets for intervention and particular types of intervention to be specified. For example, in clients who are depressed a state of 'depressive interlock' is believed to be operating through cognitive, attentional processes, somatic and behavioural feedback loops leading to the maintenance of low mood. Cognitive behavioural psychotherapists would therefore target the content and processing found in depression. Interventions for depression thus might include distraction to reduce the negative propositional processing, cognitive restructuring or behavioural activation to remodel implicational negative models of the self (Barnard, 2004).

In health anxiety, maintenance of the problems is hypothesised to have occurred as a perpetuation of idiosyncratic models, where the self or others are viewed as diseased, and naturally occurring physical symptoms and physical arousal have become encoded as threatening (Barnard, 2004; Teasdale and Barnard, 1993). In the case of health anxiety, physical arousal, physical symptoms or bodily changes, mood, attention processes, and behavioural configurations have all become encoded together.

CASE INTRODUCTION

Anne (a pseudonym) is a 36-year-old white female client who was seen at a specialist cancer service. Prior to referral, a consultant cancer specialist had carefully assessed and investigated her symptoms. The assessment and investigations had not detected any cancer-related reasons for her symptoms. She had also been given supportive counselling and psycho-education from a specialist breast cancer care nurse about the relationship between anxiety and physical symptoms. That had produced a minimal effect in reducing her anxiety and she continued to seek regular reassurance regarding her symptoms. She was therefore referred to a cognitive behavioural psychotherapy service for people with health anxiety.

Following her referral, an initial screening assessment was carried out and provided all the subsequent therapeutic interventions. The assessment indicated that Anne was an appropriate candidate for cognitive behavioural psychotherapy. This decision was made on the grounds that she had a distressing problem that could be conceptualised in psychological terms (Brown, 2006).

Presenting complaint

Anne's presenting problem was preoccupation and fear that she had breast cancer. Five days a week she would spend up to 80 per cent of her day thinking about the possibility that she might have cancer or that she had the symptoms of cancer in her breasts. On the other two days she would have fleeting ideas that she might have cancer, but was able to dismiss them and continue with her normal activities. She sought reassurance from her husband at least ten times a day and visited her general practitioner, again for reassurance, at least once a fortnight. She was unable to look at herself in the mirror as these evoked images of herself with cancer, and was also unable to examine her own breasts as this would evoke an automatic fear response. She consequently avoided all forms of appropriate self-examination for months at a time. However, every three to four months she would become so overwhelmed and self-focused on the possibility that she had cancer that she would spend several hours examining her breasts and armpits. This would lead to tenderness in these areas which she interpreted as a sign of cancer. Every six months she would ask for a referral for a private consultation with a consultant cancer specialist.

Anne's history

Anne had no problems with health anxiety up to the age of 27. She did however have a history of generalised anxiety symptoms at times of prolonged stress. For example, she reported high levels of anxiety during examinations at school, college and university. Despite this, she did well at university leaving with a first class honours degree in business studies. She had one young child and had been married for 17 years. She had worked full-time and then changed to part-time work with the same company after her child was born.

Her problems with health anxiety started several months after her mother died from breast cancer. Anne had been the main carer for her mother as her father had been unable to cope at the time with his wife's illness. She coped through this difficult and distressing time by throwing herself head long into caring for her mother, making her death as comfortable and stress free as she could by reassuring her and comforting her and other family members. She also provided support for her father and was the point of contact for all healthcare staff involved. Finally, she provided some of the physical care for her mother in the later stages of the disease and made all the funeral arrangements following her death.

Following her mother's death, she was unable to grieve due to feeling isolated, detached and depressed. Her mother had died three years prior to initial assessment. When seen for assessment she was tearful and talked about her guilt for being unable to cry for her mother. Her health anxiety had started during routine breast self-examination. Around this time she had been feeling low in mood due to work pressures and looking after her daughter. At the time she recalled thinking 'I have cancer' and 'I am going to die like my mum'. She subsequently experienced an image of herself lying on a hospital bed with cancer.

She made an immediate appointment with her general practitioner who did not detect any abnormality but referred her to a breast cancer specialist in order to reassure her that everything was normal. Anne then waited a few weeks for the appointment, during which time she carried out daily examinations and felt very low and anxious. She became increasingly worried that she might have cancer and she spent most of the day preoccupied with this possibility. She also began to think that 'something must be wrong' because the general practitioner referred her to a specialist. Subsequent investigation by the cancer specialist did not indicate any problems and she was referred to the breast care nurse for follow-up and reassurance.

Assessment

The assessment process took place over four interlinked and overlapping stages. The first stage consisted of a cognitive behavioural analysis of the main presenting problem (guidelines for cognitive behavioural analysis can be found in Mulhern et al. (2004), Hawton et al. (1989) and Chapter 2 of this book). A cognitive behavioural analysis was carried out in order to develop an ideographic understanding of cognitive, attentional, emotional, behavioural, physical factors and their interplay maintaining Anne's health anxiety. Both motivational and mental status assessment was also carried out – the former to identify any potential problems around engagement with psychological therapy and the latter to help rule out any contraindications to therapy. It was also important to assess the role of any depression that may have predated health anxiety, examine its possible maintenance role, and to rule out psychosis or identify any other co-morbid problems.

The final stage of the assessment process consisted of taking a psychiatric, developmental and personal history. This process, while similar to general psychiatric practice, differs in one important way. The information is collected in order to identify key events or life stages that might have influenced or predisposed the person to develop health anxiety through learning processes and any associated meaning. In particular, early learning about illness and illness experiences as a child or adolescence were assessed and her experience of her mother's death later in life was particularly important. Finally, assessment measures were also administered to the client, the details of which are outlined below.

Measures

Ideographic and nomothetic screening and outcome measurement were an important feature of work with this client and were used throughout the therapeutic process.

A useful screening tool was the Somatoform Symptom-7 Scale (Rief and Hiller, 2003). This is a self-report instrument that provided information about the presence and severity of 53 commonly found somatic symptoms.

Ideographic measures included Problem and Target statements (Marks, 1986) and a specific two-item strength of belief (SB) scale and subjective units of discomfort (SUD) scale. The SB scale utilised 0–100 per cent quantitative measurement, where 0 per cent implied that she had not believed in the last week that she had cancer and 100 per cent that she believed without doubt she had cancer over the course of the previous week. The SUDs were also rated using a 0–100 per cent scale, where 0 per cent implied that she had not been distressed in the last week that she had cancer and 100 per cent that her distress was as bad as it could possibly have been.

Nomothetic measures included the Fear Questionnaire (Marks, 1986), which was used to assess both phobic avoidance and dysphoria and the Work and Social Adjustment Scale (WASA) (Marks, 1986) to assess and measure the effect of the health anxiety on the client's wider life.

Case conceptualization

Anne's preoccupation with breast cancer, or the belief that she had breast cancer, was reported as being triggered by a number of internal (felt) and external triggers. A speculative hypothesis was formed during the assessment that her physical symptoms, emotional responses, avoidance, checking and reassurance-seeking behaviours had occurred due to the development of an implicational system related to the danger posed by the physical symptoms. This can be predicted by ICS theory (Barnard, 2004; Barnard and Teasdale, 1991) where the following subsystems – proprioceptive (feeling tense), imagery (images of cancer), visual (observation of self in a mirror), acoustic (hearing or saying the word cancer), peripheral, articulatory (repeated checking) and morphonolexical (what was said to her about cancer) – were all feeding into the two main subsystems of moment by moment meaning and higher order implication meaning.

The ICS interaction hypothesis was supported by the case conceptualisation, as Anne would often experience immediate negative automatic thoughts such as 'I have cancer'. These thoughts were underpinned by implicational beliefs that any physical symptoms were a sign of serious illness which would lead to her inevitable death. Once her implicational level of meaning had been triggered, her global sense of being in danger would elicit an emotional response of fear. This was accompanied by a physiological response of increased palpitations, muscle tension and hyperventilation. She would then become preoccupied and ruminate about her symptoms, with an internal self-focused attention on how her breasts felt.

The unhelpful cycles relating to her health beliefs and anxiety therefore included:

- Preoccupation with her health, increasing the conviction that she was in fact seriously ill; the more time she spent thinking about this the stronger the beliefs became.
- Attentional patterns of both automatic and purposeful scanning for evidence that her health beliefs were true.
- A biased view of her symptoms and autonomic arousal.
- Behavioural reactions of checking, reassurance seeking and avoidance, which further maintained her problem through both negative reinforcement and prevented her from recognising that her beliefs were false.

These processes in ICS terms are shown below.

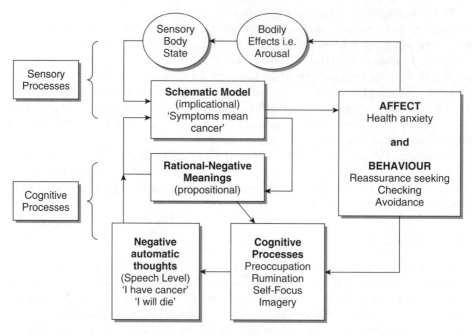

Figure 13.3   Idiosyncratic conceptualisation for Anne's health anxiety based on Interacting Cognitive Subsystems theory (adapted from Teasdale, *Clinically Relevant Theory*, reproduced from Salkovskis (ed.), 1996: 33. Reprinted with permission © Guilford Press.)

STRUCTURE OF THERAPY AND ASSESSMENT OF PROGRESS

The model of therapy used to work with Anne was based on the theoretical premises of ICS. The framework of the therapy followed a weekly structure of:

1 Pre-therapy assessment including intrinsic motivation, risks posed, decision for suitability for cognitive behavioural therapy and measures completion.
2 Weeks 1–2: A full cognitive behavioural assessment, mental status assessment, measures and individual conceptualisation and socialisation to cognitive behavioural psychotherapy.
3 Weeks 3–4: Further assessment of Anne's medical and psychiatric history and a personal and developmental history were carried out. While this is similar to a psychiatric history, its purpose is to understand the formation of her now unhelpful beliefs and behaviour within a developmental context. Work also took place during this time with the identification of internal and external triggers for health beliefs and behaviours through functional analysis, with homework using self-monitoring diaries.

   During these sessions, psycho-education, the developing conceptualisation and the idea of 'interlock' from ICS was also introduced to help to explain in full her belief systems, hot and cold cognitions and her now almost constant preoccupation with her health.

4   Weeks 5–6: Thought records were used in order to recognise unhelpful thinking and the early recognition of physical tension, autonomic arousal and bodily states. Cognitive therapy during this stage was linked to behavioural experiments targeted to reduce her reassurance seeking and checking behaviours and monitor the effects of these behaviour changes on her anxiety and belief conviction.

5   Weeks 7–10: More detailed identification and understanding of physiological, behavioural and cognitive responses during periods of low mood that increased her self-focus and strengthened her beliefs was carried out. This phase was a continuation of cognitive restructuring with links made to her propositional and implicational systems. Attention control training was also introduced. This consisted of breathing control whilst focusing on the word relax on the exhale. This technique was not framed as a relaxation strategy but as a way of helping to train her to switch her attention away from her physical symptoms and thus break the 'interlock' cycle.

6   Week 11: The focus during this week was on consolidating therapy, with a problem solving focus and further homework.

7   Weeks 12–15: The conceptualisation was updated as to the structure and content of the implication system and its lifeline formation through prior learning experiences. Her experience of caring for her mother and her family's response were particularly important. Positive data logging, and challenging unhelpful beliefs and rules were used to strengthen her new implication systems through continuation and recording of behavioural experiments and flashcards. The development of a relapse prevention blueprint, to consolidate the new implicational model and prevent future reoccurrences of the health anxiety, was also developed.

PROCESS AND ENGAGEMENT IN THERAPY

Anne's response to cognitive behavioural therapy was good. This was probably because she engaged fully and worked hard to overcome her difficulties. Regular reviews with Anne indicated that she found therapy helpful. She also fed back that having a formulation helped her to begin to recognise what the problem was rather than what it was not, and indicated that the cognitive interventions, behavioural experiments and exposure all helped her to develop more helpful beliefs and behaviours.

In some cases of health anxiety, and related problems within the category of medically unexplained symptoms, engagement in therapy can be a problem. This occurs simply because the client believes so strongly that their problem is physical and can therefore see no reason to engage in psychological therapy (Townend et al., 2002). This form of resistance can helpfully be managed by the following:

1   NEVER arguing with the client about their beliefs; instead, engage in discussion with the client as to the reasons for their very real concerns.

2   Gently probing for any doubts that they might have about their illness beliefs.

3   The therapist feeding back his acceptance of the real symptoms that the client is experiencing, being careful not to link those with the disease the client believes is the cause of the symptoms. Again, it can be helpful to ask if they think that other normal processes could have produced the symptoms.

4   Using behavioural experiments in the session to illustrate or demonstrate the effects of preoccupation, self-focused attention, repeated checking or reassurance seeking,

or manipulation or repeated contact with areas of the body that the person believes are diseased.

5   Asking the client if they would be willing just to engage with psychological therapy for a short trial – of say 6 sessions – to consider alternative, anxiety-based, explanations of their problem to rule them out.

Case management considerations

In the above case study, as in all cases of functional symptoms, it is an imperative that physical explanations for the symptoms have been ruled out (Bass, 1990). In this case, close liaison with the referring cancer team was essential, and all necessary investigations had been concluded and a short period of supportive psychotherapy had been provided by the referring team. Following referral, it was agreed with both the referring team and the client's general practitioner that no further investigations would be carried out for the specific presenting symptoms until the psychological therapy had been concluded (Brown, 2006). Relapse and set backs are also not uncommon in people with functional symptoms (Bass, 1990), so a relapse plan was put in place to help her manage future problems.

Follow-up

After completion of therapy, a follow-up period was initiated as part of her relapse plan. This consisted of the client being seen at 1 month, 3 months, 6 months and 12 months after discharge. At each of these sessions the outcome measures were completed to check progress against baseline measures, and reviews and problem-solving of any difficulties was carried out.

THERAPY AND FORMULATION IMPLICATIONS OF THE CASE

Anne's presentation was typical of cases of health anxiety seen by cognitive behavioural psychotherapists. The multi-level approach to formulation used here was useful in that it helped to explain to her why her belief conviction ratings fluctuated, and the relationship of these with mood changes. It also helped to explain the internal or introspective cues for anxious thoughts or images as well as situational cues.

Implications for clinicians

The ICS theory of the cognitive behavioural approach underpinning this case study specifically targets meanings, sensory elements and cognitive processes of health beliefs and behaviours. The distinction between propositional and implicational meanings subsystems is important in conceptualising in terms of two important and sometimes puzzling elements for both the clinician and the client respectively. These are the tendency for the health preoccupation behaviour to occur immediately following an internal or external trigger (directly via the implicational route) or after a delay following a period of dysphoria and preoccupation (indirectly via the propositional route). It can also help clinicians to understand beliefs held by the client which are clearly unhelpful but which go without question by the person with medically unexplained symptoms.

Conceptualisation is at the heart of the therapeutic process; when a comprehensive conceptualisation is developed in a way that seems to fit the presentation and responses of the client, alternative implicational models can be built through cognitive restructuring, behavioural changes and the development of more adaptive coping strategies.

Summary

1   Health anxiety (also variously referred to as hypochondriasis, functional somatic symptoms, and medically unexplained symptoms) is a common and disabling problem in both primary and secondary care services.

2   Interacting Cognitive Subsystems is a framework that can help to understand, assess and formulate health anxiety.

3   A good outcome was achieved by targeting key cognitions and behaviours with empirically validated approaches.

4   Follow-up indicated maintenance of progress, after therapy was completed.

Activities

1   Consider your own practice with health anxious individuals, and how you engage with people in therapy who believe their problem is physical and dismiss psychological factors.

2   Review your approach to formulation and consider if using Interacting Cognitive Subsystems as a framework can help you to understand health anxiety and its maintenance further.

Further reading

Barnard, P. (2004) 'Bridging between basic theory and clinical practice', *Behavior Research and Therapy*, 42: 977–1000.
This article, part of a tribute to John Teasdale, lays out the value of Interacting Cognitive Subsystems as both a cognitive and clinical framework.

Brown, R. J. (2006) 'Medically unexplained symptoms', in N. Tarrier (ed.), *Case Formulation in Cognitive Behaviour Therapy. The Treatment of Challenging and Complex Cases*. Hove: Routledge.
This chapter applies the principles of case formulation to medically unexplained symptoms using a cognitive behavioural approach.

A case study and formulation of chronic depression in a client with high self-criticism

14

Michael Townend

Learning objectives

After reading this chapter and completing the activities at the end of it you should be able to:

1 Recognise the similarities and differences between Beckian, behavioural models of cognitive behavioural therapy, and compassionate mind training based on the three circles model.

2 Understand the importance of a client's history and background in the onset, development and maintenance of depression from a biopsychosocial perspective.

3 Understand and appreciate the key elements of assessment and formulation as it applies to depression.

4 Recognise the importance of linking formulation to empirically validated interventions.

THEORY AND RESEARCH BASE

Clients who are chronically depressed pose a challenge to even the most experienced cognitive behavioural psychotherapist. Such clients are likely to have been within the mental health system for many years or be well known to the primary healthcare team due to repeated consultations and prescriptions of antidepressants. Clients with such severe and chronic difficulties frequently evoke a heart sink reaction amongst clinicians (Scott, 1998), due to a cycle of helplessness and hopelessness for both clients and clinicians.

Depression is a common problem with a high risk of relapse even in recovered individuals (Segal et al., 2001). There is an added complication that only around half of people with severe or chronic depression respond to either pharmacotherapy or psychological therapy, although combined approaches do offer a better outcome (NICE, 2004; Scott, 1998).

Traditional cognitive behavioural approaches to therapy are based on the assumption that disorders of anxiety or depression are mediated by consciously accessible meanings. These meanings are partly linked to internal information processing systems that form schema, core beliefs and dysfunctional assumptions which develop and evolve through life experience (Beck et al., 1979; James et al., 2004).

This, so-called 'cognitive mediation' theory has also been at the heart of cognitive behavioural formulation since the beginning of cognitive and behavioural psychotherapy in late 1960s and early 1970s. It has been enormously influential in driving forward the 'cognitive revolution' within psychological therapy practice and research. However, recent research suggests that cognitions and meanings can be the product of emotional and non conscious-processing (Teasdale, 1997), and that people can also generate thoughts and meanings to fit their feelings (Haidt, 2001).

There are also the familiar phenomena clinicians frequently describe as the emotions cognition mismatch (Gilbert, 1992), sometimes referred to as the head-heart lag (Lee, 2005). The client is able to generate realistic and balanced thoughts and beliefs, yet this does not influence affect: 'Although I know X, I continue to feel Y'. Quite simply, at an intellectual level, while the client understands that his beliefs and thoughts are biased, they feel no different at an emotional or 'gut feeling' level.

This separation or multi-level representation of cognition is described in the previous chapter of this book and can be understood in terms of propositional and implicational meaning systems within ICS theory (Barnard and Teasdale, 1991). The importance of this theory is that it suggests that it is change in the emotional belief (implicational system) that is the necessary condition for recovery from emotional problems such as chronic or severe depression, rather than the propositional system or automatic thought level meaning that standard cognitive therapy typically emphasises.

Another important theory that addresses cognitive-emotional mismatch has been developed by Gilbert (1984, 1992). He suggests that depression is linked to the triggering of an innate affect regulation system that tones down positive affect and confidence, and tones up threat-focused negative affect in the contexts of loss and defeat. Those affect regulation systems or psychobiological response patterns underpin depression in animals as well as humans (Gilbert, 1984). Once the affect systems are triggered, they pull affect and thinking in particular ways. The key to severity, chronicity and recovery in depression is thus the psychosocial resources the individual has available to them to turn off these patterns. For one person it may be developing new supportive relationships, while for another it may be the ability to utilise positive memories and styles of thinking. Depression is also more likely to become accentuated in the contexts of having few positive memories (via a history of abuse or neglect), and thinking styles which are ruminative, focusing on inferiority and shame, and become highly categorical (black and white thinking).

Gilbert's approach draws upon elements of traditional cognitive and behaviour therapies, but also addresses change in terms of innate affect processing systems (Gilbert, 2005). Thus depression can be seen as an interplay between genes, physiological systems, a life history which gives rise to emotional memories (for example, a self as

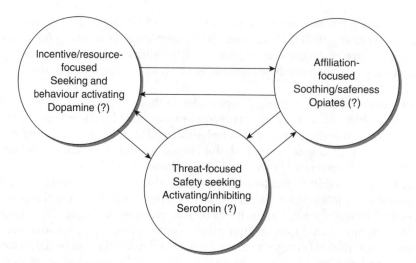

Figure 14.1   Types of affect-regulation system (reproduced from Gilbert, 2005: 26; © London and New York: Routledge)

rejected and threatened), affect regulation strategies, self-other schema and current social relationships.

The key to this approach is the finding that humans have two types of positive affect system. One is focused on drive, doing and achieving, and the other is focused on soothing contentment and social connectedness. Depressed people seem to lose the ability to maintain drive and self-sooth. Instead of being able to be self-nurturing and self-supportive in difficult contexts, depressed people typically become self-critical and highly threat- sad safety strategy-focused as a way of trying to cope with adversity.

The therapeutic task is therefore to try to reactivate drive and engagement and reduce avoidance and also to develop a self-nurturing and compassionate approach to self. Both systems need to be addressed, since depressed people may not be able to feel reassured by alternative thoughts or changed behaviours if the affect systems under-pinning the feelings of reassurance (the soothing systems) are toned down. It is this aspect which generates the cognition-emotion mismatch of 'I know it in my head but this does not reassure me or change how I feel'. An approach to helping people activate these self-soothing, positive affect systems has been called *compassionate mind training and compassion focused therapy* (Gilbert, 2000, 2007; Gilbert and Irons, 2005).

Compassion based formulations for depression are based on the hypothesis that depressed individuals have switched to threat processing and are unable to access self-soothing. Instead they engage in repeated self-attacking as a form of coping and safety behaviour. The formulation is therefore based on four key domains:

1   *Historical influences. Key early vulnerabilities* related to the thwarting of innate needs, for example, for early love, care and protection which give rise to emotional memo-ries of soothing and self as loved and acceptable, and *traumas*, which might have taken the form of repeated criticism, abuse, bullying or neglect.
2   *Innate and basic fears.* As a result of these backgrounds, children develop core fears and concerns to avoid rejection or harm from others. These fears and concerns can be

internally focused – such as feelings of anxiety, shame, guilt, depression and anger, while simultaneously trying to stop these emotions from emerging. They are also externally focused in terms of the possible ways in which the external world might harm the individual. These fears can be acquired in various ways including conditioning.

3 *Safety strategies* develop to try to cope with key fears and concerns. These are non-consciously chosen, automatic strategies which constitute the way that the person has learned to protect themselves. They include avoidance, withdrawal or controlling unwanted emotions through suppression, dissociation or self-attacking. So, for example, a person who grows up fearful of bullying might become overly submissive. Equally, a person who is fearful of anger, in case others are rejecting, might learn to inhibit this emotion and become fearful of it. Vigilance to inner cues of anger and efforts to inhibit expression then become safety strategies to protect the self from rejection and to also maintain a consistent self-identity.

4 *Unintended consequences.* These can occur because the person has become threat- and safety-focused, and lacks abilities for self-soothing or emotional memories of others as supportive and loving. For example, attempts at thought or emotion suppression might leave the individual feeling less in control, while being passive or avoidant means that the person might be ignored or develop a cycle of fear/discomfort with continued avoidance. This leads, in turn, to the person never learning that they can cope in feared situations.

Over time, and through vicious circles, the above biopsychosocial factors combine with meta-cognitive processes. A cycle of affective-behavioural patterns thus develops which maintains an individual's cycles of self-criticism, low self-warmth and safety strategies, which all serve in turn to hinder recovery or maintain chronic depression. The key aspect of this formulation at the level of the problem is to help people see the connections between fears, safety strategies and unintended consequences. This helps to 'depathologise' people's symptoms and efforts, avoids labelling, and makes plain the therapy plan in terms of engaging with safety strategies, acknowledging the fear and ambivalence of giving them up, and the importance of developing self-compassion (to stimulate the soothing system) as a regulator of threat systems.

The process of compassion focused therapy will now be described through a case formulation of chronic and recurrent depression.

CASE INTRODUCTION

'Paul' is a 63-year-old married, retired white professional male with a 40-year history of chronic and recurrent depression. He had requested a referral for psychological therapy following a visit to his general practitioner, who had discussed this possibility with him on a previous consultation. Paul had recently started to feel depressed following a two-year period of remission and had been taking antidepressants on and off for the last 20 years, with a very limited effect. He also had irritable bowel syndrome (IBS), uncontrollable shaking, and panic and avoidance of leaving his home for long periods of time.

Following Paul's referral, I carried out the initial screening assessment and provided all the subsequent therapeutic interventions. The assessment indicated that Paul was an appropriate candidate for compassionate mind training. This decision was made on the grounds that he had a problem that could be conceptualised in self-attacking terms and had difficulties with self-compassion. He accepted the rational for this form of therapy when this was explained to him. He was also given a client handout to further reinforce the principles of therapy (reproduced at the end of this chapter with permission of the author and copyright holder).

Presenting complaint(s)

Assessment was based on carrying out a functional analysis of key cognitions, cognitive processes, behaviours and their unintended proximal and distal consequences. This indicated that Paul had been depressed on this occasion for six months prior to referral. His general practitioner had given him a trial of SSRI antidepressants which he had been unable to tolerate due to side effects of increased agitation and shaking. His mood was low and he scored 42 on the Beck Depression Inventory (Beck, 1996), indicating a severe depression. He felt low in mood constantly throughout the day, with increased anxiety in the evenings. His IBS had worsened so that he was unable to leave his house for longer than 30 minutes without visiting the toilet. His stools were always semi-loose and he had pain for short periods of the day in his stomach. These symptoms had been investigated by his general practitioner and other physicians and a diagnosis of IBS had been made several years previously. Paul also had bouts of uncontrollable shaking and panic every few days, precipitated by fleeting ideas that something serious must be wrong with him. He had no friends, but he and his wife were happy with their own company. He also had a dependent family member, who had been in residential care for many years, who he visited every week, and helped several local elderly neighbours with shopping and other assistance when needed. He had recently found all of this increasingly difficult, due to reduced energy and anxiety, but felt very guilty if he was not able to visit.

Paul's history

Paul had experienced significant criticism, abuse and dismissive behaviours towards him when he was both a child and during adolescence. He had a dependent sibling who required a lot of care and attention from his mother, while his father showed no interest in either son. He had memories from an early age of his father's drunken behaviour and verbal abuse of his mother. Paul was also verbally abused by his father, who would say things like 'you are useless', 'you can't do anything properly' and 'I wish you had never been born'. Paul thus had many, easily accessible, threat-based emotional memories, but few of feeling soothed, protected and loved. He also described situations when his achievements were not acknowledged and he was told 'you should be doing even better'. He did well at school, but had a particular memory of receiving his final school examination results. They were just put to one side and not acknowledged and he felt rejected and useless.

After school, he entered a profession and did further professional examinations but always felt that he was not good enough and was worried about making mistakes (key threats and fears). He described feeling tense at work, being rather unassertive and being very cautious, and having great difficulty in making decisions. He had repeated periods of depression, with occasional periods of a few months off work throughout his career. From the beginning of his career, he had felt that he could not advance in his job and remained in the same role throughout his professional life (submission and avoidance in order to reduce threat). He eventually took redundancy and retired early.

He met and married his wife when he was in his early 20s. He described her as a quiet shy woman. Although they loved each other, there was little affectionate display between them and sexual contact was minimal. Paul had never had any close friends, but he did meet up with relatives or friends of his wife on occasions for dinner. He found such occasions difficult due to anxiety and concern over his IBS. Thus his current relationships did not provide 'inputs' of affection and warmth.

His key memory, evoked when he was either in a situation were he might be criticised or he had to make a decision, was an image of his fathers' face which he described as being 'tight, contorted and filled with rage'. When he experienced this image he felt small and insignificant, with an overwhelming emotion of shame.

ASSESSMENT

During the functional analysis, the aim was to try and collect a specific pattern of information. In this case it was important to understand the current status of Paul's problems, including what was happening around him when he felt depressed (environmental triggers); what he was thinking about before, during and after the experience of the problem (cognition and memories) and how he then responded (behaviours); how depressed he felt when the problem was at its worst and also generally about the difficulty (emotional); and what physical or somatic sensations he experienced (physical) and where he experienced those in his body.

While assessing Paul through the functional analysis, it was also important to consider what he was doing to try to cope with the problem and consider how this might be maintaining his difficulties. It was also important to consider the role of prescribed medication or non-prescribed substances that he might be using such as alcohol or other drugs.

Next, a full history of the development of the problem was undertaken through a detailed and systematic interview. Here it was important to ask when the problem first started, why it might have started when it did, assessment of any changes over time, or periods when it might have got better or worse. Part of this process also included assessment of previous interventions and a full prescribed drug history was also undertaken.

The specific theories that underpin compassion focused therapy also lead to other maintenance and contributing factors being assessed. These included habitual strategies that Paul used to keep himself safe and reduce threats, such as being threat-focused and watching others for signs of criticism. His ability to take risks was also assessed, given that he led a life of rigid routines. He was also unable to assert himself in many areas of his life, responding with automatic withdrawal or a submissive strategy at times of conflict. Paul held high moral standards which functioned to keep him safe from the threat of being seen by others as worthless, and from feelings of worthlessness which might be evoked. It was also important to assess any unintended consequences of his attempts to cope as, within a functional analysis, these are causal in maintaining a depressed mood.

Finally a full family, psychological, social and physical history was taken, and information about others in the family with anxiety and depression was also gathered to identify any potential genetic, social learning and attachment-based contributing factors.

The interview and functional analysis was used to begin to develop a working alliance which modelled a non-critical and compassionate stance. This included an emphasis that the problem was not Paul's fault, but could be seen as important attempts to cope with difficult life events, low mood and anxiety.

His goals for therapy were also assessed and these were defined and agreed within a compassionate framework as:

- Recognise self-attacking and become more compassionate and warm to myself.
- Recognise and feel that the responses were not my fault.
- Take some risks and enjoy life.

MEASURES

As well as overall subjective feedback, ideographic and nomethetic measures were used throughout the therapeutic process. Ideographic measures included problem and target statements (Marks, 1986) and self-monitoring diaries to record the frequency of visits to the toilet each day to open his bowels.

Nomothetic measures included the forms of self-criticism/attacking and self-reassurance scale (FSCRS) (Gilbert, 2004), the Beck Depression Inventory (BDI II) (Beck, 1996), the Rathus Assertiveness Schedule (Pearson, 1979) and the Work and Social Adjustment Scale (WASA) (Marks, 1986; Mundt et al., 2002).

CASE CONCEPTUALISATION

Standard, Beckian cognitive therapy focuses on the content of thoughts and changing cognitive processes or behaviours hypothesised to be causing the depression or maintaining the cognitive-negative emotion cycle. In contrast, compassion focused therapy focuses on emotions generated by self-criticism or hostile self-self relationships, the function that they serve and how they have developed (Gilbert, 2007; Gilbert and Irons, 2005). A diagrammatic representation of Paul's case conceptualisation is in Figure 14.2. This puts explicit and implicit processing and affect regulation at the heart of the model (Gilbert and Irons, 2005).

STRUCTURE OF THERAPY AND ASSESSMENT OF PROGRESS

Psychoeducation

Following from the initial assessment process, the ideas and principles underpinning compassion focused therapy were discussed with Paul, as follows:

> **The idea of compassionate mind training is to help you refocus your thoughts and feelings and behaviours on being supportive, helpful and caring of yourself. In practising doing this it can help you access an aspect of yourself that can help tone**

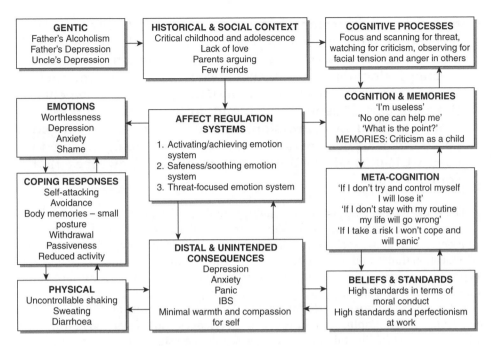

Figure 14.2   Biopsychosocial formulation for Paul

down more negative feelings and thoughts and build up a more helpful way of feeling and responding. The approach that we take will also help you to recognise that the negative thoughts and feelings that you have about yourself are not your fault, but are the product of your previous experiences and natural attempts to cope that have not worked as you would have hoped. Part of the therapy will help you to understand why these might not have worked. We will work together on the idea that when you are feeling down or perhaps being self-critical you might learn to recognise the triggers for this, such as making a mistake, having set too high a standard, experiencing a loss, or a particular fear or worry. In these situations, maybe being self-critical is a way you have learned to cope when you feel under threat or take your frustration out on yourself, but this is not a kind or supportive thing to do. It does not help you deal with disappointment, loss or fear, so we need to be understanding and compassionate about these. We will also work together on helping you recognise automatic behaviour patterns that you have learned to use to protect yourself from unpleasant feelings and experiences, and other safety strategies that you have been using to cope. In your therapy we will work on you trying

to develop compassion for your feelings and behaviours. If you are having powerful feelings of hopelessness, pessimism, anger or anxiety then you will be able to learn how to compassionately recognise and work with these emotions. We will also work together on accepting that negative emotions are part of being human and, although they can seem more powerful in depression, they do not make you a bad person or a useless person – just a human being trying to cope with difficult feelings and situations. How does that sound to you?

The above dialogue helped with socialising Paul into compassion focused work and the development of a compassion-based working alliance which, at its core, stressed that depression and associated problems were not Paul's fault. It also began a process of education that would hopefully lead to Paul's greater understanding of the nature of depression, shame, role relationships, fear of emotion and the nature and consequences of self-attacking.

Later, an explanation of the affect regulation systems was also given (below), with a particular emphasis on how social experiences and interactions throughout his life, particularly in childhood and adolescence, can stimulate one or more of the systems to become overused, whilst other systems remain underdeveloped. In the case of his depression it was identified that the activating/achieving and threat-focused emotion systems had been overdeveloped, whilst the safeness/soothing emotion system had not been developed in a way that balanced out the other two systems.

This discussion served a number of purposes. It again stressed that the depression and related experiences were not Paul's fault. It also helped to link his childhood experiences to his habitual pattern of self-attacking, safety strategies and his current low mood and recurrent depression over many years.

The next phase was similar to standard cognitive therapy in that self-monitoring was introduced. The aim was to identify triggering situations, events or images and to use guided discovery to elicit self-attacking and shame experiences. This followed the guidelines of Gilbert and Irons (2005), with shame being broken down into two types: external shame, consisting of thoughts about the attacks and put downs from others; and internal shame, consisting of self-to-self attacking thoughts. An example can be seen in the first column of the compassion diary in Figure 14.3.

Useful questions which helped Paul elicit self-attacking and shame were:

1 What were you thinking when you felt low?
2 What did that experience mean to you?
3 What did that event imply to you in terms of key threats?
4 Did you have any thoughts about what others might be thinking about you?
5 Did you have any thoughts about yourself?
6 Did you feel or sense things about yourself?
7 Did you feel anything in your body in that situation or during that event?

Following elicitation of self-attacking and shame/depression related thinking, further guided discovery followed in order to identify unintended consequences and habitual/conditioned patterns of responding. The aims were to make the links between self-attacking and the unintended consequences, to help Paul to begin to think about compassion-based alternatives and, again, to reinforce the idea that these responses were not his fault. Figure 14.3 shows a completed compassion record sheet, from relatively early on in the therapeutic process.

Compassion focused therapy differs from standard cognitive therapy in that restructuring or re-appraisal of the content of the thoughts does not take place. Instead, Paul was continually invited to reflect on the emotions and behaviours that were emerging. A similar strategy was used later to address meta-cognitive beliefs. What appears to happen through compassion focused therapy is that when connections are made, some people experiment and test out what happens when they don't engage in self-attacking or the blocking of emotions and usually feel far better as a consequence. In this respect, Paul was no exception and he felt far less anxious and depressed as he began to drop his safety strategies.

The central role of the affect regulation systems was also important with Paul's therapy. Part of the conceptualisation was that Paul's affiliation-focused soothing/safeness system was underdeveloped. Therefore in order to develop or stimulate this system he was taught mindfulness exercises (Segal et al., 2001). He found body scan mindfulness difficult, but with practice was able to engage with mindful breathing. He also wrote down on flashcards a number of self-accepting statements that he used when he noticed self-criticism.

Further work was also undertaken to develop a compassionate soothing image, again this was to try and develop the affiliation-focused soothing/safeness system (Gilbert and Procter, 2008). Imagery work of this type may also act as a rebuttal to the habitual self-attacking strategies previously used by the client. The image developed should also have a 'mind'. Gilbert and Procter (2008) suggest the importance of this, so that the image can communicate the qualities of warmth, understanding and compassion (a client information sheet and form that can be useful in this process are reproduced at the end of this chapter on page 209).

In Paul's case, he initially tried to develop an image of an omnipotent being, but had great difficulty in developing this into a compassionate image despite practice. Religious imagery in this context must also be used with caution for a variety of reasons (see Gilbert and Irons, 2005); in Paul's case, he held an existing idiosyncratic view of God that seemed to be of a relatively inflexible nature in terms of its form and content.

Paul then tried a soothing image of a still and calm lake and attempted to develop within it the qualities of warmth, wisdom and compassion, but again found this difficult as the critical self overwhelmed him. This apparent lack of success frustrated Paul considerably and he again became very self-critical. This was handled through re-stating the role of self-attacking in depression to normalise his experiences. A discussion followed about how many people had these difficulties with imagery, even many people who are not depressed.

Further assessment also indicated that Paul's difficulty with imagery was in part due to intrusive images of his father's face. It was therefore agreed to tackle this instead through imaginal rescripting. Imaginable rescripting is a strategy frequently used with survivors of trauma and child sexual abuse (Ehlers and Clark, 2000). The function that the intrusive memories were serving was first discussed

Triggering Events, Feelings or Images	Beliefs and Key Thoughts	Feelings	Compassion Focused Alternatives to Self-Critical Thoughts	Understanding and change in feelings
Key questions to help you identify your thoughts. What actually happened? What was the trigger?	What went through your mind? What are you thinking about others, and their thoughts about you? What are you thinking about yourself, and your future?	What are your main feelings and emotions?	What would you say to a friend? What compassionate alternatives might there be? What is the evidence for new view? (How) are these examples of compassion, care and support? Can you think these through with warmth?	Write down any change in your feelings
Feeling that I have let my family down and not achieved much in my life when I think about my life. Triggered by seeing an old work colleague	**External shame** (what I think others think about me): *My wife thinks I can't cope. She is disappointed in me. None of my family respects me.* **Consequences:** Detachment, avoidance of taking risks and avoiding telling my wife that I love her.	World feels against me, anxious and panicky	*Empathy for own distress:* It is not my fault that I feel this way; it is understandable given all the criticism I had during my childhood. Anyone would feel this way. I did try hard and have done so all through my life. I have simply been trying to cope. I can be ok about myself and I am slowly learning how to do this. I think I will try my meditation practice. The images are natural and part of my past, not who I am now.	*I feel more in control, but I don't yet believe the compassionate ideas – although this might be just me criticising myself again. I will stick with it. See how it goes.*
		Weak, pathetic and valueless	*Compassionate:* In order to go easier on myself I could switch my attention to times where I have given and received love and remind myself and feel how wonderful those feelings are. I will be accepting and warm to myself. I am ok.	
	Internal shame (what I think about me): *I have never achieved anything, people only put up with me, I am a failure. No one can love me. If I try anything it will go wrong or the anxiety will overwhelm me.* **Consequences:** Preoccupation with my failures and physical symptoms. **Image and emotion:** Image of father shouting at me and telling me how useless I am. Feel pathetic. **Function:** Stops me trying new things or changing my life.	Feeling tired, with urges to go to the toilet	*Attention:* It is understandable and natural to think about past difficult events, ruminate and think about my past bad experiences. My therapist called this being threat focused. Repeat the information on my flashcards. *Thinking:* Preoccupation and going over things in my mind is me simply trying to solve a problem. This is natural but unhelpful if I feel low or worried. *Compassionate Behaviour:* I ought to discuss how I have been feeling with my wife. If I buy myself that new car and take the risk, after initially feeling anxious I will probably feel good. Nobody is perfect but I can like myself more if I do other things that give me pleasure. I will practise my meditation and breathing regularly and not just when I feel unhappy. I will think about the caring I have done for my family and neighbours and how I used to look out for new people starting at work to help them settle in. *Function:* To help me cope with feeling low and anxious and help me to feel loved.	

Figure 14.3 Using thought forms in compassion focused therapy (form used and reproduced with the permission of Professor Paul Gilbert
© University of Derby, UK)

and framed as a threat signal. Time was also spent assessing the image characteristics and meanings and it was noted that Paul felt like a 'vulnerable child' when he experienced the image.

In Paul's case, he was continually attempting to block out the images or push them away. Time was thus spent on discussing how memories and images are stored, and how they retain their original context – in his case, experiencing them again and again as if he were a distressed and vulnerable child. Guided discovery was then used as a way to explore what a compassionate response to such an image might entail. This included accepting the image, with Paul accepting the idea of the image being an empathic friend warning of danger rather than an enemy. He also found it useful to remind himself that an image is simply that – an image – and not his current reality. At this point, we discussed how he might soothe himself when he noticed the images and he decided to use mindful breathing which he had worked on previously.

The next stage involved discussing how he might soothe and be empathic and accepting of himself as a child. We discussed options and agreed that this could be achieved by his adult self, dialoguing, supporting and expressing warmth and empathy for his child self in imagery. The strategy used was for the adult self in imagery to return to the child in a critical situation and help them to understand that they are not to blame, and to help them to be self-accepting and soothing to themselves.

In carrying out this strategy, the guidelines of both Smucker et al. (2002) and Lee (2005) were carefully followed. Detailed assessment also took place of the precise situations and experiences that were evoked in imagery through functional analysis, including the specifics of how the experience of acceptance and soothing might be experienced in terms of thinking, feelings and behaviours, combined with mindful breathing. Time was also spent on the development of flashcards and a fully detailed narrative script about how he would communicate with his child self. This included what he would say, his tone of voice, his posture and how he would respond to the child's distress by hugging, and coaching his child self to be more accepting. He also decided to tell his child self that his experiences and responses were not his fault, that he was not to blame, that adults such as his parents could sometimes do and say things that were hurtful, but, importantly, that he would get through his current difficulties and learn to feel good about himself. The dialogue and practice of the above continued for four sessions, until Paul was able to successfully sooth his child self. He later tackled experiences from his adolescence.

Work of this type, and imagery work more generally, can be a very useful intervention. However, in unskilled hands it can result in therapeutic problems and should not be undertaken without appropriate supervision and training. Guidance on using imagery as described above can be found in a number of cognitive therapy texts (Beck, 1995; Lee, 2005; Smucker et al., 2002).

In addition to the compassionate mind strategies used, a number of standard cognitive behavioural psychotherapy approaches were also used to help Paul cope with, and overcome, his IBS (Thornton, 1989). This involved bowel retraining, graded exposure and assertiveness training. As he improved, increased exercise was also encouraged.

Over the later sessions, further exposure to risk-taking was also encouraged. This included making rapid and spontaneous decisions to do certain activities, or visit family members without careful planning. In part, this was to assist Paul with practising feeling anxiety and panic without resorting to safety strategies or self-attacking.

Table 14.1   Summary of interventions and rationale for the intervention

Interventions	Rationale for the Intervention
Education regarding the nature of depression, shame, role relationships, fears and self-attacking and early experiences	–Socialisation into CMT –Development of working alliance –Emphasis 'this is not your fault'
Education regarding three circles (affect regulation). Internal and external cues with self-monitoring and safety behaviours in their various forms	–Setting the scene for therapy and further emphasis of 'this is not your fault' –Further information and recognition of safety strategies
CMT monitoring sheets to identify self-attacking, safety behaviours and their unintended consequences	–Emphasises links between safety behaviours and unintended consequences
Development of the formulation and continuation of CMT monitoring sheets	–To notice/be mindful of the feelings associated with memories. –Development of understanding through guided discovery that it is not the cognitive distortions *per se* that are the issue but understanding the safety strategies as conditioned responses (thus emphasising again this is not my fault) –The influential role of meta-cognition in the development and maintenance of the perception of internal and external threats
Learn compassionate acceptance, mindfulness and empathy for self through recognition of the above natural processes, reminding self 'this is not my fault' and dropping of safety behaviours	–Reduction in self-criticism –Reduction in anxiety and depression –Recognition and acceptance of emotions –Development of the affiliation system
Compassionate Image Training	–Reframe self-criticisms and development of a more compassionate self and warm self-to-self relationship
Empathy for own distress through imaginal rescripting	–Development of empathy for self as a child and as an adolescent (in this case)
Compassionate practice with breathing exercises	–Early recognition of self-attacks –Place the attack in its historical context –Refocus with compassionate attention –Engage in compassionate behaviours to bring compassion into action between session –Record any further self-criticism
Graded exposure, assertiveness and bowel training (whilst not a formal feature of CMT these were essential in this case due to avoidance of risk and the need to enhance skills not learned in earlier life)	–Tackling avoided situations, learning to take risks (and enjoy the process – linked to affect regulation, and allowing self to become angry and to feel anxiety) –Bowel retraining to regain a sense of self-efficacy
Prevention of the return of self-attacking	–Development of a relapse blueprint to continue to practise self-compassion

Over the last two sessions a relapse blueprint was developed that summarised the work that had been undertaken during therapy and future practice that would be needed.

COMPLICATING FACTORS

Paul had experienced bouts of depression for 40 years. One of the recurrent issues during therapy was that he continuously expressed doubt as to the value of the compassionate mind training work. He also asked the relevant question 'how I will know if this is helping me?' and stated that 'I will probably relapse in a few years time – so why bother?' While some of these issues were framed within compassionate mind work as a defensive response, and an understandable feature of his depression, my honesty was also important with regard to his chances of success. This was outlined as:

1 The CFT approach is experimental and may or may not help you, but if we both keep an open mind and give it a try at least we will learn one way or another.
2 Achieving a cure might be being a bit optimistic but, even with limited success, you might gain some relief from your anxiety and depression.
3 I want to work with you to learn about your experiences and see if together we can work out how best to help you (and others with similar problems).
4 I have a commitment to work with you to help you over the longer term. So, even if you have setbacks and relapses we can work together to help you to learn from them and overcome them.

   An added problem was that Paul found compassionate imagery difficult. One reason for this was that he seemed to be a narrative (word-based) rather than an image-based thinker, although he may also have had an unrecognised fear of compassion. Therefore, rather than using imagery, writing as therapy might have worked better for Paul. Writing, or narrative therapy, is seen very much as part of compassionate mind training (Gilbert and Irons, 2005). However, it wasn't until after Paul had been discharged into follow-up that this possibility was considered during a supervision case review process. It may be relevant to try this approach later if he begins to relapse, or if new issues surface that require further psychotherapeutic work.

CASE MANAGEMENT CONSIDERATIONS

The compassionated mind training programme, developed for people with depression such as described in this case study, may open up the opportunity for a significant number of such people in the future. The programme as discussed above does however remain experimental and as such is not widely available within the United Kingdom or abroad at this stage. It is advised that further training should be sought for those interested in the approach, details of which are available from the Compassionate Mind Foundation (www.compassionatemind.co.uk).

OUTCOME AND FOLLOW-UP

Paul made good progress over the 20 sessions of assessment and therapy (see outcome measures overleaf). He was followed up at 1 month, 3 months and 6 months following compassionate mind training. Follow-up was arranged both to track his progress and offer booster sessions if required. At each follow-up session, measures of progress were administered, progress was reviewed and the relapse prevention plan reconsidered and updated.

Overall, the outcome of Paul's therapy was good in that he was no longer phobic and he did not experience any panic. His IBS had improved to the point where he only opened his bowels 1–2 times each day, although he continued to experience irregular stomach pain following eating rich foods. Importantly however, he did not allow this to restrict his life. His mood throughout the follow-up period remained in the mild range (BDI II score of 13–17). There had also been a significant reduction in self-criticism and an increase in self-reassurance on the FSCRS with scores of 14–16 during the follow-up period. He was also making significant progress on his pre-therapy goals and the work and social adjustment scale further indicated broader improvements in quality of life.

Table 14.2   Outcome of Paul on the outcome measures © Using thought forms in compassion focused therapy (CFT) (reproduced from Gilbert (2007) *Counselling and Psychotherapy for Depression.* © London: Sage)

	Pre	Post	1-mfu	3-mfu	6-mfu
Main Problem (Range 0–8)	8	4	3	3	2
Main Target 1 (Range 0–8)	8	4	4	2	3
Main Target 2 (Range 0–8)	8	3	3	3	4
Forms of self-criticism/ attacking and self-reassurance scale (FSCRS) (Range 0–88)	44	24	16	20	14
Beck Depression Inventory (BDI II) (Range 0–63)	42	20	16	14	17
Work and Social Adjustment Scale (WASA) (Range 0–40)	30	25	15	10	10
Daily frequency of open bowels	12	4	2	2	1

Key
Pre   = Pre-therapy Scores
Post   = Post-therapy Scores
1-mfu = 1 month follow-up
3-mfu = 3 month follow-up
6-mfu = 6 month follow-up

THERAPY AND FORMULATION IMPLICATIONS OF THE CASE

This study is relevant because it demonstrates the effectiveness of compassionate mind training in someone experiencing severe depression relapses, with complications of IBS and panic. The outcome of this case study shows an improvement on a number of reliable and valid indicators. However, caution is also required in the interpretation of its value. Compassionate focused therapy has not been subject to rigorous controlled evaluation against existing empirically validated therapies and, as such, the approach remains experimental.

Further implications for clinicians

An implication for the clinician is the value of working to a process-based therapy programme such as compassion focused therapy. The approach gives the clinician the flexibility to work on an individualised basis with the client while ensuring that the interventions chosen are theory- and formulation-based (Gilbert and Procter, 2008). The results from this case study may contribute to the further development of compassionate mind training and the addition of case study data is valuable to the developing body of research and practice evidence.

DEVELOPING QUALITIES OF INNER COMPASSION (CLIENT HANDOUT)[1]

As we have seen from our work together, being self-critical can be very stressful and make us feel worse. One way of coping with disappointment and our 'inner bully' is to learn to be compassionate to the self. This requires a number of things of us, as follows:

1   *Valuing compassion.* Some people are worried that if they are compassionate with themselves they may somehow be weak or lack the drive to succeed. Thus, they don't really value compassion. However, if we think about people who are renowned for their compassion, such as Buddha, Jesus, Ghandi, Florence Nightingale and Nelson Mandela, they can hardly be regarded as weak or 'unsuccessful'. Learning to be compassionate can actually make us stronger and feel more confident.

2   *Empathy.* Empathy means that we can understand how people feel and think, see things from their point of view. Similarly, when we have empathy *for ourselves* we can develop a better *understanding* for some of our painful feelings of disappointment, anxiety, anger or sadness. This can mean we may need to learn when to be *gently sensitive* to our feelings and distress – rather than try not to notice them or avoid them. Sometimes we tell ourselves that we shouldn't feel or think as we do, and try to deny our feelings rather than working with them. The problem with this is that we don't explore them to understand them and then they can be frightening to us.

3   *Sympathy.* Sympathy is less about our understanding and more about feeling and wanting to care, help and heal. When we feel sympathy for someone, we can feel sad or distressed with them. Learning to have sympathy for *ourselves* means that we can learn to be sad, without being depressed e.g. without telling ourselves that there is something wrong or bad about feeling sad. We can also focus on feelings of *kindness in our sympathy.*

[1]Reproduced from Gilbert, 2007; Appendix 5; © London: Sage

4   *Forgiveness*. Our self-critical part is often very unforgiving, and will usually see any opportunity to attack or condemn as an opportunity not to be missed! Learning the art of forgiveness however, is important. Forgiveness allows us to learn how to change; we are open to our mistakes and learn from them.

5   *Acceptance/tolerance*. There can be many things about ourselves that we might like to change, and sometimes it is helpful to do that. However, it is also important to develop acceptance of ourselves as human beings 'as we are' with a full range of positive and negative emotions. Acceptance isn't passive resignation, such as feelings of being defeated, or not bothering with oneself. It is an *open-heartedness* to all our fallibilities and efforts. It is like having the flu and accepting that you have to go to bed perhaps, but also doing all you can to help your recovery.

6   *Developing feelings of warmth*. This requires us to begin to experience and practise generating *feelings* of warmth for the self. To do this we can use images and practise feeling warmth coming into us. When we are depressed this feeling may be very toned down and hard to generate – so we will have to practise. It can seem strange and sometimes even frightening – so we can go one step at a time.

7   *Growth*. Compassion is focused on helping people grow, change and develop. It is life enhancing in a way that bullying often is not. When we learn to be compassionate with ourselves, we are learning to deal with our fallible selves, such that we can grow and change. Compassion can also help us face some of the painful feelings we wish to avoid.

8   *Taking responsibility*. One element of compassionate mind work is taking responsibility for one's self-critical thinking. We can learn to understand how and why we became self-critical, often because we felt threatened in some way. Becoming empathic means coming to see the threats that lay behind self-criticism. To do this we can learn to recognise when it's happening and then use our compassionate side to provide alternative views and feelings.

9   *Training*. When we attack ourselves we stimulate certain pathways in our brain but when we learn to be compassionate and supportive to our efforts we stimulate different pathways. Sometimes we are so well practised at stimulating inner attacks/criticisms that our ability to stimulate inner support and warmth is rather underdeveloped. Hence, now that we have seen how we can generate alternatives to our self-attacking thoughts, we can explore ways to help them have more emotional impact. It does not take away painful realities but it can help us to cope in a different way. The training part can be like going to a physiotherapist, where you learn to do exercises and build up certain strengths. The compassion systems in your brain are the ones we are trying to strengthen with our exercises.

BUILDING A COMPASSIONATE IMAGE[2]

This exercise is to help you *build* up a compassionate image for you to work with and develop (you can have more than one if you wish, and they can change over time). Whatever image comes to mind, or you choose to work with, note that it is *your* creation and therefore your own personal ideal – what you would really like from feeling cared

---

[2]Reproduced from Gilbert, 2007. Appendix 6 © London: Sage

for and cared about. However, in this practice it is important that you try to give your image certain qualities. These will include *wisdom, strength, warmth* and *non- judgement.* So in each box below think of these qualities (wisdom, strength, warmth and non-judgement) and imagine what they would look, sound or feel like.

If possible we begin by focusing on our breathing, finding our calming rhythm and making a half smile. Then we can let images emerge in the mind – as best you can – do not too try to hard – if nothing comes to the mind, or the mind wanders, just *gently* bring it back to the breathing and practise compassionately accepting.

Here are some questions that might help you build an image: would you want your caring/nurturing image to feel/look/seem old or young; male or female (or non-human looking e.g., an animal, sea or light). What colours and sounds are associated with the qualities of wisdom, strength, warmth and non-judgement? Remember your image brings compassion to you and for you.

How would you like your ideal caring-compassionate image to look – visual qualities?	
How would you like your ideal caring-compassionate image to sound (e.g., voice tone)?	
What other sensory qualities can you give to it?	
How would you like your ideal caring-compassionate image to relate to you?	
How would like to relate to your ideal caring-compassionate image?	

USING COMPASSION TO CHANGE OUR MINDS[3]

In helping people work with distressing thoughts, feelings and behaviours, compassion focused approaches, and compassionate mind training or CMT, follows a fairly standard CBT format in some ways. One helps clients to identify triggering events, explore current feelings and then the meanings and thoughts associated with them. However, compassionate mind work also varies in a number of ways.

1   CMT suggests that negative automatic thoughts are related to threat-focused automatic reactions. For thoughts associated with negative moods CMT distinguishes between *external* and *internal* threats. External threats are what the world/or people in it will do to the self; internal threats are related to thoughts and feelings that arise within the self. People can of course then worry that they will be criticised or shamed for those internal reactions. Thus, thought forms will reflect this as in the compassionate form on the next page. However, the one we provide here is quite complicated and is useful for demonstration. Whether or not you would need to have a much simpler form but one which captures the essence of the compassionate approach is a clinical judgement.

2   Not only can people feel frightened by the emergence of powerful feelings, but they can experience their own self-evaluations in a frightening way. Thus in CMT we focus on the emotions that can be generated within a self-critical or self-attacking sequence. The consequences of feeling attacked by one's own negative thoughts may be to feel beaten down. So, CMT spends time exploring the *emotions of the self-attack*, e.g., frustration, anger, or aggressive or submissive contempt. We explore the *function* of the self-attacking, possible *origins*, why *submit/agree* with it (e.g. habit, or fear based). The client can be asked to imagine the self-attacking part as if it were a person, 'What would it look like?', 'What emotions would it be directing at you?' This can help people recognise the power of their self-critical side.

3   CMT helps people recognise self-attacking as a component of their *threat* systems. Commonly when people become threatened about making mistakes or being shamed, there is a kind of inner panic and frustration which becomes weaved into a self-attacking focus. Sometimes however, the self-criticism is a memory of being attacked and one can identify the critical 'voice' as the voice of a parent or authority figure. When the client plays this in their mind they may adopt the same submissive postures they did as a child. Either way, threat powers the self-attacking system. One can work on that by revisiting the authority, credentials or legitimacy of the critic. This helps people to see that they often maintain this bullying out of fear of change rather than logic.

The New Emotional Experience

4   Mindfulness approaches work by helping people become better observers and attentive to the flow of their thoughts rather than being rushed along with them. The idea is to change the relationship with thoughts, rather than the thoughts themselves. CMT utilises this approach but suggests that some people will find it easier, at least in the early stages, if they can deliberately re-focus their attention in a compassionate way to be with themselves.

---

[3]Reproduced from Gilbert, 2007: Appendix 7: © London: Sage

5 Some cognitive-based approaches are focused on trying to generate alternative evidence to counteract negative thoughts. CMT may do this but this approach does not believe that focusing on evidence will necessarily be sufficient to help people change. Rather we need to get 'processing' from a different emotional source and create a new emotional experience in one's thinking that counteracts the emotional experience of their frustration, anger or contempt of the self-criticism. Rational and evidence-based re-evaluations are useful in so far as they help to do this.

The first steps

6 The first movement into change is developing *empathy for one's own distress*. This is directing the patient's attention to why this distress is understandable (though obviously undesirable). This does require understanding rather than just acceptance. Many patients have a sense of shame and feeling that they are not coping because of their distress. Empathy for one's distress can take a lot of work therapeutically, but it is key for the person to begin to work with their distress rather than avoid it. Explore how patients think and feel when they do this. Empathic understanding can also be extended to self-criticism because we can see it as threat based.

7 CMT will then try to recruit attention, memory, meta-cognitive reasoning, behaviour and emotion systems, in the service of being nurturing and caring of oneself. CMT tries to integrate these different elements and focus them all on development of compassion.

Compassionate attention involves the way in which we focus our minds, what we choose to attend to. The exact focus of attention will be worked out with the client but it may involve a focus on a compassionate image, an object, a smell, a smiling face of someone who was caring, a compassionate memory. Compassionate attention focuses on the sensory modalities.

Compassionate thinking is related to the process of reasoning and meta-cognition. It will focus on many cognitive therapy elements such as bringing balance to thinking, de-personalising and de-shaming, developing multi-causal ideas of responsibility, seeing each event as unique rather than overgeneralising, common humanity thinking (to tackle negative social comparisons). When compassionate thinking is fused with compassionate feeling we move towards the position of wisdom. Wisdom emerges because we have deep insight into the nature of things.

Compassionate behaviour focuses on what people feel would be the most helpful, nurturing, supportive or encouraging thing to do. As noted in the behavioural approaches actions are important. There needs to be clarity on the distinction between compassionate behaviour and submissiveness. Compassionate behaviour is also more than being 'nice to oneself', it must focus on the quality for growth, development and flourishing. Compassionate behaviour can focus on immediate behaviours or on longer-term goals.

Compassionate emotion focuses on trying to generate a certain emotional tone in the whole process of change and growth. The emotions that we are interested in are therefore warmth, kindness, gentleness and soothing. Hence when we create thoughts in our mind we deliberately try to make them warm, gentle and soft in tone. This of course does not in any way preclude more excitement emotions and feelings of joy when we succeed or our children succeed at certain things. Joy is a part of compassion too, although probably has more activation in it. The key of the compassionate emotions is that they are focused on well-being and flourishing.

8   I am going to offer a rather complex thought form that you would simplify for certain people. Certainly for very depressed people this may be a bit much although if you go through it with them and do the writing for them it can be useful for them to have as an overview. You will need to use your clinical sensitivity and judgement here. The idea is to give you a certain flavour of the whole thing put together. You will note that we include images and functions of self-criticisms and the images and functions of self-compassion. Various thought forms can be used, ideally these should be quite simple. So, these types of thought forms should be done first with the therapist, gradually building up understanding and knowledge. They may be simplified to one or two columns. Independent work should be straightforward and understandable.

RELAPSE PREVENTION PLAN

What have I learned during therapy?

That if I am kind to myself I feel better about me.
Criticism can help drive you forward but can also lead to feeling low
It is not my fault when I feel low
Not taking risks
Avoidance hinders my life and helps to keep my problems going
Taking risks can be enjoyable
Emotions are OK
Exposure to situations leads to my anxiety decreasing
I can cope with my IBS

How can I build upon what I have learned?

Practise my breathing
Notice my thoughts and feelings and learn to be OK with them
Stop criticising myself and keep being kind especially when I don't feel like it
Doing things just for me from time to time
Keep taking risks

What might lead to a setback?

Feeling low or anxious
Feeling I am responsible for other people
Death or injury to a family member
Remembering my past
Criticising myself too much

How will I manage a setback?

Practise my meditation breathing
Use my diaries to help me spot and work on self-criticism and safety strategies
Get out my flashcards and use them again

Do exposure practice
Plan my day and do things I usually enjoy
Ask for help and support from my wife (this is a strength not a weakness)
Contact my therapist
Do compassionate things

Summary

1   Depression (with self-attacking) is a common and disabling problem in both primary and secondary care services.

2   An understanding of human threat, goal orientated and self-soothing systems is a biopsychosocial framework that can help therapists understand, assess and formulate depression.

3   A good outcome was achieved by targeting cognitive and behaviour processes using a compassion focused approach.

4   Follow-up indicated maintenance of progress after therapy was completed.

Activities

1   Consider your own practice with clients who self-attack and experience shame as part of their difficulties and how you assess their difficulties.

2   Review your approach to formulation and consider if using a biopsychosocial model adds anything to your existing approaches to assessment, formulation and therapy.

Further reading

Gilbert, P. (2005) *Compassion: Conceptualisations, Research and Use in Psychotherapy.* Hove: Routledge.
This book draws together the theory and practice of compassion and its role in psychotherapy from a range of perspectives. A definitive text for professionals interested in shame and compassion.

Gilbert, P. (2007) 'Evolved minds and compassion in the therapeutic relationship', in P. Gilbert, and R.L. Leahy (eds), *The Therapeutic Relationship in the Cognitive Behavioural Psychotherapies.* Hove: Routledge.
This chapter will provide the reader with further information about the theory underpinning compassionate mind training, as well as the therapeutic relationship aspects that are so important to the success of therapy using this approach.

Part III
Concluding Reflections

It has been clear to us while writing this book that whilst case formulation has the potential to be the cornerstone of effective practice, particularly at a time characterised by the continued empirical investigation and refinement of cognitive behavioural psychotherapy, it also sits in an era further characterised by the rapid developments of the so-called 'third wave' approaches to thinking about and working with client problems, such as mindfulness-based cognitive therapy (Segal et al., 2001), compassion focused therapy (Gilbert, 2007), acceptance and commitment therapy (Pierson and Hayes, 2007), all within a far more explicitly therapeutic relation-focused context (Gilbert and Leahy, 2007).

We use the word 'potential' here to make it clear that, as discussed within this text, the empirical support for case formulation remains relatively weak. However, our assessment is that on balance it shows great promise, hence our commitment to this way of working. Our view is that case formulation is important in the context of psychological therapies research where each individual has their own unique set of experiences, idiosyncratic meanings and emotions and behaviours, which can't readily be addressed through traditional randomised controlled trials or meta-analytic techniques. We therefore urge researchers in the field to consider issues of process and formulation more readily within their research designs for the future.

Developments in computer software may also, in the future, help cognitive behavioural psychotherapists to make better decisions about assessment, formulation and interventions, or enable the more effective teaching of both the process and the 'how to do' of formulation. We have found it helpful to use mind mapping software already in our own practice, and are aware of clinical decision tools being developed in certain areas of medical practice which in time will doubtless be considered suitable for application in the psychological therapies fields.

We are also aware that there are some obvious tensions between the constraints of working in mental health services and providing good, effective cognitive behavioural psychotherapy. This is an ever-present moral dilemma that cannot be ducked by therapists and their managers. In a climate that is often more about image management and defensive working than therapeutic excellence, reflective practice, clinical supervision and reflective organisational learning is all too often talked up rather than being part of the real day-to-day experience of clients and clinicians (Grant and Townend, 2007).

In this context, we argue that further change is needed, with organisations having a clear ethical charge to live the image of supporting cognitive behavioural practitioners in the delivery of formulation-based, empirically supported interventions. Senior practitioners in cognitive behavioural psychotherapy – no matter what their professional background – have a responsibility to role model and promote good quality case formulation and assessment through clinical supervision and development of practice, which includes reflective practice (Sutton et al., 2007; Townend et al., 2002).

In our view, we further argue that the future will need to involve extending the case formulation approach to identify 'dysfunctional' organisational aspects, as illustrated in this text (see also Grant et al., 2004a, 2006), and support and promote positive organisational change. Although potentially threatening for all parties involved in this endeavour, such a marriage of reflexive professional and corporate organisational learning could only be to the betterment of our clients through enhancing support for practitioners and a sense of real individual and organisational integrity.

In related terms, we also suggest that mental health organisations need to become more strategic in the development of planned, coherent services that maximise the uptake of cognitive behavioural psychotherapy and support student practitioners of the approach (Poole and Grant, 2005). This may well mean services which are balanced between professionals who use, under close supervision, protocol-based interventions with defined and carefully selected client groups, and those more rigorously trained who not only supervise but deliver case formulation-based interventions within the context of complex casework (Centre for Economic Performance, 2006). Strategic development is not, however, without its dangers, given that managers and service planners may look for the cheapest option under the guise of efficiency. If this were to happen, it would lead to an unhealthy relationship between levels of therapist competency and the possibility of formulation-driven practice becoming usurped by standardised and mechanistic approaches.

We would also be pleased if those cognitive behavioural psychotherapists who often seem to defensively hide behind the 'evidence-based practice' slogan became more aware of the, sometimes polarised and contradictory, dialogues within the evidence-based psychotherapy movement at a national and international level (Mace et al., 2001; Norcross et al., 2005; Rowland and Goss, 2000). We urge them to bring themselves up to date with theoretical and integrative developments in the broad psychotherapy field and begin to use these developments in the context of client-centred case formulation.

We make a further plea for all cognitive behavioural psychotherapists to role model optimal engagement with opportunities for practice development and reflective practice by supporting 'real time equivalent' (video/DVD of their own practice with systematic self and peer appraisal) rather than 'retrospective reporting' forms of clinical supervision (Grant and Townend, 2007; Townend et al., 2002).

Much of the above is the stuff of continuous professional development which, hopefully, subject to approval of the proposed series, will be a forthcoming Sage text in the not to distant future. We live in great hope that both this book and the proposed new text will be helpful to our cognitive behavioural communities in taking the field forward.

Alec Grant, Michael Townend, Jem Mills, Adrian Cockx

January 2006 – July 2007

Appendix 1

Five Aspect case formulation (Adpated from Greenberger and Padesky, 1995: 4;
© 1986 Center for Cognitive Therapy, Newport Beach, CA

Client: _____ Date of Birth: _____ Therapist: _____

Supervisor: _____ Diagnosis (DSM IV or ICD 10): (i) _____ (ii) _____

Relevant History:

Behavioural:

Physiological/Biological: Emotional:

Cognitive:

Environmental: Reinforcing Life Experiences:

Appendix 2

Compassion focused therapy formulation sheet

Client: _____ Date of Birth: _____ Therapist: _____

Supervisor: _____ Diagnosis (DSM IV or ICD 10): (i) _____ (ii) _____

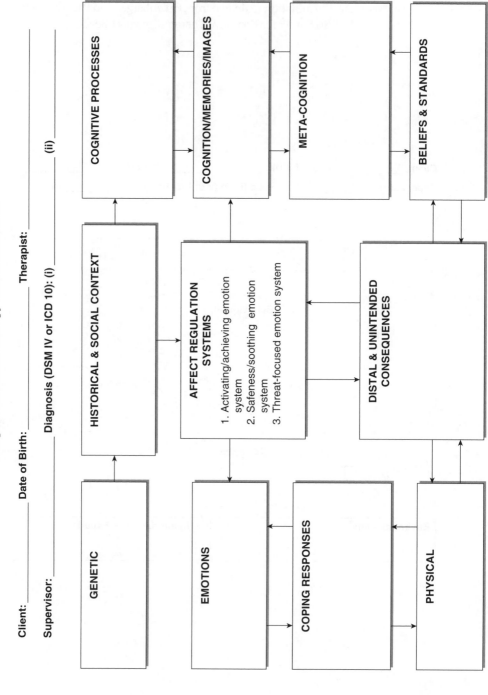

Appendix 3

Three system – case formulation

Client: _____ Date of Birth: _____ Therapist: _____

Supervisor: _____ Diagnosis (DSM IV or ICD 10): (i) _____ (ii) _____

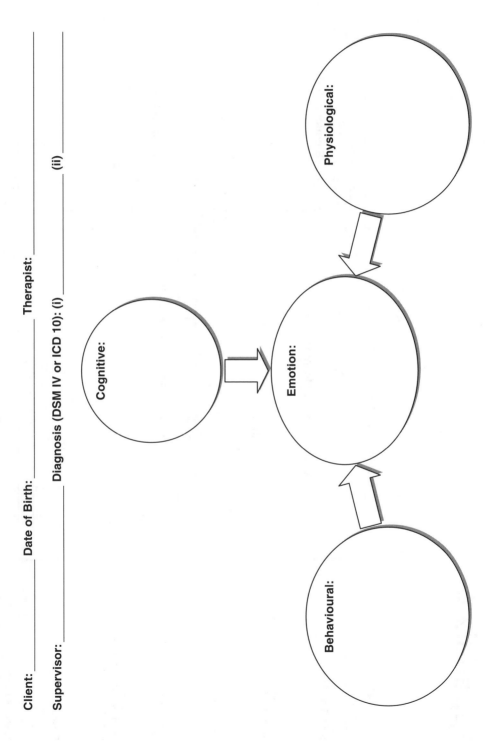

Appendix 4

Interacting cognitive subsystems – case formulation

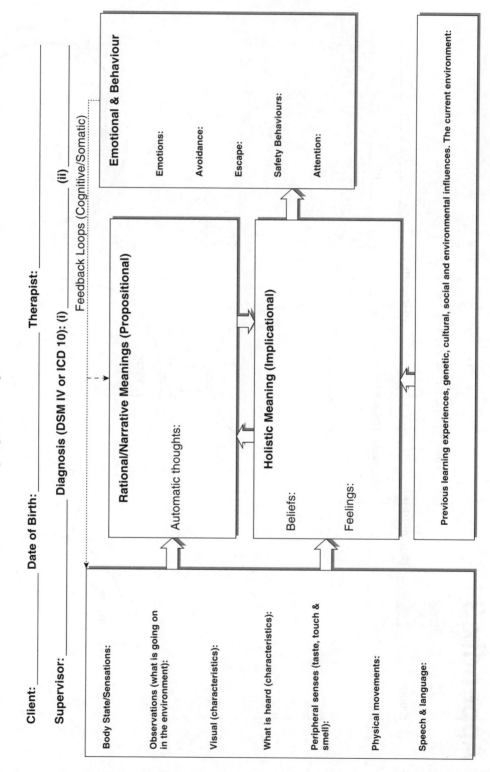

Client: _____ Date of Birth: _____ Therapist: _____

Supervisor: _____ Diagnosis (DSM IV or ICD 10): (i) _____ (ii) _____

Feedback Loops (Cognitive/Somatic)

Rational/Narrative Meanings (Propositional)

Automatic thoughts:

Holistic Meaning (Implicational)

Beliefs:

Feelings:

Emotional & Behaviour

Emotions:

Avoidance:

Escape:

Safety Behaviours:

Attention:

Body State/Sensations:

Observations (what is going on in the environment):

Visual (characteristics):

What is heard (characteristics):

Peripheral senses (taste, touch & smell):

Physical movements:

Speech & language:

Previous learning experiences, genetic, cultural, social and environmental influences. The current environment:

Appendix 5

SPAARS – case formulation (adpated from Power and Dalgleish, 1999: 178; © Wiley. Reproduced with permission).

Client: _____ **Date of Birth:** _____ **Therapist:** _____

Supervisor: _____ **Diagnosis (DSM IV or ICD 10): (i)** _____ **(ii)** _____

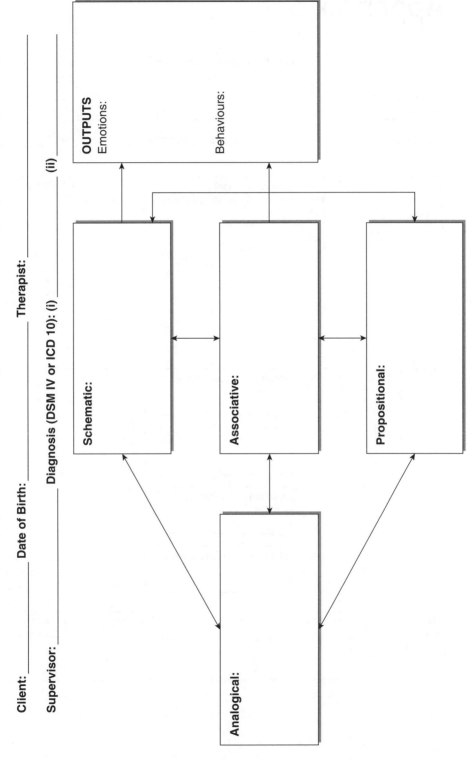

Appendix 6

Meta-cognitive – case formulation

Client: _____ Date of Birth: _____ Therapist: _____

Supervisor: _____ Diagnosis (DSM IV or ICD 10): (i) _____ (ii) _____

Critical Incidents (what started the problem off):

Relevant History (early life):

Proximal Trigger (internal or external):

Assumptions:

Automatic Thoughts & Images:

Meta-thoughts and Beliefs:

Physical and Somatic Symptoms:

Behaviour:

Emotion(s):

Attention and Reasoning:

Thought Control Strategies:

Appendix 7

Clinical cognitive model – case formulation (adapted from Beck, 1995: 139; © 1993 Judith Beck)

Client: _____ Date of Birth: _____

Therapist: _____ Supervisor: _____

Diagnosis (DSM IV or ICD 10): (i) _____ (ii) _____

Childhood and Early Information

Core Beliefs

Conditional Assumptions and Rules

Compensatory Strategies

Description of Situation 1	Description of Situation 2	Description of Situation 3
Negative Thoughts and Images	Negative Thoughts and Images	Negative Thoughts and Images
Meaning	Meaning	Meaning
Thinking Processes	Thinking Processes	Thinking Processes
Emotion(s)	Emotion(s)	Emotion(s)
Behaviour	Behaviour	Behaviour

References

Alford, B. and Beck, A.T. (1997) *The Integrative Power of Cognitive Therapy*. New York and London: The Guilford Press.

Antony, M.M. and Barlow, D.H. (2002) *Handbook of Assessment and Treatment Planning for Psychological Disorders*. New York: Guildford Press.

APA (American Psychiatric Association) (2000) *Diagnostic and Statistical Manual of Mental Disorders (DSM IV)*, 4th edn, text revision. Washington DC: American Psychiatric Association.

Augoustinos, M., Walker, I. and Donaghue, N. (2006) *Social Cognition. An Integrated Introduction*, 2nd edn. London: Sage Publications Ltd.

Bandura, A. (2004) 'Model of causality in social learning theory', in A. Freeman, M.J. Mahoney, P. Devito and D. Martin. (eds), *Cognition and Psychotherapy*, 2nd edn. New York: Springer Publishing Company.

Barnard, P. (2004) 'Bridging between basic theory and clinical practice', *Behavior Research and Therapy*, 42: 977–1000.

Barnard, P. and Teasdale, J. (1991) 'Interacting cognitive subsystems: a systemic approach to cognitive-affective interaction and change', *Cognition and Emotion*, 5: 1–39.

Bass, C. (ed.) (1990) *Somatization: Physical Symptoms and Psychological Illness*. London: Blackwell Science.

Beck, A.T. (1964) 'Thinking and depression: II. theory and therapy', *Archives of General Psychiatry*, 10: 561–71.

Beck, A.T. (1967) *Depression: Clinical, Experimental and Theoretical Aspects*. New York: Hoeber.

Beck, A.T. (1976) *Cognitive Therapy and the Emotional Disorders*. New York: International Universities Press.

Beck, A.T. (1996) *Beck Depression Inventory*. San Antonio: The Psychological Corporation.

Beck, A.T. and Steer, R.A. (1990) *Beck Anxiety Inventory Manual*. San Antonio, TX: The Psychological Corporation.

Beck, A.T., Weissman, A., Lester, D. and Trexler, L. (1974) 'The measurement of pessimism: The Hopelessness Scale', *Journal of Consulting and Clinical Psychology*, 42: 861–5.

Beck, A.T., Rush, A.J., Shaw, B.F. and Emery, G. (1979) *Cognitive Therapy for Depression*. New York: Guilford Press.

Beck, A.T., Epstein, N., Brown, G. and Steer, R. (1988) 'An inventory for measuring clinical anxiety: psychometric properties', *Journal of Consulting and Clinical Psychology*, 56: 893–7.

Beck, A.T., Freeman, A., Pretzer, J., Davis, D.D., Fleming, B., Ottaviani, R., Beck, J., Simon, K.M., Padesky, C., Meyer, J. and Trexler, L. (1990) *Cognitive Therapy of Personality Disorders*. New York: The Guilford Press.

Beck, J.S. (1995) *Cognitive Therapy. Basics and Beyond*. New York and London: The Guilford Press.

Beiling, P.J. and Kuyken, W. (2003) 'Is cognitive case formulation science or science fiction?', *Clinical Psychology: Science and Practice*, 10(1): 52–69.

Bennett-Levy, J. (2006) 'Therapist skills: a cognitive model of their acquisition and refinement', *Behavioural and Cognitive Psychotherapy*, 34: 57–78.

Bennett-Levy, J. and Thwaites, R. (2007) 'Self and self-reflection in the therapeutic relationship: a conceptual map and practical strategies for the training, supervision and self-supervision of interpersonal skills', in P. Gilbert and R.L. Leahy (eds), *The Therapeutic Relationship in the Cognitive Behavioural Psychotherapies*. Hove: Routledge.

Bennett-Levy, J., Turner, F., Beaty, T., Smith, M., Paterson, B. and Farmer, S. (2001) 'The value of self-practice of cognitive therapy techniques and self-reflection in the training of cognitive therapists', *Behavioural and Cognitive Psychotherapy*, 29: 203–20.

Bennett-Levy, J., Lee, N., Travers, K., Pohlman, S. and Hamernik, E. (2003) 'Cognitive therapy from the insider: enhancing therapist skills through practising what we preach', *Behavioural and Cognitive Psychotherapy*, 31(2): 143–58.

Bennett-Levy, J., Butler, G., Fennell, M., Hackmann, A., Mueller, M. and Westbrook, D. (2004) *The Oxford Guide to Behavioural Experiments in Cognitive Therapy*. Oxford: Oxford University Press.

Bentall, R.P. (2004) *Madness Explained: Psychosis and Human Nature*. London: Penguin Books.

Bernard, J.M. and Goodyear, R.K. (2004) *Fundamentals of Clinical Supervision*, 3rd edn. New York: Pearson.

Blackburn, I.M., James, I.A., Milne, D.L., Baker, C., Standart, S., Garland, A. and Reichelt, F.K. (2001) 'The Revised Cognitive Therapy Scale (CTS-R): psychometric properties', *Behavioural and Cognitive Psychotherapy*, 29(4): 431–46.

Bogels, S.M., Mulkens, S. and De Jong, P.J. (1997) 'Task concentration training and fear of blushing', *Clinical Psychology and Psychotherapy*, 4: 251–8.

Bohart, A., Elliott, R., Greenberg, L.S. and Watson, J.C. (2002) 'Empathy', in J.C. Norcross (ed.), *Psychotherapy Relationships that Work*. New York: Oxford University Press. pp. 89–108.

Bordin, E.S. (1979) 'The generalizability of the psychoanalytic concept of the working alliance', *Psychotherapy: Theory, Research & Practice*, 16: 252–60.

Borkovec, T.D. and Inz, J. (1990) 'The nature of worry in generalized anxiety disorder: a predominance of thought activity', *Behaviour Research and Therapy*, 28: 153–8.

Borkovec, T.D. and Roemer, L. (1995) 'Perceived functions of worry among generalized anxiety disorder subjects: distraction from more emotionally distressing topics?', *Journal of Behavior Therapy and Experimental Psychiatry*, 26: 25–30.

Brewin, C.R., Dalgleish, T. and Joseph, S. (1996) 'A dual representation theory of posttraumatic stress disorder', *Psychological Review*, 103: 670–86.

Brown, T.A., Di Nardo, P.A. and Barlow, D.H. (1994) *Anxiety Disorders Interview Schedule for DSM-IV (ADIS-IV)*. San Antonio, TX: Psychological Corporation.

Brown, R.J. (2006) 'Medically unexplained symptoms', in N. Tarrier (ed.), *Case Formulation in Cognitive Behaviour Therapy*. Hove: Routledge.

Bruner, J. (1990) *Acts of Meaning*. Cambridge, MA and London: Harvard University Press.

Buber, M. (1958) *I and thou*, 2nd edn. New York: Charles Scribner's Sons.

Burns, D. and Auerbach, A. (1996) 'Therapeutic empathy in cognitive-behavioural therapy: Does it really make a difference?' in P. Salkovskis (ed.), *Frontiers of Cognitive Therapy*. New York: Guilford Press.

Burr, V. (1995) *An Introduction to Social Constructionism*. London: Routledge.

Capella, J.N. and Street, R.L. Jnr. (1985) 'Introduction: a functional approach to the structure of communicative behaviour', in R.L. Street, Jnr and J.N. Capella, *Sequence and Pattern in Communicative Behaviour*. London: Edward Arnold.

Cecchin, G. (1992) 'Constructing therapeutic possibilities', in S. McNamee and K.J. Gergen (eds), *Therapy as Social Construction*. London: Sage.

Centre for Economic Performance, London School of Economics and Political Science (2006) *The Depression Report. A New Deal for Depression and Anxiety Disorders*. Website: http://cep.lse.ac.uk/research/mentalhealth

Chadwick, P. (2006) *Person Based Cognitive Therapy for Distressing Psychosis*. Chichester: John Wiley & Sons.

Chadwick, P., Birchwood, M. and Trower, P. (1996) *Cognitive Therapy for Hallucinations, Delusions and Paranoia*. Chichester: John Wiley & Sons.

Chase Grey, J. and Grant, A. (2005) 'Cognitive behavioural therapy: helping the client find her voice', *Mental Health Practice*, 8(8): 34–7.

Cheavens, J.S., Feldman, D.B., Woodward, J.T. and Snyder, C.R. (2006) 'Hope in cognitive psychotherapies: on working with client strengths', *Journal of Cognitive Psychotherapy: An International Quarterly*, 20(2): 135–45.

Clark, D.M. (1988) 'A cognitive model of panic attacks', in S. Rachman and J.D. Maser (eds), *Panic: Psychological Perspectives*. Hillsdale, NJ: Erlbaum.

Clark, D.M. and Fairburn, C.G. (2005) *Science and Practice of Cognitive Behaviour Therapy*. Oxford: Oxford University Press.

Clark, D.M. and Wells, A. (1995) 'A cognitive model of social phobia', in R. Heimberg, M. Liebowitz, D.A. Hope and F.R. Schneier (eds), *Social Phobia. Diagnosis, Assessment and Treatment*. New York: Guildford Press.

Clark, D.M., Ball, S. and Pape, D. (1991) 'An experimental investigation of thought suppression', *Behaviour Research and Therapy*, 29: 253–7.

Cowie, H. and Rivers, I. (2000) 'Going against the grain: supporting lesbian, gay and bisexual clients as they "come out" ', *British Journal of Guidance and Counselling*, 28(4): 503–13.

Dalgleish, T. (2004) 'Cognitive approaches to posttraumatic stress disorder: the evolution of multirepresentational theorizing', *Psychological Bulletin*, 130(2): 228–60.

Datilio, F.M. (2004a) 'Cognitive-Behavioural family therapy: a coming-of-age story', in R.L. Leahy (ed.), *Contemporary Cognitive Therapy: Theory, Research and Practice*. New York: Guilford Press.

Datilio, F.M. (2004b) 'Family therapy', in R.L. Leahy (ed.), *Roadblocks in Cognitive-Behavioral Therapy: Transforming Challenges into Opportunities for Change*. New York: Guilford Press.

Dobson, K.S. and Dozois, D.J.A. (2001) 'Historical and philosophical bases of the cognitive-behavioral therapies', in K.S. Dobson (ed.), *Handbook of Cognitive Behavioral Therapies*, 2nd edn. New York and London: The Guilford Press.

du Gay, P., Evans, J. and Redman, P. (eds) (2000) *Identity: A Reader*. London: Sage in association with The Open University.

Dummett, N. (2006) 'Processes for systemic cognitive-behavioural therapy with children, young people and families', *Behavioural and Cognitive Psychotherapy*, 34: 179–89.

Duncan-Grant, A. (2001) *Clinical Supervision Activity among Mental Health Nurses: A Critical Organizational Ethnography*. Portsmouth: Nursing Praxis International.

Eells, T.D. (1997) 'Psychotherapy case formulation: history and current status', in T.D. Eells (ed.), *Handbook of Psychotherapy Case Formulation*. New York and London: The Guilford Press.

Ehlers, A. and Clark, D.M. (2000) 'A cognitive model of posttraumatic stress disorder from different sources of trauma', *Behaviour Research and Therapy*, 38: 319–45.

Ellis, A. (1962) *Reason and Emotion in Psychotherapy*. New York: Lyle Stuart.

Epstein, S. (1994) 'Integration of the cognitive and the psychodynamic unconscious', *American Psychologist*, 49(8): 709–24.

Erikson, E. (1950) *Childhood and Society*, 2nd edn. New York: WW Norton.

Farrington, A. and Telford, A. (1996) 'Naming the problem – assessment and formulation', in S. Marshall and J. Turbull (eds), *Cognitive Behaviour Therapy: An Introduction to Theory and Practice*. London: Bailliere Tindall.

Fennell, M. (1998) 'Low self esteem', in N. Tarrier, A. Wells and G. Haddock, *Treating Complex Cases The Cognitive Behavioural Therapy Approach*. Chichester: Wiley.

Fennell, M. (2004) Round Table discussion. European Association for Behavioural and Cognitive Therapies XXXIV Annual Congress, September.

Fennell, M. (2006) *Overcoming Low Self-Esteem, Self Help Course, A 3-part Programme Based on Cognitive Behavioural Techniques*. London: Constable & Robinson.

Fineman, S. (ed.) (1996) *Emotion in Organizations*. London: Sage.

Flitcroft, A., James, I., Freeston, M. and Wood-Mitchel, A. (2007) 'Determining what is important in a good formulation', *Behavioural and Cognitive Psychotherapy*, 35(3): 352–34.

Foa, E.B. and Kozak, M.J. (1986) 'Emotional processing of fear: exposure to corrective information', *Psychological Bulletin*, 99(1): 20–35.

Fowler, P., Garety, P. and Kuipers, L. (1995) *Cognitive Behaviour Therapy for Psychosis: A Clinical Handbook*. Chichester: John Wiley & Sons.

Freeman, A. and Martin, D.M. (2004) 'A psychosocial approach for conceptualizing schematic development', in A. Freeman, M.J. Mahoney, P. Devito and D. Martin (eds), *Cognition and Psychotherapy*, 2nd edn. New York: Springer Publishing Company.

Freeman, A., Pretzer, J., Fleming, B. and Simon, K.M. (2004) *Clinical Applications of Cognitive Therapy*, 2nd edn. New York: Kluwer Academic/Plenum Publishers.

Freeston, M.H., Rheume, J. and Ladouceur, R. (1996) 'Correcting faulty appraisals of obsessional thoughts', *Behaviour Research and Therapy*, 34: 433–46.

Freiheit, S.R., Vye, C., Swan, R. and Cady, M. (2004) 'Cognitive-behavior therapy for anxiety: is dissemination working?', *The Behavior Therapist*, 27(2): 25–32.

Freund, B., Steketee, G.S. and Foa, E.B. (1987) 'Compulsive Activity Checklist (CAC): psychometric analysis with obsessive-compulsive disorder', *Behavioral Assessment*, 9: 67–79.

Frost, R.O. and Shows, D.L. (1993) 'The nature and measurement of compulsive indecisiveness', *Behaviour Research and Therapy*, 31: 683–92.

Gergen, K. (1999) *An Invitation to Social Construction*. London: Sage.

Gilbert, P. (1984) *Depression: From Psychology to Brain State*, Hove: Erlbaum.

Gilbert, P. (1989) *Human Nature and Suffering*. London: Lawrence Erlbaum Associates.

Gilbert, P. (1992) *Depression: The Evolution of Powerlessness*. Hove: Erlbaum.

Gilbert, P. (2000) 'Social mentalities: internal "social" conflicts and the role of inner warmth and compassion in cognitive therapy', in P. Gilbert and K.G. Bailey (eds), *Genes on the Couch: Explorations in Evolutionary Psychotherapy*. Hove: Brunner-Routledge.

Gilbert, P. (2004) 'Depression: a biopsychosocial, integrative and evolutionary approach', in M. Power (ed.), *Mood Disorders: A Handbook of Science and Practice*. Chichester: Wiley.

Gilbert, P. (2005) 'Compassion and cruelty. A biopsychosocial approach', in P. Gilbert (ed.), *Compassion: Conceptualisations, Research and Use in Psychotherapy*. London and New York: Routledge.

Gilbert, P. (2006) 'A biosocial and evolutionary approach to formulation with a special focus on shame', in N. Tarrier (ed.), *Case Formulation in Cognitive Behaviour Therapy*. London: Routledge.

Gilbert, P. (2007) 'Evolved minds and compassion in the therapeutic relationship', in P. Gilbert and R.L. Leahy. (eds), *The Therapeutic Relationship in the Cognitive Behavioural Psychotherapies*. Hove: Routledge.

Gilbert, P. and Irons, J. (2005) 'Focussed therapies and compassionate mind training for shame and self-attacking', in P. Gilbert (ed.), *Compassion, Conceptualisation, Research and Use in Psychotherapy*. London: Routledge.

Gilbert, P. and Leahy, R.L. (eds) (2007) *The Therapeutic Relationship in the Cognitive Behavioural Psychotherapies*. Hove: Routledge.

Gilbert, P. and Procter, S. (2008) 'Compassionate mind training for people with high shame and self-criticism: overview and pilot study of a group therapy approach', *Clinical Psychology and Psychotherapy*.

Goffman, E. (1969) *The Presentation of Self in Everyday Life*. Reading: Pelican.

Goldstein, A.P. and Myers, C.R. (1988) 'Relationship enhancement techniques', in F.H. Kanfer and A.P. Goldstein (eds), *Helping People Change*, 3rd edn. Oxford: Pergamon.

Goodman, W.K., Price, L.H., Rasmussen, S.A., Mazure, C., Fleischmann, R.L., Hill, C.L., Heninger, G.R. and Charney, D.S. (1989) 'The Yale-Brown obsessive compulsive scale. I. Development use and reliability', *Archives of General Psychiatry*, 46: 1006–11.

Gowlett, A. and Townend, M. (2007) MSc in Cognitive Behavioural Psychotherapy e-learning resources. Unpublished document. University of Derby.

Grant, A. (2005) 'Developing reflective skills through the use of cognitive change methods', Workshop presentation at the 10th Annual Learning and Teaching Conference, University of Brighton.

Grant, A. and Townend, M. (2007) 'Clinical supervision in mental health nursing: rescuing practice within cultural and organisational dynamics, *Journal of Psychiatric and Mental Health Nursing*, 14: 609–14.

Grant, A., Mills, J., Mulhern, R. and Short, N. (2004a) 'The therapeutic alliance and case formulation', in A. Grant, J. Mills, R. Mulhern and N. Short, *Cognitive Behavioural Therapy in Mental Health Care*. London: Sage.

Grant, A., Mills, J., Mulhern, R. and Short, N. (2004b) *Cognitive Behavioural Therapy in Mental Health Care*. London: Sage.

Grant, A., Mills, J., Bridgeman, A., Mulhern, R. and Short, N. (2006) 'Mental health services: a suitable case for treatment?', *Mental Health Practice*, 10(2): 30–3.

Greenberg, L.S. (2007) 'Emotion in the therapeutic relationship in emotion-focussed therapy', in P. Gilbert and R.L. Leahy, *The Therapeutic Relationship in the Cognitive Behavioural Psychotherapies*. Hove: Routledge.

Greenberger, D. and Padesky, C.A. (1995) *Mind over Mood: A Cognitive Therapy Treatment Manual for Clients*. New York: Guilford Press.

Gumley, A. and Power, K.G. (2000) 'Is targeting cognitive therapy during relapse in psychosis feasible?', *Behavioural and Cognitive Psychotherapy*, 28: 161–74.

Haidt, J. (2001) 'The emotional dog and its rational tail: a social intuitist approach to moral judgement', *Psychological Review*, 108(4): 814–34.

Haarhoff, B.A. (2006) 'The importance of identifying and understanding therapist schema in cognitive therapy training and supervision', *New Zealand Journal of Psychology*. 35(3): 126–31.

Hammack, P.L. (2003) 'The question of cognitive therapy in a postmodern world', *Ethical Human Sciences and Services*, 5(3): 209–24.

Harvey, A., Watkins, E., Mansell, W. and Shafran, R. (2004) *Cognitive Behavioural Processes Across Psychological Disorders: A Transdiagnostic Approach to Research and Treatment*. Oxford: Oxford University Press.

Hawton, K., Salkovskis, P.M., Kirk, J. and Clark, D.M. (1989) *Cognitive Behaviour Therapy for Psychiatric Problems: A Practical Guide*. Oxford: Oxford University Press.

Hebblethwaite, P. (2002) 'Helping people change, part 2', *Accord* (Summer): 20–2.

Hodgson, R. and Rachman, S. (1974) 'Desynchrony in measures of fear', *Behaviour Research and Therapy*, 2: 19–326.

Holeva, K., Tarrier, N. and Wells, A. (2001) 'Prevalence and predictors of acute PTSD following road traffic accidents (RTAs). Thought control strategies and social support', *Behaviour Therapy*, 32: 65–83.

Holstein, J.A. and Gubrium, J.F. (2000) *The Self We Live By. Narrative Identity in a Postmodern World*. New York and Oxford: Oxford University Press.

Hoshmand, L.T. (2006) *Culture, Psychotherapy, and Counselling. Critical and Integrative Perspectives*. London: Sage.

Hubble, M.A., Duncan, B.L. and Miller, S.D. (1999) 'Directing attention to what works', in M.A. Hubble, B.L. Duncan and S.D. Miller (eds), *The Heart & Soul of Change. What Works in Therapy*. Washington, DC: American Psychological Association.

Hugdahl, K. (1981) 'The three-systems-model of fear and emotion – a critical examination', *Behaviour Research and Therapy*, 19: 75–85.

Ingram, R.E. and Snyder, C.R. (2006) 'Blending the good with the bad: integrating positive psychology and cognitive psychotherapy', *Journal of Cognitive Psychotherapy: An International Quarterly*, 20(2): 117–22.

James, I.A. (2001) 'Schema therapy: the next generation but should it carry a health warning?', *Behavioural and Cognitive Psychotherapy*, 29: 401–7.

James, I.A., Blackburn, I.-M. Reichelt, F.K. in collaboration with Garland, A. and Armstrong, P. (2001) *Manual of the Revised Cognitive Therapy Scale (CTS-R)*. Unpublished Document. University of Newcastle-upon-Tyne.

James, I.A., Southam, L. and Blackburn, I.-M. (2004) 'Schemas revisited', *Clinical Psychology and Psychotherapy*, 11: 369–77.

Katzow, A.W. and Safran, J.D. (2007) 'Recognising and resolving ruptures in the therapeutic alliance', in P. Gilbert and R.L. Leahy, *The Therapeutic Relationship in the Cognitive Behavioural Psychotherapies*. Hove: Routledge.

Kitchiner, N. and Short, N. (2004) 'Working with people who have psychological problems because of a physical illness', in A. Grant, J. Mills, R. Mulhern and N. Short, *Cognitive Behavioural Therapy in Mental Health Care*. London: Sage.

Kumar, N. (2007) 'Challenges faced within the emergent Indian Economy in the delivery of evidence based psychological therapy', paper delivered at the World Congress of Behavioural and Cognitive Therapies, Barcelona, 11–14 July.

Kuyken, W. (2006) 'Evidence-based case formulation, is the emperor clothed?', in N. Tarrier (ed.), *Case Formulation in Cognitive Behaviour Therapy: The Treatment of Challenging and Complex Cases*. Hove: Routledge.

Kuyken, W., Fothergill, C.D., Musa, M. and Chadwick, P. (2005) 'The reliability and quality of cognitive case formulation', *Behaviour Research and Therapy*, 43(9): 1187–201.

Lambert, M.J. and Barley, D.E. (2002) 'Research summary on the therapeutic relationship and psychotherapeutic outcome', in J. Norcross (ed.), *Psychotherapy Relationships that Work: Therapist Contribution and Responsibility to Patients*. Oxford: Oxford University Press.

Lang, P.J. (1968) 'Fear reduction and fear behavior: problems in treating a construct', in J.M. Shilen (ed.), *Research in Psychotherapy, Vol. III.* Washington, DC: American Psychological Association.

LaTaillade, J. (2006) 'Consideration of treatment of African American couple relationships', *Journal of Cognitive Psychotherapy: An International Quarterly*, 20(4): 341–58.

Layden, M.A., Newman, C., Freeman, A. and Morse, S. (1993) *Cognitive Therapy of Borderline Personality Disorder*. Boston: Allyn and Bacon.

Leahy, R.L. (2001) *Overcoming Resistance in Cognitive Therapy*. New York and London: The Guilford Press.

Leahy, R.L. (2004) *Cognitive Therapy Methods*. New York and London: The Guilford Press.

Leahy, R.L. (2007) 'Schematic mismatch in the therapeutic relationship: a social cognitive model', in P. Gilbert and R.L. Leahy, *The Therapeutic Relationship in the Cognitive Behavioural Psychotherapies*. Hove: Routledge.

Lee, D. (2005) 'The perfect nurturer: a model to develop a compassionate mind within the conext of cognitive therapy', in P. Gilbert (ed.), *Compassion: Conceptualisations Research and Use in Psychotherapy*. London: Brunner-Routledge.

Liotti, G. (2007) 'Internal working models of attachment in the therapeutic relationship', in P. Gilbert and R.L. Leahy, *The Therapeutic Relationship in the Cognitive Behavioural Psychotherapies*. Hove: Routledge.

Lyddon, W.J. and Weill, R. (1997) 'Cognitive psychotherapy and postmodernism: emerging themes and challenges', *Journal of Cognitive Psychotherapy. An International Quarterly*, 11(2): 75–89.

McAdams, D.P. (1993) *The Stories We Live By. Personal Myths and the Making of the Self.* New York and London: The Guilford Press.

McFall, M.E. and Wollersheim, J.P. (1979) 'Obsessive-compulsive neurosis: a cognitive-behavioural formulation and approach to treatment', *Cognitive Therapy and Research*. 3: 333–48.

Mace, C., Moorey, S. and Roberts, B. (2001) (eds) *Evidence in the Psychological Therapies. A Critical Guide for Practitioners*. Hove: Brunner-Routledge.

Mahoney, M.J. (2003) *Constructive Psychotherapy: A Practical Guide*. New York and London: The Guilford Press.

Mahoney, M.J. (2004) 'Human change processes and constructive psychotherapy', in A. Freeman, M.J. Mahoney, P. Devito and D. Martin, *Cognition and Psychotherapy*. 2nd edn. New York: Springer Publishing Company, Inc.

Marks, I.M. (1986) *Maudsley Pocket Book of Clinical Management*. Bristol: Bristol Wright.

Marks, I.M. (1987) *Fears, Phobias and Rituals: Panic, Anxiety and their Disorders*. Oxford: Oxford University Press.

Marks, I.M. and Mathews, A.M. (1979) 'Case histories and shorter communications: brief self-rating for phobic patients', *Behaviour Research and Therapy*. 17: 263–7.

Marshall, S. (1996) 'The characteristics of cognitive behaviour therapy', in S. Marshall and J. Turnbull, *Cognitive Behaviour Therapy: An Introduction to Theory and Practice*. London: Bailliere Tindall.

Martell, C.R., Safren, S.A. and Prince, S.E. (2004) *Cognitive-Behavioral Therapies with Lesbian, Gay, and Bisexual Clients*. New York: Guildford.

Marzillier, J. (2004) 'The myth of evidence-based psychotherapy', *The Psychologist*, 17(7): 392–5.

Milgram, S. (1983) *Obedience to Authority: An Experimental View*. New York: Harper Collins.

Mills, J. (2006) 'Dealing with voices and strange thoughts', in C. Gamble, and G. Brennan (eds), *Working with Serious Mental Illness: A Manual for Clinical Practice*, 2nd edn. London: Balliere Tindall in association with the Royal College of Nursing.

Mills, J., Grant, A., Mulhern, R. and Short, N. (2004a) 'Working with people who have complex emotional and relationship difficulties (borderlines or people?)', in A. Grant, J. Mills, R. Mulhern and N. Short, *Cognitive Behavioural Therapy in Mental Health Care*. London: Sage.

Mills, J., Grant, A., Mulhern, R. and Short, N. (2004b) 'Cognitive behavioural interventions: understanding techniques in the context of theory', in A. Grant, J. Mills, R. Mulhern and N. Short, *Cognitive Behavioural Therapy in Mental Health Care*. London: SAGE Publications Ltd.

Mills, J., Mulhern, R., Grant, A. and Short, N. (2004c) 'Working with people who hear voices and have strange beliefs', in A. Grant, J. Mills, R. Mulhern and N. Short, *Cognitive Behavioural Therapy in Mental Health Care*. London: Sage.

Miranda, R. and Andersen, S.M. (2007) 'The therapeutic relationship: Implications from social cognition and transference', in P. Gilbert, and R.L. Leahy (eds), *The Therapeutic Relationship in the Cognitive Behavioural Psychotherapies*. Hove: Routledge.

Mooney, K.A. and Padesky, C.A. (2000) 'Applying client creativity to recurrent problems: constructing possibilities and tolerating doubt', *Journal of Cognitive Psychotherapy*, 14(2): 149–61.

Moorey, S. (2007) 'Cognitive therapy', in W. Dryden (ed.), *Dryden's Handbook of Individual Therapy*, 5th edn. London: Sage.

Morgan, G. (1997) *Images of Organization*, 2nd edn. Thousand Oaks, CA: Sage.

Morse, S.B. (2002) 'Letting it go. Using cognitive therapy to treat borderline personality disorder', in G. Simos (ed.), *Cognitive Behaviour Therapy. A Guide for the Practising Clinician*. Hove: Brunner-Routledge.

Mulhern, R., Short, N., Grant, A. and Mills, J. (2004) 'Key skills of assessment', in A. Grant, J. Mills, R. Mulhern and N. Short, *Cognitive Behavioural Therapy in Mental Health Care*. London: Sage.

Mulkens, S., Bogels, S.M. and De Jong, P. (1999) 'Attentional focus and fear of blushing', *Behavioural and Cognitive Psychotherapy*, 27: 153–64.

Mumma, G.H. and Smith, J.L. (2001) 'Cognitive-behavioral-interpersonal scenarios: interformulator reliability and convergent validity', *Journal of Psychopathology and Behavioural Assessment*, 23: 203–31.

Mundt, J.C., Marks, I.M., Shear, M.K. and Griest, J.H. (2002) 'The work and social adjustment scale: a simple measure of impairment in functioning', *British Journal of Psychiatry*, 180: 461–4.

Needleman, L.D. (1999) *Cognitive Case Conceptualization. A Guidebook for Practitioners*. Mahwah, NJ: Lawrence Erlbaum Associates.

Neimeyer, R.A. and Mahoney, M.J. (1999) *Constructivism in Psychotherapy*. Washington, DC: American Psychological Association.

Newman, C.F. (1984) 'Understanding client resistance: methods for enhancing motivation to change', *Cognitive and Behavioural Practice*, 1: 47–69.

Newman, C.F. (2007) 'The therapeutic relationship in cognitive therapy with difficult-to-engage clients', in P. Gilbert and R.L. Leahy (eds), *The Therapeutic Relationship in the Cognitive Behavioural Psychotherapies*. Hove: Routledge.

Nezu, C.M., DelliCarpinni, L. (1998) 'An Interview with Jeremy Safran', in: J.D. Safran *Widening the Scope of Cognitive Therapy. The Therapeutic Relationship, Emotion, and the Process of Change*. Northvale, NJ and London: Jason Aronson Inc.

NICE (2004) 'Depression – management of depression in primary and secondary care', *Clinical Guideline 23*. Web accessed 8 November 2006. http://www.nice.org.uk/guidance/CG23/niceguidance/pdf/English

Norcross, J.C. (2002) *Psychotherapy Relationships that Work: Therapist Contributions and Responsiveness to Patients*. New York: Oxford University Press.

Norcross, J.C., Beutler, L.E. and Levant, R.F. (eds) (2005) *Evidence-Based Practices in Mental Health. Debate and Dialogue on the Fundamental Questions*. Washington, DC: American Psychological Association.

OCCWG (Obsessive-Compulsive Cognitions Working Group) (1997) 'Cognitive assessment of obsessive-compulsive disorder', *Behaviour Research and Therapy*, 35: 667–82.

Ohman, A. and Soares, J.J.F. (1994) 'Unconscious anxiety: phobic responses to masked stimuli', *Journal of Abnormal Psychology*, 103: 231–40.

Ornstein, R. (1992) *The Evolution of Consciousness*. New York: Simon & Schuster.

Padesky, C.A. (1989) 'Attaining and maintaining positive lesbian self-identity: a cognitive therapy approach', *Women & Therapy*, 8(1,2): 145–56.

Padesky, C.A. (1993) 'Socratic questioning: changing minds or guiding discovery, a keynote address delivered at the European Congress of Behavioural and Cognitive Therapies', 24 Sept, London.

Padesky, C.A. (1994) 'Schema change processes in cognitive therapy', *Clinical Psychology and Psychotherapy*, 1(5): 267–78.

Padesky, C.A. (1996) 'Developing cognitive therapy competency: teaching and supervision models', in P.M. Salkovskis (ed.), *Frontiers of Cognitive Therapy*. New York and London: The Guilford Press.

Padesky, C.A. (1998) 'When there's not enough time: innovation in cognitive therapy', Workshop handout. Imperial College, London.

Padesky, C.A. (1999) *Therapist Beliefs: Protocols & Personalities (CD)*. Center for Cognitive Therapy (see www.padesky.com).

Padesky, C.A. (2003) 'Cognitive therapy unplugged: fine-tuning essential therapist skills', two-day workshop by Cognitive Workshops (www.cognitiveworkshops.com), Institute of Education, London, 17–18 June.

Padesky, C.A. (2006a) 'Constructing a new self', two-day workshop by Cognitive Workshops (www.cognitiveworkshops.com), Institute of Education, London, 23–4 May.

Padesky, C.A. (2006b) Personal communication to Grant.

Padesky, C.A. and Mooney, K.A. (1990) 'Clinical tip: Presenting the cognitive model to clients', *International Cognitive Therapy Newsletter*, 6: 13–14.

Pearson, J.C. (1979) 'A factor analytic study of the items in the Rathus Assertiveness Schedule and the Personal Report of Communication Apprehension', *Psychological Reports*, 45: 491–7.

Pennebaker, J.W. (2004) *Writing to Heal. A Guided Journal for Recovering from Trauma & Emotional Upheaval*. Oakland, CA: New Harbinger Publications, Inc.

Persons, J.B. (1989) *Cognitive Therapy in Practice. A Case Formulation Approach*. New York and London: W.W Norton & Company.

Persons, J.B. (1995) 'Why practicing psychologists are slow to adopt empirically-validated treatments', in S.C. Hayes, V.M. Follette, R.M. Dawes and K.E. Grady (eds), *Scientific Standards of Psychological Practice: Issues and Recommendation*. Reno, NV: Context Press.

Persons, J. and Bertagnolli, A. (1999) 'Inter-rater reliability of cognitive behavioural case formulations: a replication', *Cognitive Therapy and Research*, 23: 271–83.

Persons, J.B. and Davidson, J. (2001) 'Cognitive-behavioural case formulation', in K.S. Dobson (ed.), *Handbook of Cognitive Behavioral Therapies*, 2nd edn. New York and London: The Guilford Press.

Persons, J.B. and Tompkins, M.A. (1997) 'Cognitive-behavioural case formulation', in T. Eels (ed.), *Handbook of Case Formulation*. New York and London: The Guilford Press.

Persons, J., Mooney, K. and Padesky, C. (1995) 'Interrater reliability of cognitive-behavioural case formulations', *Cognitive Therapy and Research*, 19: 21–34.

Pfeffer, J. (1981) *Power in Organizations*. Marshfield, MA: Pitman.

Pierson, H. and Hayes, S.C. (2007) 'Using acceptance and commitment therapy to empower the therapeutic relationship', in P. Gilbert and R.L. Leahy, *The Therapeutic Relationship in the Cognitive Behavioural Psychotherapies*. Hove: Routledge.

Poole, J. and Grant, A. (2005) 'Stepping out of the box: broadening the dialogue around the organizational implementation of cognitive behavioural psychotherapy', *Journal of Psychiatric and Mental Health Nursing*, 12(4): 456–63.

Power, M. and Dalgleish, T. (1997) *From Cognition and Emotion: From Order to Disorder*. Hove: Psychology Press.

Power, M.J. and Dalgleish, T. (1999) *Handbook of Cognition and Emotion*. Chichester: Wiley.

Preston, S.D. and de Waal, F.B.M. (2002) 'Empathy: it's ultimate and proximate bases', *Behavioural and Brain Sciences*, 25: 1–72.

Rachman, S. and de Silva, P. (1978) 'Abnormal and normal obsessions', *Behaviour Research and Therapy*, 16: 233–48.

Rachman, S. and Shafran, R. (1997) 'Cognitive and behavioural features in obsessive-compulsive disorders', in R.P. Swinson, M.M. Antony, S. Rachman and M.A. Richter (eds), *Obsessive-Compulsive Disorder: Theory, Research & Treatment*. New York: Guilford Press.

Ramsay, J.R. (1998) 'Postmodern cognitive therapy: cognitions, narratives and personal meaning-making', *Journal of Cognitive Psychotherapy*, 12(1): 39–55.

Rief, W. and Hillier, W. (2003) 'A new approach for the assessment of the treatment effects of somatoform disorders', *Psychosomatics*, 44: 492–8.

Rogers, C.R. (1959) 'A theory of therapy, personality and interpersonal relationships, as developed in the client-centered framework', in S. Koch (ed.), *Psychology. A Study of Science*, Vol 3. New York: McGraw-Hill.

Rosenberg, M. (1989) *Society and the Adolescent Self-Image*, revised edn. Middletown, CT: Wesleyan University Press.

Roth, A.D. and Fonagy, P. (1996) *What Works for Whom?: A Critical Review of Psychotherapy Research*. New York: Guilford Press.

Rowland, N. and Goss, S. (eds) (2000) *Evidence-Based Counselling and Psychological Therapies. Research and Applications*. London and Philadelphia: Routledge.

Rudd, M.D. and Joiner, T.J. (1997) 'Countertransference and the therapeutic relationship: a cognitive perspective', *Journal of Cognitive Psychotherapy: An International Quarterly*, 12(1): 39–55.

Safran, J.D. (1997) 'The relational turn, the therapeutic alliance, and psychotherapy research. Strange bedfellows or postmodern marriage', in L.R. Greenberg, L.N. Rice and R. Elliott (eds), *Facilitating Emotional Change: The Moment-by-Moment Process*. New York: The Guilford Press.

Safran, J.D. (1998) *Widening the Scope of Cognitive Therapy: The Therapeutic Relationship, Emotion and the Process of Change*. Northvale, NJ: Jason Aronson.

Safran, J.D. and Messer, S.B. (1997) 'Psychotherapeutic integration: A postmodern critique', *Clinical Psychology: Science and Practice*, 4: 140–52.

Safran, J.D. and Muran, J.C. (2000) '*Negotiating the Therapeutic Alliance: A Relational Treatment Guide*. New York: The Guilford Press.

Safran, J.D. and Segal, Z. (1996) *Interpersonal Process in Cognitive Therapy*. Lanham, MD: Jason Aronson Inc.

Salkovskis, P.M. (1985) 'Obsessive-compulsive problems: a cognitive behavioural analysis', *Behaviour Research and Therapy*, 23: 571–83.

Salkovskis, P.M. (1989) 'Cognitive behavioural factors and the persistence of intrusive thoughts in obsessional problems', *Behaviour Research and Therapy*, 27: 677–82.

Salkovskis, P.M. (1991) 'The importance of behaviour in the maintenance of anxiety and panic: a cognitive account', *Behavioural Psychotherapy*, 19: 6–19.

Salkovskis, P.M. (1996) *Frontiers of Cognitive Therapy*. New York: Guildford Publishing.

Salkovskis, P.M. (2002) 'Empirically grounded clinical interventions: cognitive-behavioural therapy progresses through a multi-dimensional approach to clinical science', *Behavioural and Cognitive Psychotherapy*, 30: 3–9.

Salkovskis, P.M. and Harrison, J. (1984) 'Abnormal and normal obsessions: a replication', *Behaviour Research and Therapy*, 22: 549–52.

Sanavio, E. (1988) 'Obsessions and compulsions: the Padua Inventory', *Behaviour Research and Therapy*, 26: 169–77.

Sanders, D. and Wills, F. (2005) *Cognitive Therapy. An Introduction*. 2nd edn. London: Sage.

Schaap, C., Bennun, A., Schindler, L. and Hoogduin, K. (1993) *The Therapeutic Relationship in Behavioural Psychotherapy*. Chichester: John Wiley & Sons.

Schon, D.A. (1983) *The Reflective Practitioner: How Professionals Think in Action*. New York: Basic Books Inc.

Scott, J. (1998) 'Where there's a will ... cognitive therapy for people with chronic depressive disorders', in N. Tarrier, A. Wells and G. Haddock (eds), *Treating Complex Cases. The Cognitive Behavioural Therapy Approach*. Chichester: Wiley.

Scott, M.J. and Sembi, S. (2006) 'Cognitive behaviour therapy treatment failures in practice: the neglected role of diagnostic inaccuracy', *Behavioural and Cognitive Psychotherapy*, 34: 491–5.

Scrimali, T. and Grimaldi, L. (2004) 'The entropy of mind: a complex systems-oriented approach to psychopathology and cognitive psychotherapy', in A. Freeman, M.J. Mahoney, P. Devito and D. Martin, *Cognition and Psychotherapy*, 2nd edn. New York: Springer Publishing Company.

Segal, Z., Williams, J.M.G. and Teasdale, J. (2001) *Mindfullness-Based Cognitive Therapy for Depression. A New Approach to Preventing Relapse*. New York: Guidford.

Shafran, R., Thordarson, D.S. and Rachman, S. (1996) 'Thought-action fusion in obsessive compulsive disorder', *Journal of Anxiety Disorders*, 10: 379–91.

Sholomskas, D.E., Syracuse-Siewert, G., Rounsaville, B.J., Ball, S.A., Nuro, K.F. and Carroll, K.M. (2005) 'We don't train in vain: a dissemination trial of three strategies of training clinicians in cognitive-behavioral therapy', *Journal of Consulting and Clinical Psychology*, 73(1): 106–15.

Short, N. (2005) 'Vocal heroes: the views of two people who experienced a cognitive behavioural approach for their difficulties. Their narratives are accompanied by a commentary from the therapist', *Journal of Psychiatric and Mental Health Nursing*, 12(5): 574–81.

Short, N., Grant, A., Mills, J. and Mulhern, R. (2004) 'Working with people who are anxious', in A. Grant, J. Mills, R. Mulhern and N. Short, *Cognitive Behavioural Therapy in Mental Health Care*. London: Sage.

Sinason, V. (1999) 'In defence of therapy for training', in C. Feltham (ed.), *Controversies in Psychotherapy and Counselling*. London: Sage.

Smucker, M.R., Dancu, C.V., Foa, E.B. and Niederee, J. (2002) 'Imagery rescripting: a new treatment for survivors of childhood sexual abuse suffering from posttraumatic stress', in R.L. Leahy and E.T. Dowd (eds), *Clinical Advances in Cognitive Psychotherapy: Theory and Application*. New York, NY: Springer Publishing.

Smucker, M.R., Grunert, B.K. and Weis, J.M. (2003) 'Posttraumatic stress disorder: a new algorithm treatment model', in R.L. Leahy (ed.), *Roadblocks in Cognitive-Behavioral Therapy: Transforming Challenges into Opportunities for Change*. New York: Guilford Press.

Snyder, C.R. (2002) 'Hope theory: rainbows in the mind', *Psychological Inquiry*, 13(4): 249–75.

Snyder, C.R., Michael, S.T. and Cheavens, J.S. (1999) 'Hope as a psychotherapeutic foundation of common factors, placebos, and expectancies', in M.A. Hubble, B.L. Duncan and S.D. Miller (eds), *The Heart & Soul of Change: What Works in Therapy*. Washington, DC: American Psychological Association.

Stevens, C.L., Muran, J.C. and Safran, J.D. (2003) 'Obstacles or opportunities?: a relational approach to negotiating alliance ruptures', in R.L. Leahy (ed.), *Roadblocks in Cognitive-Behavioral Therapy: Transforming Challenges into Opportunities for Change*. New York: Guilford Press.

Strong, S.R. and Matross, R.P. (1973) 'Change processes in counselling and psychotherapy', *Journal of Counselling Psychology*, 30: 25–37.

Summerfeldt, L.J. and Antony, M.M. (2002) 'Structured and semistructured diagnostic interviews', in M.M. Antony and D.H. Barlow, *Handbook of Assessment and Treatment Planning for Psychological Disorders*. New York: Guildford Press.

Sutton, E., Townend, M. and Wright, J. (2007) 'The experience of reflective learning journals by cognitive behavioural psychotherapy students', *Reflective Practice*, 8(3): 387.

Tarrier, N. (ed.) (2006) *Case Formulation in Cognitive Behaviour Therapy: The Treatment of Challenging and Complex Cases*. Hove: Routledge.

Tarrier, N., Wells, A. and Haddock, G. (eds) (1998) *'Treating Complex Cases: The Cognitive Behavioural Therapy Approach*. Chichester: Wiley.

Teasdale, J. (1997) 'The relationship between cognition and emotion: the mind-in-place in mood disorders', in D.M. Clark and C.G. Fairburn (eds), *Science and Practice of Cognitive Behaviour Therapy*. Oxford: Oxford University Press.

Teasdale, J. and Barnard, P. (1993) *Affect Cognition & Change. Re-modelling Depressive Thought*. Hove: Lawrence Erlbaum Associates.

Thornton, S. (1989) 'Irritable Bowel Syndrome', in S. Pearce and J. Wardle, *The Practice of Behavioural Medicine*, Oxford: Oxford Scientific Publications.

Thwaites, R. and Bennett-Levy, J. (2007) 'Conceptualizing empathy in cognitive behaviour therapy: making the implicit explicit', *Behavioural and Cognitive Psychotherapy*, 35(5): 1–22.

Townend, M. and Grant, A. (2006) 'Integrating science with practice and reflexivity: cognitive therapy with driving phobia', *Journal of Psychiatric and Mental Health Nursing*, 13: 554–61.

Townend, M., Iannetta, L. and Freeston, M.H. (2002) 'UK study of the supervision practices of behavioural, cognitive and rational emotive behavioural psychotherapists', *Behavioural and Cognitive Psychotherapy*, 30: 485–500.

Waddington, L. (2002) 'The therapy relationship in cognitive therapy', *Behavioural and Cognitive Psychotherapy*, 30(2): 179–91.

Weiss, D. and Marmar, C. (1997) 'The impact of event scale-revised', in J. Wilson and T. Keane (eds), *Assessing Psychological Trauma and PTSD*. New York: Guildford.

Wells, A. (1997) *Cognitive Therapy of Anxiety Disorders: A Practice Manual and Conceptual Guide*. London: Wiley.

Wells, A. and Carter, K. (1999) 'Preliminary tests of a cognitive model of generalized anxiety disorder', *Behaviour Research and Therapy*, 37: 585–94.

Wells, A. and Carter, K. (2001) 'Further tests of a cognitive model of generalized anxiety disorder: metacognitions and worry in GAD, panic disorder, social phobia, depression, and non-patients', *Behavior Therapy*, 32: 85–102.

Wells, A. and Papageorgiou, C. (1995) 'Worry and the incubation of intrusive images following stress', *Behaviour Research and Therapy*, 33: 579–83.

Wells, A. and Papageorgiou, C. (1998) 'Relationships between worry, obsessive-compulsive symptoms and meta-cognitive beliefs', *Behaviour Research and Therapy*, 36: 899–913.

Wells, A., White, J. and Carter, K. (1997) 'Attention training: effects on anxiety and beliefs in panic and social phobia', *Clinical Psychology and Psychotherapy*, 4: 226–32.

Whittal, M.L., Rachman, S. and McLean, P. (2002) 'Psychosocial treatment for OCD. Combining cognitive and behavioural treatments', in G. Simos (ed.), *Cognitive Behaviour Therapy. A Guide for the Practising Clinician*. Hove: Brunner-Routledge.

WHO (World Health Organistion) (2002) *International Classification of Disease, Mental and Behavioural Problems Version 10*. Geneva: World Health Organisation.

WHO (World Health Organisation) (2006) http://www3.who.int/icd/currentversion/fr-icd.htm/, accessed 18 Sept. 2006.

Wolfgang, G.J. (2001) 'Cultural factors in psychiatric disorders', paper presented at the 26th Congress of the World Federation for Mental Health, July.

Young, J. (1990) *Cognitive Therapy for Personality Disorders: A Schema-Focused Approach*, 3rd edn. Sarasota, FL: Professional Resource Exchange.

Young, J.E., Klosko, J.S. and Weishaar, M.E. (2003) *Schema Therapy. A Practitioner's Guide*. New York and London: The Guilford Press.

Zimmerman, M. and Mattia, J. (1999) 'Psychiatric diagnosis in clinical practice: is comorbidity being missed?', *Comprehensive Psychiatry*, 40(3): 182–91.

Index

Please note that references to non-textual matter such as Figures or Tables will be in *italic* print